A FIELD GUIDE TO CHANNEL STRATEGY:
BUILDING ROUTES TO MARKET

www.ChannelFieldGuide.com

First Edition

Anne T. Coughlan
Northwestern University
Kellogg School of Management

Sandy D. Jap
Emory University
Goizueta Business School

A Field Guide to Channel Strategy:
Building Routes to Market

First Edition
December 2016
ISBN-10:   1539987744
ISBN-13:   978-1539987741

Copyright © 2016, Anne T. Coughlan and Sandy D. Jap. All rights reserved. Printed in the United States of America by CreateSpace, an Amazon.com Company. This publication is protected by copyright and permission should be obtained from the copyright holders prior to any prohibited reproduction, storage in a retrieval system, or transmission in any form or by any means, electronic, mechanical, photocopying, recording, or any other. For information regarding permission(s), contact:

Anne T. Coughlan
a-coughlan@kellogg.northwestern.edu
or
Sandy D. Jap
sjap@emory.edu

For Chuck especially, and for Catherine, C.J. and Courtney, who make it all worthwhile – ATC

For Jenny and Alex, the joys of my life, and the students who have taught me so much -- SDJ

About the Authors

Anne T. Coughlan is the Polk Bros. Chair in Retailing, and Professor of Marketing, at the Kellogg School of Management at Northwestern University. She has been at Kellogg since 1985. Her research interests are in the areas of distribution channel management and design; sales force management and compensation; pricing to end-users and through the channel; and competitive strategy. She has worked with dozens of companies on these issues over the years, and is the Academic Director of the Distribution Channel Strategies program at Kellogg's Allen Center for Executives. Her writings include many academic articles as well as business cases and books. She has been on the editorial boards of several leading journals and is the Editor of Social Science Research Network's Marketing e-Journals. She also taught at the University of Rochester's business school (1981-85) and INSEAD (1997-98). She earned a Ph.D. in Economics from Stanford University. She enjoys family, travel, and growing exotic plants from around the world in her greenhouse.

www.distribunomics.wordpress.com , @annecoughlan

Sandy Jap is Professor of Marketing at the Goizueta Business School at Emory University. She joined the school in 2001 and was a co-founder of the Emory Marketing Analytics Center (MAC). Her research centers on the development and management of interorganizational relationship and multichannel strategy as well as e-procurement design of industrial reverse auctions. She has won numerous awards for her impact on the field and her research efforts have been conducted in a number of industries, including the aerospace, automotive, chemical, petroleum, high-tech and consumer product industries. Her work has received significant attention from the academic community and the marketplace, and she is the author of *Partnering with the Frenemy*. She is an editorial board member at leading marketing journals and serves as President of the American Marketing Association's Foundation and is on their Board of Directors. She was on the faculty at the Sloan School of Management at the Massachusetts Institute of Technology from 1995-2001 and was a visiting Associate Professor of Marketing at the Wharton School at the University of Pennsylvania. She received her Ph.D. from the University of Florida (Go Gators!), and enjoys life with her kids. Tennis, red wine, and New England summers come in a very close second.

http://sandyjap.com, @SandyJap

Acknowledgments

We appreciate our colleagues who particularly influenced the direction and development of this book, including Mark Bergen, Alex Chernev, and Gary Lilien. We also thank Nancy Long of 11 Fingers, who provided graphic art design and web development; David Raney, who copy-edited the book; and Chuck Jameson, who contributed photographic and technical expertise.

- Sandy and Anne.

This book is the result of many years of teaching MBA and executive MBA students the ins and outs of channel strategy at Northwestern University. You may all think I taught you (and I hope that is so!), but you also taught me a great deal, by sharing new case ideas, providing research revision insight, and sharing your infectious excitement about learning. Outside companies and speakers have generously provided their time, data, and research sponsorship and I am grateful for all of them.

The Kellogg School supported my work on this book. I'd like to thank my colleagues in the Marketing Department for many insightful conversations that helped shape the book's content and tenor. Particular thanks are due to Greg Merkley, Henry Lowell Carrigan, Mike Mazzeo, and Alex Chernev. I am also grateful to my assistant, Susan Triforo, who has managed book production logistics and cheered me on to the finish line.

- Anne.

This book would not have been possible without the many graduate, undergraduate, and executive students in my channel strategy classes at MIT and Emory over the past two decades as well as the countless guest speakers who have shared their valuable time. There are many corporations who have graciously hosted me and my classes on site and these experiences have proven invaluable in informing and shaping the content of this book.

This book was also made possible by the support of the Goizueta Business School and Emory's Center for Faculty Development and Excellence. Frédéric Dalsace influenced the direction and development of this book. And of course, Amy Clark, my invaluable assistant who helps juggle everything that I can't.

- Sandy.

TABLE OF CONTENTS

PREFACE 7
   Doing Channel Strategy 7
   Our Philosophy 9
   Why Should We Care? 10
   The Structure of This Book 11
      Part 1: What Should My Route to Market Be? 11
      Part 2: How Do I Execute? 12
      Part 3: How Do I Incentivize? 13
   The Whole is More Than the Sum of Its Parts 13

PART 1: WHAT SHOULD MY ROUTE TO MARKET BE? 15

Chapter 1: A FRAMEWORK FOR CHANNEL STRATEGY 17
   1 in 5 Before 5 17
   Getting the Channel On Board 18
   The Structure of a Solution 19
      Supply and Demand Principles of Channel Strategy 19
      Channel Strategy and Value Creation 22
      Making it Work 22
   Key Take-Aways 23

Chapter 2: IDENTIFYING AND CAPTURING EXPLOSIVE CHANNEL VALUE 25
   How Do You Buy Shoes? 25
   Identifying Explosive Value 26
   A Framework for Creating Channel Value 27
   A Checklist for Diagnosing Channel Value Opportunities 29
   A Redux on Explosive Value: the 6pm.com Case 31
   Explosive Channel Value in B2B 31

Chapter 3: HOW DO CUSTOMERS WANT TO BUY? 35
   Solve the Customer's Purchase Problem 35
   Channel Benefits Defined 36
   BB&B's Benefit Delivery 37
   Channel Benefits at Lockheed Martin 40
   Channel Formats Create Different Benefits 41
   Price is Not a Channel Benefit 42
   Determining Channel Benefits 42
   Strategic Implications 43

Chapter 4: HOW CAN I AUDIT MY CUSTOMERS' CHANNEL BENEFIT PREFERENCES? 45

Steps in the Analysis.. 45
Application of the Analysis to Zappos.com and 6pm.com 46
    Identify the Target Segment(s) and the Product of Interest 46
    List and Define the Channel Benefits Demanded by Each Target Segment 47
    Encode the Relative Intensity of Demand for Each Channel Benefit 47
    Identify Channels that Sell Your Product to Your Target Segments 49
    Report and Interpret Grades for Each Channel 49
What About Multi-Channel Shopping?... 52
Repeat Purchase: Same Person, Different Channel Benefit Segment 53
Some Insights from the Analysis 55

Chapter 5: WHAT FUNCTIONS AND COSTS ARE THE RESPONSIBILITY OF EACH CHANNEL MEMBER? 57

What is the Work of the Channel?... 57
The Necessary Functions: SIFCO... 58
Autotrader: Monetizing Function Bundles 61
Solving Darren's Dilemma 62
Functions and Strategic Channel Design 64
The Zero-Based Channel Structure 65

Chapter 6: HOW TO AUDIT THE WORK OF THE CHANNEL? 67

Elements and Purpose of a Function Audit 67
Steps in Your Function Audit.. 67
    Identify and Describe Channel Members 68
    Define Functions and Assign Them Relative Weights 68
    Assess Performance of Channel Functions by Each Member 70
    Calculate the Share of Total Costs Borne by Each Channel Member 70
A Function Audit of Darren's Flooring Distribution Channel 71
    Darren's Baseline Situation and What He Knows 71
    Darren's Analysis.. 72
    Darren's Insights from the Function Audit 74
Summary: What Can We Learn From a Function Audit? 76

Chapter 7: HOW CAN YOU ALIGN CHANNEL ACTIVITIES AND BENEFITS?... 79

Aligning the Channel 79
    Demand-Side (Mis)Alignment: Drugstore.com.. 80
    Supply-Side (Mis)Alignment 82
Implications 84
Solutions for Misalignment 85
Alignment Constraints 86

    A Final Word 87

PART 2: HOW DO I EXECUTE? 89

Chapter 8: BECOME A STRATEGIC SKEPTIC! 91

    Flanders Wallcovering Inc. 91
    Paradise Lost... And a Possible Map 92
        Channel Conflict 93
        Channel Power 94

    The Strategic Skeptic 96
        What Do They Need to Know? 98
        What's In It for Them? 99
        Can They Do Less Than They Should? 100
        Can They Take Advantage of Me or Other Channel Partners? 101

    The Vertical Integration Solution 103
    The Strategic Skeptic's Kit 103

CHAPTER 9: HOW CAN I REDUCE OR PREVENT OPPORTUNISM? 105

    What Could Go Awry – And How To Keep It From Happening? 105
    Rodan + Fields: How Some Key Rules of Conduct Govern Distributor
        Performance in Direct-Selling Channels 107
        Promoting R+F Products and Business Opportunity 109
        Managing Channel Function Costs in the R+F Channel 109
        Contracting and Relationship Management Rules in the R+F Channel ... 110

    R+F's Rules Improve Channel Protection for Both Consultants and Itself ... 110
        Communicating the Consequences 111

    Monitoring Activities in a Direct Selling Channel 112
    Enforcement of Penalties 113
    Imperfect Governance is the Norm: Monitoring and Enforcement Efforts in Other
        Contexts 114
    From "What Could Go Awry?" to "How to Keep It from Happening" 115

Chapter 10: HOW TO THRIVE WITH A POWERFUL CHANNEL PARTNER? 117

    Asymmetric Power, or How to Dance with Elephants 117
    Invest to Build and Leverage Power 118
        How Small Players Can Have Big Power 118
        Building Power 119

    The Benevolent Dictator 121
    The Nature of Power 121
    Balanced Power and Dancing with Equals 123
        Targeting Homeowners at John Deere 123
        Diagnosing Power Sources 124

    Assessing Potential Conflict 126
    The Solution 128

Final Thoughts 129
Summary Insights 130

Chapter 11: WHY DO I NEED A CHANNEL "RELATIONSHIP"? 131

Types of Channel Relationships 132
When Does a Collaborative Relationship Make Sense? 133
How Do I Build a Collaborative Relationship Over Time? 134
Management Implications 136
Getting the Balance Right 137
    Step 1: Determine the economic potential of a closer relationship 138
    Step 2: Evaluate the current state of the relationship 140
    Step 3: Analyze next steps 141

Chapter 12: WHEN SHOULD I TAKE THE LEAP TO STRATEGIC PARTNERING? 147

Recreating Flower Distribution 147
Conditions for Success 148
    Persuading the Channel 148
    The Growers 149
    The Shipper 149
The Engine that Makes it Work 150
    Complementary Competencies 150
    Mutual Investments 151
    Trust Between Partners 152
    The Dark Side of Partnering 153
Strategic Partnerships as a Source of Competitive Advantage 154
A Checklist for Strategic Partnering Management 155

PART 3: HOW DO I INCENTIVIZE THE CHANNEL? 157

Chapter 13: HOW DO I PRICE THROUGH THE CHANNEL? 159

End-User Price Generally Cannot be Set by the Manufacturer 159
Developing a Channel Pricing Strategy 160
Pricing Challenges 161
    Retaining Ownership: Vertical integration 162
Challenge #1: Ownership Transfer 163
    DigiGadgets: End-User Pricing Chaos 163
    Why Is Ownership Transfer a Problem? 164
    Solutions to Loss of Pricing Control 164
        The Use of a Sales Representative Firm 165

- Sell on Consignment, Make-to-order, or Drop-ship 165
- MAP Policies and Unilateral, Voluntary Price Maintenance Agreements with Channel Partners 166

Challenge #2: Channel Margin Math, or the Tendency Toward Double Marginalization 168

- The "Self"-Publishing Author's Dilemma: DIY, or Use a Channel Partner Like Dogear Publishing? 168

What's the Problem Here? … The Tendency Toward Double Marginalization . 168

- How to Solve the Double Marginalization Problem 169

Challenge #3: Asymmetric Partners 170

- Pricing to Asymmetric Partners in the Retail Book Industry 170
- What's the Problem with Asymmetric Partners? 171
- Solution to the Asymmetric Partner Challenge: Functional Discounts Linked to Performance of Valued Functions 171

Challenge #4: Motivating Multiple Partner Behaviors 172

- Selling Health Insurance to Corporations and Their Employees 172
- The General Problem: Creating the Right Incentives for Performance of Multiple, Specific Functions 173
- Solutions to the Problem of Incentivizing Performance of Multiple Functions: Vertical Integration, Functional Discounts, and SPIFFs 174

Summary of Pricing Challenges 175

Chapter 14: HOW SHOULD I COMPENSATE MY SALES FORCE? 177

- Wells Fargo's Cross-Selling Scandal 177
- The Sales Compensation Breakdown 177
- Repercussions Throughout the Business 179
- Implications For Channel Design and Implementation 180
- How to Use Compensation Effectively 181

ENDNOTES 185

BOOK INDEX 193

PREFACE

During the Internet boom years, many students dropped out of MBA programs to become entrepreneurs and make their millions in a Silicon Valley startup. What they all learned was the need to make a sale: in other words, they needed a go-to-market strategy. It was not enough to have invented a better mousetrap. One executive student running a venture capital fund told us that among all the entrepreneurial ventures he vetted, his major reason for declining to fund a startup was a lack of vision about how to generate robust sales to end-users through a viable channel strategy.

Channel strategy is foundational for every business and a key source of competitive advantage. Not only is it useful for generating sales, its conceptual value goes beyond organizational strategy; channel thinking can generalize to virtually every encounter that contains a transactional element. Anytime there is a give-and-take between two parties, whether in a business or a personal relationship, understanding others' motivations and knowing how to create innovative value for both parties is a key to success. We would go so far as to say that "channels is life," a statement that we have even made boldly in our classrooms. One student, Charles, laughed loudly (he had a booming voice) and asked how one could think that any topic was so useful. But after Charles and his classmate, Tony, graduated and began interviewing for jobs, they recounted that during an interview at a prestigious consulting firm, they recognized the case scenario as a channels problem and solved it accordingly. They were ultimately given a prize for the most innovative solution to the case problem.

This is the outcome that we strive for in our teaching and in this book. We believe that knowing and successfully implementing channel strategy is fundamental to business survival, and a key differentiator of any MBA holder or business executive. Despite this, there is too little practical teaching material available on channel design and management. Without real-world problem motivation, channel analysis becomes harder to understand and less compelling for students. As a result, some students think business-to-business problems are boring, or believe they will never encounter these issues in the business world. But we respond by asking, how in the world did that product reach my local store's shelf? And how does Amazon deliver seemingly anything in the world to my doorstep in two days? Many find channels discussions impenetrable and full of jargon; part of the motivation for this book is therefore to demystify and simplify marketing channel strategy, with the goal of spreading its insights more broadly both in the classroom and in business. *Our colleagues who teach in the academy are a big reason we wrote this book.*

Doing Channel Strategy

The other major reason is to focus on the *doing* of channel strategy. Most startups face a daunting and confusing array of options and often conflicting interests in forming their route to market. Not surprisingly, then, the channel strategy of many startups is typically disjointed, fraught with misinformation, and pieced together in an *ad hoc* manner, often with programs, processes, and systems being developed one initiative at a time. Many channel programs in established firms are equally problematic. Some firms that "hit a wall" in sales growth turn to additional channels such as big box retailers – but with no strategic vision for how that might create added customer value instead of simply intensifying competition among a greater number of channel partners. Other firms suffer from the inaccurate perception that creating a channel endows them with the absolute right to dictate all aspects of its operation: "This is my channel and they *will* do as I direct!!" In actuality, all channel partners have some form of power, but cooperation cannot be achieved by edict. Instead, the strategic channel manager, or channel strategist, uses all the resources and incentives in his arsenal, rather than just threats, to achieve desired outcomes.

Many channel strategies are built like the wood towers used in popular stacking games. Each block in the tower is like the many pieces of your channel strategy, including your choice of partners, a pricing program, channel promotions, and the contributions of a variety of intermediaries. These are built into the plan when you initially design your channel. The tower is (we hope) sturdy and strong, with no missing walls or floors. Then another strategist may come along and make changes. Perhaps your successor takes out a piece and moves it elsewhere or removes it altogether. Partners are replaced and added, routes are subtracted or extended, and new programs are added to the mix. Over time, the structure is surprisingly robust, remaining standing and apparently capable of absorbing many adjustments. However, is the ever-eroding structure the strongest or most efficient use of the pieces within? How long will it be before the removal of one more block causes the whole structure to collapse, as it inevitably does in this game? In the same way, all channel strategies, while made of an array of similar building blocks, come with varying tradeoffs. What is the impact of these tradeoffs and what can the structure afford – or not? A wood block structure is seemingly simple to construct (kids can play this game at a very young age). But growing it and making changes to it over time requires both skill and strategy, and often, a delicate hand.

In this book, our goal is to share our learnings across many industries and contexts about the best channel strategies and their tradeoffs. It turns out that some systematic patterns and properties of channels hold; these can be thoughtfully managed and their limitations addressed. We like to refer to this book as our Field Guide because its goal is to introduce you to the channels landscape, help you understand the various species of building block options, and begin to understand the physics of adding and subtracting elements in a dynamically changing market. Channel management is a wild and woolly world, and our goal as your guides is to help you make sense of it.

Our Philosophy

Every firm faces growth challenges. This is why firms spend a lot of resources and effort to develop new products. But innovation in value does not have to be limited to the "product" element of the 4Ps of marketing. Innovation can also come from "place," the distribution element. A cornerstone of this book is that new sources of value come from asking, "*How* do my customers want to buy?" You will learn that the greatest source of value creation comes from simply making it easier for customers to find, purchase, and return your products. They are willing to pay for lower transaction costs, i.e. convenience, intelligence, and robustness. Our systematic process for identifying these opportunities and monetizing them will improve your managerial go-to-market decisions.

In our minds, it is not enough to teach students and executives the 60-story-view of channel strategy through descriptions and definitions of various institutional routes such as those using distributors, wholesalers, franchisors and retailers. While extremely informative for understanding the grand scheme of channels, at the end of the day it does not help managers *get the job done*. It begs several questions: How should a channel manager assess specific routes to market? How will a specific channel system resolve conflict or more efficiently assign tasks and processes? How should the channel manager link channel structure to channel member compensation and motivation? And once all of this is in place, how can a firm make sure that channel partners don't rob it blind?

So while we think that an entire chapter devoted to the topic "Why does a channel exist?" is existentially valuable, we also want managers to *manage* this key strategic variable better. Our students have been able to distinguish themselves in the firms they have worked in through application of the principles, techniques, and frameworks that we offer in this book. This book is the bread and butter of what we've shared with hundreds of students and executives for the nearly 60 combined years that we have served as faculty at our respective institutions.

Our motives are also self-interested. We think channels of distribution should be taught differently across all business school programs, to highlight its position and importance as a key "P" of the 4Ps of the marketing mix. The most consistent comment we get from students and executives who take our courses is that they had no idea that how a firm places its product in the market, with whom the product is placed, and how intermediaries are motivated could be such a fantastic source of competitive advantage and innovation. We hope that this book ignites a fire for readers, too.

Why Should We Care?

When we teach undergraduate or graduate classes whose students have little or no work experience, the first issue we must tackle is why channels are important. The simple answer is: money, and lots of it. As of 2015, wholesale distribution revenues in the United States totaled $5.35 *trillion*. This is serious coin – in fact, it represents nearly 30% of the nation's nominal GDP, or gross domestic product.[1] If we add retailing activities to these numbers, then one can truly get a sense of why channel strategy matters. U.S. retail sales topped $5.13 trillion in 2015, representing 29% of the country's nominal GDP.[2] All in all, channel strategy activities represent 57%, or more than half, of the economic activity of our economy. This is a staggering fact.

Our graduate students with work experience and every executive we have ever taught understand the importance of channel management and the go-to-market problem facing every firm. Many of them deal with resource constraints for channel investments and rising sales force costs (which can easily run three or more times the cost of advertising). Many of these students are asked by their firms to manage customer channel shifting, run incentive programs, and evaluate the benefits of adding or subtracting a specific route to market. Others must regularly resolve conflicts with their firm's distributors, develop new sales programs and promotions for retail customers, and run the analytics to determine exactly what the ROI is on each channel member in their system.

In other words, individuals with work experience understand that most business is B2B, not B2C. In fact, a more realistic view of the world is that business is B2B2C. There's a whole lot of B2B underlying that B2C effort. We like to illustrate this in our classes with the graphic below:

**Figure P-1:
The World of B2B2C**

This is the "work" of the channel. It is not just supply chain coordination and logistics – the tower's blocks must fit together and that channel implementation analogously requires coordination of the activities of two or more players. This requires more than a cost minimization emphasis: it requires a strategy for *motivating the channel* to perform value-added processes and activities at the right place and time.

Marketing curricula that focus only on how marketing impacts individual and end consumers don't prepare and equip students and managers for the challenges they will face. Much of marketing is about working through and with intermediaries in order to reach the final individual consumer. We aim in this book to preparing the reader for real-world marketing decision making.

The Structure of This Book

In keeping with our emphasis on *doing* channel management, our field guide approach demystifies the most common challenges that any marketer or channel manager might face while helping you make sense of the channel challenges before you. First, we provide a lay of the land. Chapter 1 presents an overall framework that underscores the need to make products, goods, and services available to customers *at the right place and time*. Chapter 2 introduces the central tenet that the right channel system is a driver of explosive value on both the cost and demand sides of your business. In this chapter, we explain how one goes about finding and identifying explosive value, the basis for your channel strategy. The rest of the book is structured in three parts. Each part and chapter builds from a question that most working students and executives have when they enter our classrooms.

Part 1: What Should My Route to Market Be?

The most common broad challenge faced by most firms is encapsulated by the question "How do I go to market?" This is the fundamental problem of which channel form is most appropriate/apposite. Do I need a wholesaler, or is a distributor better? Should I own a sales force or just rent one? The simple answer is that it will depend on *how customers want to buy*, which is the topic of Chapter 3. In this chapter, you will learn a framework for identifying and quantifying what benefits customers seek from channels. This may be post-purchase services, transaction convenience, wide assortments, and package sizes, to name a few. In Chapter 4, we provide an audit tool to guide this activity and show how to think about the key tradeoffs and weaknesses of any identified option. The answer to the "how do I go to market" question is that you must match the channel demands of customers to the supply of channel functions that assist in creating explosive value. These two chapters essentially help managers determine the "demand side" of any channel strategy. What benefits do downstream customers want? Which benefits are the most important to deliver, and which are less vital?

The next two chapters (5 and 6) tell managers how to determine the supply side of their channel strategy – that is, to attack the question "How should I organize my channel partners so that I can get them to do more for less?" Chapter 5 identifies the key activities or functions that intermediaries perform to create customer value. Having identified those activities, the next task is to assign and evaluate them. Chapter 6 ("How Can I Audit the Work of the Channel?") features an audit framework that can be used to organize and prioritize these key functions. Most importantly, it provides guidelines for costing out channel member efforts, which is a necessary condition for determining how to compensate those members.

Finally, Chapter 7 brings the customer's demands and the channel's supply activities together to ensure that a profit can be made. This is the critical process of channel alignment – of ensuring that the necessary supply side activities are in place at the most effective cost levels and that a business creates only the most critical benefits valued by downstream customers. The optimal channel alignment occurs when the matching of benefits demanded and functions supplied are also achieved *at the lowest possible cost*. This chapter's analyses help us understand what service levels the channel must offer, and at what price, in order to ensure profitability.

Part 2: How Do I Execute?

The next section of the book deals with the greatest challenge of channel strategy, which is executing and creating value *day in and day out*. This is not an issue of what customers want or what channel functions are available; it is entirely about how the firm should structure and govern its relationships with each channel member to make these exchanges work. The goal of this section is to improve the ability of the entire channel *system* to execute on the channel design derived from the analysis in Part I. Before delving into the tools and techniques available, it is important to understand the fundamental motivation and drivers of channel member behavior. Chapter 8 underscores the need to become a "strategic skeptic," i.e. to understand fundamental incentive challenges that all channels face. A motivational problem that every channel captain faces is the reality that most channel members, given the opportunity, will take advantage of them. Like pirates, rogues, and thieves, channel partners have the capacity and often the incentive to rob you blind. We discuss the opportunism problem and the options open to a channel strategist to minimize it. We also outline for you the various safeguards that can be put in place (and it takes more than one!) to reduce a channel partner's incentive to cheat, freeload, and shirk. This is followed by a chapter on channel governance, "How can I reduce or prevent opportunism?" (Chapter 9). We discuss how to establish rules of conduct, communicate consequences, monitor compliance, and manage violations.

A key issue in execution is the need for channel relationship management, which the next three chapters address. Channel conflict is endemic in just about all channel systems. Two or more channel partner firms that are completely self-interested and pursuing very different goals and objectives will find it virtually impossible to avoid conflict. The truth about conflict is that it is never a question of whether it will occur, but when. And when it happens, every manager must understand the options.

Most firms, particularly those who must partner with a 400-pound-gorilla partner, fail to realize that in fact they do have sources of power. We frequently hear channel managers ask Chapter 10's question, "How Can I Thrive with a Powerful Channel Partner?" The real question, though, is "How do I deal with a channel partner who is more powerful than I am?" Most are not aware that it is also possible to *thrive* as the less powerful partner. Chapter 10 shows how it is done.

Learning how to effectively work with a channel partner is the next key executional challenge. "Why Do I Need a Channel Relationship?" (Chapter 11) addresses the decision to work in either a transactional or relational manner with a channel member. Many managers believe that strong interpersonal relationships are always better for business, but in fact there are many conditions under which a focus on pay-for-performance is a better route. Relationships are useful, but developing them is costly and there will never be enough bandwidth to create relationships with everyone. This means that firms must think very carefully about when to build close relationships and with whom. It also follows that firms should never enter a strategic partnership with a channel member lightly. Chapter 12 ("When Should I Make the Leap to Strategic Partnering?") is designed to help firms understand the tradeoffs and investments that must accompany this decision.

Part 3: How Do I Incentivize?

The last section of the book addresses what we all want to know: "How Do I Get My Channel Partners to Do What I Want?" The good news is that the firm has options; most just aren't aware of what these are. For example, most managers believe that pricing through the channel – getting the channel member furthest downstream to offer the end customer the optimal price – is next to impossible. What most managers discover is that every channel member in between the supplier and the end user wants to charge too much for what they do. This can result in an end-user price that few consumers are willing to pay. Chapter 13, on "How to Price through the Channel," identifies the levers available to a channel captain to help ensure that the final price to consumers is one that they *are* willing to pay for the value being delivered. This is no minor feat; U.S. suppliers must be careful in seeking to control prices to downstream channel members who buy the manufacturer's products to resell downstream. As an example, the food and supply channel to restaurants and cafeterias have historically operated on very thin margins. For the first half of 2016, U.S. Foods, a $23 billion dollar firm with 62 distribution centers, had an operating profit margin of 4%, adjusted to exclude interest, taxes, and other one-time expenses.[3] Chapter 14 discusses how to compensate the sales force to incentivize it to execute on the channel's promotional strategy.

Parts 2 and 3 of this book may be its most distinguishing features. Few channel management books address *both* the fundamental channel partner motivation problem *and* the solutions that address this. However, a definitive understanding of these options will serve every firm and channel captain well.

The Whole is More Than the Sum of Its Parts

Obviously, each chapter represents a different moving part in the channel strategy wheelhouse. None, in and of itself, is impossible to do. The real test is in knowing how to apply each block in your channel strategy structure to make it solid. The payoff of a well-built channel strategy is that it is a largely *inimitable* source of competitive advantage. And unlike advantages like product development or market reach, which rely on specific competencies or size, channel strategy is an option that is available to all firms of any size and capability. Like education, it is a great equalizer among those with different resources and opportunities. Channel strategies are also difficult (if not impossible) to observe, as the negotiations and specific organization of channel activities, processes, and functions are not easily seen and therefore duplicated. It's not easy to understand a channel strategy through reverse engineering of its parts.

It is a useful reminder that although we have presented the channel "tower" block by block, the reality is that all of the blocks impact, and are impacted by, choices made elsewhere. In other words, conflict is conditioned by what channel activity is assigned to which channel member. Motivation and cheating are impacted by the price levels that are targeted. Channel activity costs can determine the final value offered to customers. Channel power can restrict or enable various options for handling conflict. Like an effective marketing mix, your mix of channel strategy choices has the potential to work synergistically and enable your route to market to substantially improve on its past performance and, most importantly, out-perform the competition. But this requires that each block, and each floor of your channel tower, be set to the appropriate level and that the overall choices align. Your go-to-market strategy will blow up when this isn't so.

Most managers have no idea what (or where) the levers are, and even those who do probably don't know the available range of options and levels of intensity. You hold our tool kit in your hand. Are you ready to build?

Part 1: What Should My Route to Market Be?

Chapter 1: A FRAMEWORK FOR CHANNEL STRATEGY

1 in 5 Before 5

To say that marketing is only about the development of goods and services is to sell the marketing function short. Marketing must also make these things available to customers **at the right place and time**, and this is the role of channel strategy. Right place, right time is a concept very easy to say, but enormously difficult to do. Consider, for example, a decades-old problem on the African continent widely known as "1 in 5 before 5." This phrase refers to the fact that one out of every five children born in many African countries will die before the age of five, and typically from preventable causes such as diarrhea and dehydration. These mortality figures have not changed much in 30 years, which suggests that current initiatives are not working.

This is a terribly depressing statistic, made even worse by the simple fact that technologies and products do exist to solve the problem. The 1 in 5 before 5 challenge is not like AIDS or cancer, for which a cure has yet to be developed. Child diarrhea is easily cured with products such as dehydration salts, a therapy that is well understood throughout the African region. Is the price of these salts too high, making them inaccessible to the population that needs them the most? Again, not the case, as dehydration salts are very inexpensive to manufacture and provide, even to the poorest of the poor.

African countries continue to be plagued by 1 in 5 before 5 because of a persistent inability to get the therapeutic dehydration salts into the hands of a mother at the time of need – when the child is suffering from diarrhea. In other words, the right product is available, *but not at the right place and time*. The 1 in 5 before 5 problem is a go-to-market, or placement, problem. How should one set up and manage a route to market that can deliver rehydration salts, with clean water, into a mother's hands at the time when her young child is suffering from diarrhea?

> *Right place, right time is a concept very easy to say, but enormously difficult to do.*

The answer is the brain child of Simon Berry, of the British Aid Programme in northeast Zambia. He recognized that there was a need to get small amounts of product, differentiated by locale and need, delivered to remote rural communities so that local health leaders could use them to prevent child mortality from dehydration. A channel strategist would immediately recognize this as a classic channel problem: the need to achieve intense distribution of a bulk-broken product, in a specific variety, to a normally inaccessible locale.

Simon Berry was not a channel strategist, but he did notice in the course of his travels that he welcomed the opportunity to enjoy a bottled Coca-Cola, and found that it was available just about anywhere, even in remote locations. He reasoned that if Coke could reach the far corners of the African continent, why couldn't rehydration salts? After all, these salts were substantially lighter than a bottle of Coke – why couldn't they be transported via the same carriers? And this is how his organization, ColaLife (http://www.colalife.org/), was begun. ColaLife noticed that 80% of all Coke product was delivered in plastic crates, with empty, interstitial spaces between the bottles. They created a novel packaging concept, called the Aidpod, which contained 4g (200 ml) sachets of oral rehydration salts (ORS), zinc supplements, soap, and an instruction leaflet. The packaging acted as the measuring device for the water needed to make the ORS. The Aidpod was specifically designed to fit into the unused space of a Coca-Cola crate. This was a brilliant insight and a breakthrough means for creating the explosive value of getting the ORS delivered that last mile into a mother's hands.

Getting the Channel On Board

Unfortunately, creating a channel is not as easy as recognizing how it must work. This is because a central challenge of any go-to-market problem is to enlist and motivate the right distribution partner. When Simon approached Coke, they had no interest in "sharing" their distribution channel. Instead, it alerted them to the fact that interstitial spaces between Coke bottles might instead be *revenue enhancing*, so they began to consider alternative uses for the spaces. How could a nonprofit aid organization like ColaLife compete with a paying customer for those spaces? ColaLife realized that they could not count on the goodwill and social conscience of their distribution partners to provide the transportation. They needed to provide their partners with monetary incentives.

Another way to incentivize Coke was to apply social pressure to the company regarding the need to address the 1 in 5 before 5 problem. So ColaLife mounted a social media campaign to build awareness in first world countries of the health needs in third world countries. This generated an enormous amount of awareness and helped to raise funds to continue supporting their effort. In other words, ColaLife created a form of "pull" power to get the products to move through the channels. Unlike consumer packaged goods, where the pull power comes from customers requesting products from retailers and other channel members, social media influencers essentially became the "sales force" for ColaLife and helped to build demand for, or pull the ORS products through, the channel to the individuals who needed them most.

The problem that ColaLife faced is no different from the problem that most firms face in going to market in every area of the world. What channel structure is needed to move products from suppliers to end users? What kind of channel partners are needed, and what activities must they perform? How can the channel captain provide incentives to perform critical functions at the right place and time? And how can all of this be done in a cost-effective manner?

In our courses, we teach that the role of marketing is to develop products and services that are valued and demanded by customers. To this end, students are taught the development of brand strategies, new product development processes, and service design activities. However, a critical component of value creation for customers that is often overlooked is how to make these products and goods available to the right customer at the right place and time. As is clear from the case of ColaLife, though the needs and tasks may be simple, implementation can be really, really hard.

> Business success does not rely only on product strategy; huge value can be found in the management of channel variables.

It isn't enough for marketers to ask what it is customers want to buy; they must also ask *how* customers want to buy. The how is what we will focus on in this book. Customer value does not reside solely in the tangible goods and services of the firm; it is also created by availability on the customer's terms – i.e. the point at which the customer is ready to consummate the transaction. Understanding how this works represents a key competitive advantage. This is because the organizational strategies and efforts of channel partners are difficult, if not impossible, for competitors to observe, and thus to duplicate. Additionally, learning to work successfully with a channel partner involves a steep learning curve, one that is challenging for rivals to follow.

The Structure of a Solution

The successful channel strategist must (1) understand the supply and demand principles of channel strategy; (2) design a value offering that is aligned with the benefits demanded and channel processes supplied; and (3) execute the strategy via a mix of incentives, contracts, and relationship management principles.

Supply and Demand Principles of Channel Strategy

Great channel strategy is not just about how firms offer value to customers at the right place and time, but how the firm can do this both *profitably* and *efficiently*. You have heard it said that efficient markets occur whenever the quantity of goods in the market supplied exactly meets the quantity of goods demanded, as shown below.

**Figure 1-1:
Supply and Demand**

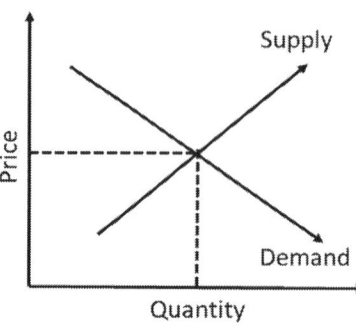

The same principle is true in channel strategy. Channel systems that supply the right level of processes, products, and value added functions to create the level of channel benefits demanded by target segments are said to be *aligned*. If the alignment is also at the point at which the costs of coordinating the channel system are at their lowest, we say that the channel is *zero-based*.

Throughout this book, we develop a framework that ensures that the goods and services offered by the firm to customers are offered in a manner that is consistent with how customers want to learn and evaluate, then access, and ultimately purchase and consume these products, as illustrated in the following graphic.

**Figure 1-2:
Channel Strategy Framework**

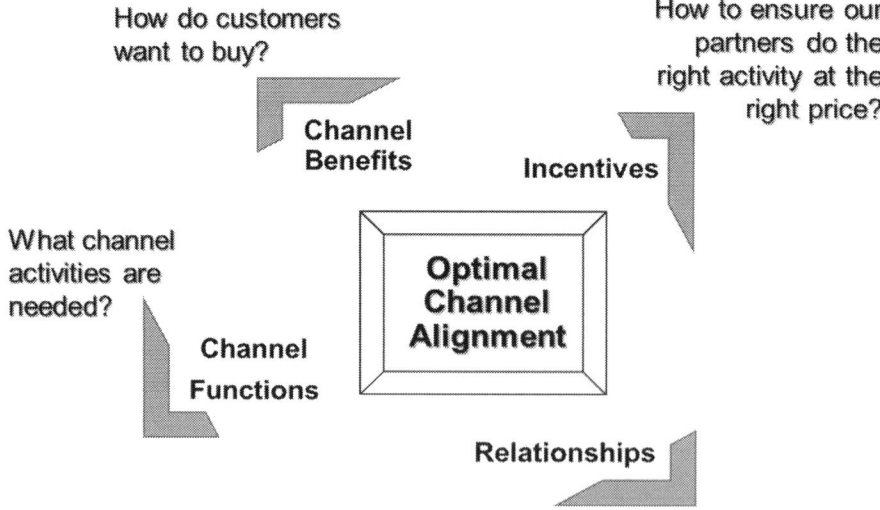

This requires a systematic understanding of the channel benefits that customers are willing to pay for, such as convenience and accessibility, product assortment and variety, education and information, etc. – in other words, the demand side of the channel system equation.

Our next step will be to configure the supply of these channel benefits. The desired benefits may require skills and activities that are beyond the scope of the firm. For example, the firm may need a channel partner to offer wide product assortment, or assembly or financing services for the goods that they sell, but would not be interested in supplying these value added functions themselves. Further, the path to profits for most firms involves the creation and sale of large quantities of goods and services. Offering these goods and services in one-off quantities or in combination with other relevant goods and services is the role of the channel. So the task of the channel strategist is to identify the operations and additional activities or service functions from outside firms and partners that can be bundled with the goods and services at a profitable price to customers. In the case of ColaLife, the organization never intended to be a charity – the idea instead was that mothers would pay for the rehydration salts, so they must be priced at a level that was affordable. This is part of a larger philosophy, called a "social conscience" model, which is often advocated by major philanthropic organizations such as the Gates Foundation. The underlying philosophy is to help improve the living and social conditions of third world countries by means other than charity alone.

The greatest challenge that ColaLife faced was structuring the supply side of the channel – identifying and incentivizing the appropriate channel partners. Ultimately, the organization created a channel that began first with a manufacturing facility where the ORS packs were assembled and packed into the kits. This was important for several reasons, the biggest being the need to ensure supply. Manufacturing outside of Zambia could be expensive; instead, by locating this process within the country, jobs were created and the supply source was close to the distribution channel.

> *Learning how to work successfully with a channel partner is a skill involving a steep learning curve and is difficult for rivals to duplicate.*

The Aidpods were then packed into boxes and a medical supply chain was used as the initial distribution point. Trucks moved the Aidpod boxes to Coke wholesalers. The wholesalers then purchased the product from the distributor and made a 20% profit on their sales to retailers. Products were delivered via Coke crates and boxes by bike and cars to retailers and vendors in local villages. Retailers controlled the ultimate pricing to the consumer. Mobile phones were used to provide an authentication system for the Aidpods and to track inventory. Prior to distribution, purchase vouchers were activated and redeemable by retailers. Retailers could then choose to offer a price discount on a customer's next purchase or other promotional incentives to customers.

Channel Strategy and Value Creation

Channel value is created when the firm can align its channel operations with customer demands regarding how they want to purchase and consume products. In short, your channel strategy is aligned when the channel benefits demanded by customers are appropriately matched with the channel operations and functions supplied by the firm and its intermediaries. Thus, the three key steps to creating channel alignment are:

1. Discover the channel benefits desired by customers in terms of how and when they want to purchase and consume your firm's goods and services
2. Identify and evaluate the necessary channel functions and operations needed in order to present the goods and services in the appropriate form and place
3. Evaluate the alignment of the benefits demanded with the operations and functions in place. *Aligned* channels occur when the costs of the necessary channel structure and delivery mechanism not only meet customer demands, but are also done at minimum cost (i.e., the channel is *zero-based*).

Making it Work

Of course, evaluating an existing channel or designing your route to market is only the first step to successful channel strategy. The ongoing challenge is to *make it work*. The vast majority of channel structures are not aligned – you must bring your channel into alignment by strategic deployment of the following levers:

1. Incentives and contracts – including pricing policies, branded variants, and fee-for-service models
2. Power asymmetries and dependence balancing – including the use of offsetting investments and the creation of bonds with other key organizations and constituents
3. Conflict management approaches – both in response to existing sources of disagreement and in anticipation of potential ones

ColaLife discovered that their channel would not work without ensuring that margins were created at every step of the channel: the distributor, the wholesaler, the transporter, and the retailer. Without fair compensation for the activities and processes that each of these channel members brought to bear on the movement and transportation of the Aidpods to far-flung locations, the ORS would never have made it into the hands of the mothers who needed them the most. Knowing how to price the Aidpod at each level of the channel and in an amount commensurate with the complexity of functions and activities that each channel must bring to bear is critical to making the entire channel system work.

---

*Channel strategy is the most inimitable source
of competitive advantage that exists in Marketing.*

More broadly, many firms also struggle with issues of power asymmetries and dependence. Some engage in activities to help offset the vulnerabilities that arise from dependence on more powerful partners. Most channel partners are organizations that are focused on different goals – for example, a manufacturer's goal is to create the greatest product volumes at the lowest cost that maximizes its capacity investment, but the retailer's goal is to provide a broad array of products in small sizes to end users. This naturally sets up conflict between the organizations, and this conflict must be managed.

Organizations working together repeatedly over time create relationships, and these can also shape and constrain the economic possibilities between them. Managing relationships well can make organizational efforts more productive, but managing them poorly can kill the exchange.

So it becomes important to understand relational phenomena – how firms together build trust and commitment, how they co-invest, and even how they break apart. Underlying this is the subtle nature of channel member perceptions, including partner suspicions and ongoing opportunism. This is hard-wired into the very nature of how channel managers and organizations perceive, respond to, and make sense of the channel environments they face daily. Managing channel partner relationships, while difficult, is a worthy investment because its success means a robust and productive go-to-market channel strategy.

Even ColaLife was not immune to relationship issues. Ultimately, ColaLife never got Coke's support. Instead, Coke later chose to support an organization called Project Last Mile, which does the same thing as ColaLife. This suggests that how we work with channel partners is critically important. It's all in the approach.

Key Take-Aways

The critical elements of any go-to-market strategy include the items in the following check-list:

1. Find the Explosive Value – determine the end user's preferences and value for channel benefits
2. Identify the ways in which potential partners perform value-added functions – this means conceiving a delivery system and roles for each partner along the channel. In the case of ColaLife, partners were needed to (1) grant access to the channel – Coke; (2) hold and move inventory – wholesalers and small retailers; and (3) co-champion the process – social media
3. Incentivize partners to perform the right activity at the right time and cost – this will include the need to be a smart skeptic and to "trust but verify" with your partners
4. Cultivate the right relationship – build a relationship that maximizes economic performance, and make sure that performance is rewarded accordingly.

Chapter 2: IDENTIFYING AND CAPTURING EXPLOSIVE CHANNEL VALUE

How can channels create value? The key difference between a channel strategy and a marketing strategy is that the product plays a central role in a marketing strategy, but is only the starting point for a channel strategy. Channels create value by focusing not on what customers want to buy, but on *how they want to buy*. By focusing on the how rather than the what, channels can offer differentiated value.

How Do You Buy Shoes?

Let's consider the purchase of a pair of shoes, a familiar event for all of us. A marketing viewpoint would ask which shoe you want to buy and what the attributes of that shoe are. A channels viewpoint would instead ask *how* you want to purchase that shoe. For example, do you need to see a lot of variety in the shoe style you are looking for? If you are shopping for a black pump, how many types of black pump pairs do you need to see before you're comfortable with a purchase decision?

Many consumers feel that it is important to touch a shoe's materials, examine the color in person, and try it on for fit before purchasing. These individuals recognize the risk of purchasing the wrong pair of shoes (e.g. poorly fitting or uncomfortable) without seeing and touching them first.

Other consumers hate to spend time shopping in a mall or shoe store. Or perhaps their lifestyle is too busy or demanding to allow time for shoe browsing. These three concerns – variety/assortment, the need to touch and feel, and convenience – are common concerns that must be dealt with when it comes to the purchase of shoes. In other words, these attributes shape *how we want to buy* our shoes. We want variety, touch, and convenience.

Explosive channel value can be found by considering how to better deliver these three benefits to consumers than is possible through any alternative offering. Enter Zappos.com. Zappos figured out a way to better deliver on all three of these shoe buying benefits, without ever having to open a single bricks-and-mortar store. How did they do this?

Variety. Physical stores limit the amount of variety that can be offered to customers. Consider a shoe style offered in four colors (black, brown, navy, and beige) and in seventeen sizes (from 5 to 11, plus half sizes) and two widths (medium and narrow). This computes to 4x17x2=136 minimum SKUs that need to be on hand in order to satisfy all customers. Holding inventory in a store is an extremely expensive use of space, since storefronts are often located in desirable or high-rent neighborhoods. Many online retailers instead hold inventory in a warehouse where real estate is relatively inexpensive. This allows them to offer much greater variety than any physical store could.

Touch and Feel. Without a physical store front, consumers could not touch and feel shoes before purchase. Zappos solved this problem by making shipping to the consumer *and* return shipping free. This meant that it was essentially costless for consumers to try on as many shoes as they liked and send back whatever they didn't want. Consumers could try on shoes in the comfort of their home, perhaps in conjunction with the outfits that they would be worn with. They could even show the potential purchases to significant others and get additional opinions before purchasing.

Convenience. Online retailers are often embraced by consumers who do not enjoy shopping in stores or battling traffic to get to one. Busy consumers want the right shoes but don't have the time or desire to shop for them in physical locations. As long as a consumer doesn't need the shoes within the next hour or two, online shopping can meet the demand for convenience within a two- or three-day delivery window (or a one-day window for a premium fee).

This is how Zappos revolutionized the channel for buying shoes. To this day, Zappos remains the dominant online shoe retailer.

Identifying Explosive Value

We know that a fundamental task of marketing is to create or improve revenue – the lifeblood of the firm. In fact, a firm's market valuation can be positively influenced by even the expectation of revenue growth. The firm's channel strategy is a driving (and often overlooked) force for creating long-term revenue growth.

How does this happen? In marketing, revenue is grown by either (1) gaining new customer segments or (2) intensifying the purchase activities of existing customers. The 4P principles of product, price, promotion, and place each contain specific levers to increase revenue through either method. In the channels realm, there are at least four chief levers by which the firm can grow revenue through new customer acquisition or better customer retention.

But first, it is important to recognize that channel strategy can create value *while holding the product strategy constant*; put differently, even if the firm does nothing to change its product features and traits, it can grow revenues via strategic channel choices. Another way to think about this is to understand that if all the products in the marketplace are standardized commodities, the firm can still create novel (we would even say explosive) differentiation value through the channel offering. Again, this goes back to our fundamental principle that there is huge value in understanding *how customers want to buy.*

If all its products are standardized commodities, the firm can still create explosive differentiation through the channel offering.

A Framework for Creating Channel Value

Like any other investment, the profit or value created by a route to market for a given product line is a function of the demand generated and the costs incurred in creating and running it. This sounds like an absurdly simple insight, based as it is on the basic profit relation:

Profit = Revenue – Costs

Creating value – or profit – through the route to market then is a "simple" task with three possible paths: increase revenue, decrease costs, or both. But of course the devil is in the details when making these options come to life, because it is usually *through* the management of value creation and cost containment that the channel attracts and keeps customers.

The first step in generating new revenue through the channel system is to gather prospective and current customers' insights into *what is missing on the demand side* in their contemplation of the firm's market offering.

Typically, these insights imply that some profit is being "left on the table" by the channel system. If the channel manager can first see where the failings are (from the customer's point of view), the next step is to reverse-engineer these insights into plans for altering the way the product goes to market. These plans involve considering a variety of ways to manage the channel system's activities, structure, and therefore costs, as illustrated in the left-hand box in Figure 2-1.

**Figure 2-1:
Generating Channel System Value**

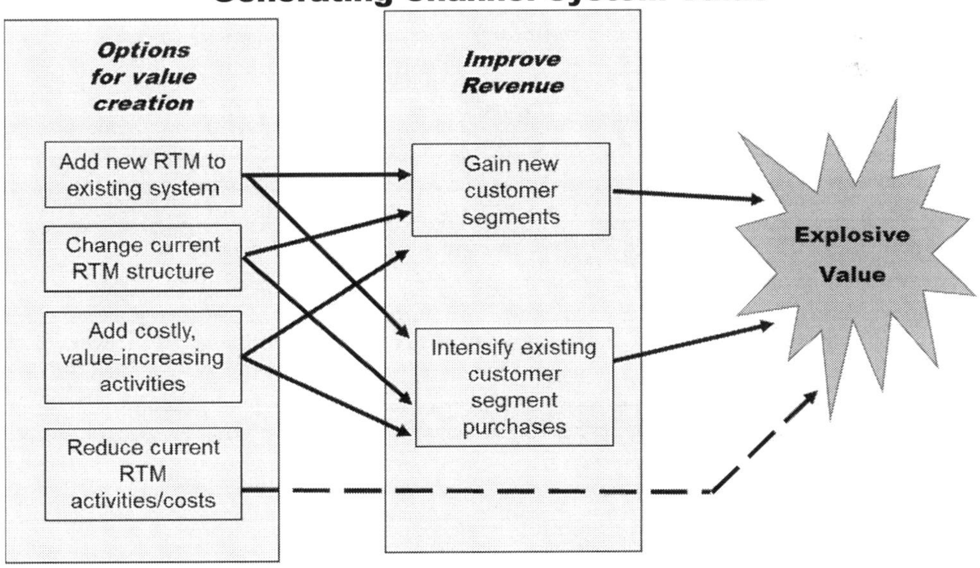

Options for value creation:
- Add new RTM to existing system
- Change current RTM structure
- Add costly, value-increasing activities
- Reduce current RTM activities/costs

Improve Revenue:
- Gain new customer segments
- Intensify existing customer segment purchases

→ Explosive Value

Any of the first three alternatives (adding a new route to market (RTM) to the channel system, changing the current structure of one RTM in the system, or adding new costly but value-added activities to one or more RTMs) can result in the acquisition of new customers or penetration of new segments, or an increase in sales from current customers and segments.

- A new route to market could include the addition of an online or physical channel. This typically requires significant resource investments and involves a serious commitment that will be difficult to alter in the short term.
- A more common response is to change existing RTMs, perhaps by expanding current coverage or modifying the players in the channel, such as adding distribution points or warehouse locations.
- The firm can also rethink the nature and scope of channel functions or value-added processes being offered in one or more RTMs. For example, sales reps who assist with product education, or kiosks and websites that enable inventory search, can increase the value of a RTM for the end user.

Zappos' approach was to add a new RTM to the existing channel system of buying shoes from brick-and-mortar outlets. By improving the benefits that consumers valued in *how they wanted to buy*, Zappos was able to acquire new customers as well as intensify sales to the shoe-shopper segment. Incremental value comes from either gaining new customers or getting current customers to buy more, and Zappos did both. By making it easier to purchase shoes, they found consumers were more likely to buy more. This is what we mean when we refer to *explosive channel value*.

A final alternative in channel system management is to reduce current RTM activities/costs and structures. Cost reduction is beneficial when an analysis of current customers' satisfaction reveals that some activities are simply wasted because they do not improve sales. In effect, such a realization creates value not through the demand side, but through a "slimming down" process on the cost side, via the shedding of wasteful and non-value-adding activities.

While cost reduction may not have a clear causal impact on growing revenue, it can nevertheless create significant channel system value and profit because it reduces wasteful expenditures on activities that do not create benefits valued by end-users. Such savings drop entirely to the channel's bottom line while not harming channel revenue generation.

> *The channel value vision is not obvious to a casual or uncommitted observer. It requires a certain discipline of thought that is best cultivated with the help of a solid, logical framework (and practice!) for attacking go-to-market problems.*

Our channels focus takes the physical product (or service) as given, and looks instead at how the channel manager successfully takes it to market. While it's possible to zig-zag between designing the route to market and designing the product that will be sold through it, our experience is that usually product line design comes first. Then it is the channel captain, or the firm with the vision for revenue growth via channel strategy levers, whose task it is to find the best route(s) to market for that product line.

A Checklist for Diagnosing Channel Value Opportunities

Ready to jump into action and fix things quickly? Not so fast. We've found that in the same way you would want a physician to first hear your symptoms, then diagnose you before recommending treatment, a thoughtful and rigorous analysis works best in channel management. A marksman follows a "Ready," "Aim," "Fire" sequence, and one who fires before aiming is showing recklessness, not skill, with his firearm.

A related reason for using the checklist below before jumping into channel redesign is that you need to be careful to avoid what's widely known as "Type 1" versus "Type 2" errors, or alternatively "false positives" versus "false negatives." A "Type 1" channel management error occurs when the channel manager erroneously identifies a flaw in channel implementation when that flaw is not present (a false positive). A "Type 2" channel management error occurs when a particular flaw exists in the channel strategy, but the channel manager fails to recognize it (a false negative). Falling prey to a "Type 1" channel error would lead a channel manager to *take action* in the mistaken belief that he is attacking a problem, while a "Type 2" channel error *prevents* a channel manager from fixing a problem that is in fact hindering the creation of explosive channel system value.

Figure 2-2 is a checklist of questions that you can use to identify viable opportunities before taking action. This checklist will increase the chances that your revised channel strategy will generate an explosive increase in channel system value, rather than a disappointing waste of your (and your channel partners') time and resources.

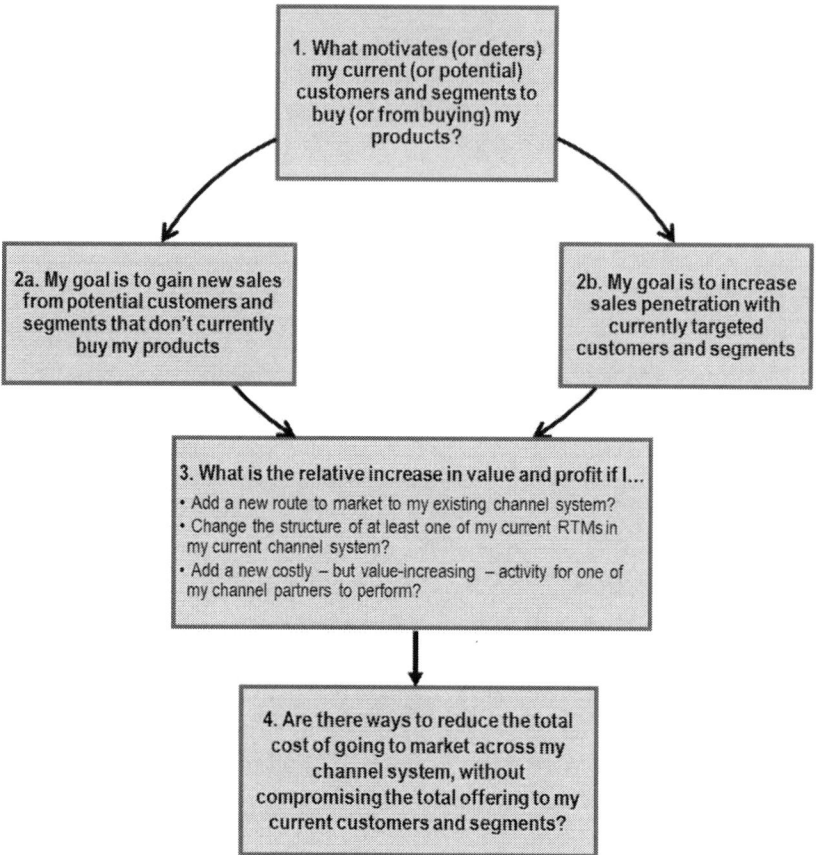

**Figure 2-2:
Checklist for Creating Explosive Value**

When considering how to improve channel system performance, the channel manager seeks both (a) to *fix what is not working well* (avoiding Type 2 channel errors) and (b) to *keep from introducing new errors into the system* (avoiding Type 1 channel errors). In other words, you might think the cost of "Firing" before you "Aim" is the monetary loss from your shortsighted channel redesign actions. That is only part of the cost. The other cost is the potential increased aggravation experienced by your customers when you fix something that isn't broken in your channel system, thereby "breaking" something that was working just fine before you took action. In short, the thoughtful channel strategist can see the best path to follow, and at the same time avoid creating new problems in the system, in the pursuit of explosive channel system value.

Channel strategists think about market opportunities and harnessing market value in a broader way than only with a product or price-reduction focus.

A Redux on Explosive Value: the 6pm.com Case

Up to now, we have stressed that thinking about how customers want to buy can create explosive channel value. This principle is robust, even when customers say they want lower prices. For example, a Stuart Weitzman shoe style sold for $275 on Zappos.com. However, Zappos still lost sales to other outlets for identical shoes, suggesting that its combined offer of shoes and service at a price point like the $275 Stuart Weitzman shoes did not appeal equally to all buyers. In particular, some consumers appeared to be willing to trade away some channel benefits such as variety, timeliness, and flexibility in sales terms for a lower price. How should Zappos respond to this? If explosive value is to be found in how customers want to buy, then Zappos needed to better understand consumer segmentation not just over products, but also over the tradeoff between price and benefits like variety, touch and feel, and convenience. Zappos noticed that another online shoe retailer, 6pm.com, offered this lower-price, lower-benefit alternative that seemed to appeal to a different segment of shoe buyers. Rather than build a clone e-tailer, Zappos acquired 6pm.com to be able to offer many of the same shoes they already sold on Zappos, but with some differences: fewer available styles, seasonal lags in offerings, email customer assistance rather than phone support, and free shipping only on the outbound (not return) side of the purchase. Zappos folded the back-end of the channel structure – warehouse activities and IT functions – around 6pm.com as well, using its economies of scale to reduce the costs of serving the 6pm.com consumer.

In terms of Figure 2-1, 6pm.com added a new RTM to Zappos' existing online channel structure. Interestingly, in contrast to the strategy of *adding* new costly but value-increasing activities, the 6pm.com acquisition *decreased* channel benefits relative to Zappos' baseline offer. In so doing, Zappos has been able to use 6pm.com to appeal to a new and different set of customers than its main Zappos.com target segment, while still growing usage and purchase frequency across its channel offerings. An additional cost-side benefit accrued from the ability to extend common channel and retailing investments from the Zappos operation to the 6pm.com business. And happily for the style-conscious but budget-constrained shoe buyer, that Stuart Weitzman shoe style sold for $109 on 6pm.com.

---

*Life is not always in the product space;
huge value can be had in the management of channel variables.*

Explosive Channel Value in B2B

Creating explosive value by considering *how* customers want to buy in tandem with *what* they want to buy is a concept that also works robustly in B2B contexts. Consider the example of a trucking company that was able to differentiate its offering to become the leading transportation option in the milk processing industry. Typically, the transporter in many industries is considered a non-differentiated and passive supplier. Its task is often to transport low-profit commodities from one location to another. In most industries, the transporter faces a race to the bottom – the winners are those who can offer the lowest price for their services.

One particular transporter began to think instead about how their customers – milk processors – wanted to buy the polyethylene pellets that were commoditized inputs to milk jug production, but nevertheless necessary for their manufacturing processes. Milk processors tended to buy at the lowest available unit price and seemed uninterested in value-added service for such a commoditized input product. However, the transporter learned that these pellets posed an environmental hazard when spilled, due to their non-biodegradability and ensuing harm to animals, birds, and fish. An unchecked pellet spill would trigger costly cleanup should the owner ever wish to sell the land.

All else equal, spill risk would be minimized if the buyer purchased the pellets in less-than-truckload lot sizes, because of the smaller inventory holdings on the processing site. However, trucking costs were minimized by shipping full truckload quantities, so they offered quantity discounts for full truckload purchases. In turn, a milk processing facility buyer that was unaware of the environmental risk and cost of full truckload purchases was unwilling to pay the higher per-unit price for a smaller bulk purchase. Further, even if the processors and transporters could have agreed on smaller shipments, the transportation costs at the system-wide level would have greatly increased due to the need for more frequent and smaller-volume purchases.

> *Your end-users are not always looking for a lower price. And if they are, it may be simply because you have failed to show them the value of buying a higher-priced but higher-value option.*

The transporter thus faced two problems. The first was to teach the milk processing buyer that its *full* costs for full-truckload purchases were higher than they thought – because those costs included not only the actual pellet price, but the expected value of costs of a pellet spill. This was the easier of the two problems; next, the transporter had to develop a channel process for providing milk processors the pellets they wanted to buy in the smaller quantities they desired, thus providing an extra channel benefit that could justify a higher (and more profitable) shipping cost. They realized that the key was to find inexpensive land closer to the milk processing facility that was relatively unproductive from a farming standpoint. This would allow them to store full truckloads of pellets for consignees. (Remember the free interstitial spaces between the Coke bottles in chapter 1? This is the B2B analogue.) It turns out that the perfect low-farming-value locations were next to railroad tracks, near the processing facilities.

So the transporter made several investments in order to better serve their customers. First, they bought the land along the railroad tracks and built rail car sidings on which rail-to-truck and full truckload-size cars could be stored. Then they redesigned some of their truck cars, dividing them into four equal-sized compartments, each of which would hold one-fourth of a full truckload of polyethylene pellets. Finally, they arranged for smaller trucks to be loaded with the one-quarter-truckload loads on a local basis that delivered directly to the processing facility with greater frequency than the original full truckload deliveries.

Importantly, since only this trucking company owned the convenient land and had made the capital equipment investments, only this trucking company could offer full truckload quantities to be delivered to the processing facility while managing to deliver the pellets one-quarter of a truckload at a time. Put differently, this was the only transporter that could offer a lowered risk of contamination of the milk processor's facility property while maintaining the same timeliness of delivery and truckload-quantity discount product pricing of other suppliers (although with a higher *shipping* cost, meaning higher revenue to the transporter). The full solution increased the loyalty of the milk-processing company consignee and the manufacturer, because the consignee demanded that any pellet supplier (remember, pellets are commodities) use this particular shipper.

> *Explosive value can be created in all sorts of contexts by any channel player.*

In this manner, by changing the current RTM structure, this transporter was able to create a significant competitive advantage in an apparently commoditized business (shipping) for the sale of a commoditized product (polyethylene pellets), as well as to increase buyer loyalty despite higher prices and margins for the shipper. It's important to emphasize that this approach did *not* generate explosive channel system value by reducing RTM costs – the transporter's costs increased significantly in the short-term. Nevertheless the total system costs over time were lower because of their costly efforts. Specifically, the lowered risk of a pellet spill on a consignee's property increased the present value of that business. In this sense, the explosive channel value that was created was not limited to the transporter, but shared with the entire channel. The extra system-wide explosive value created benefited the consignee in a lower risk of environmental hazards and costs, and benefited the shipper in higher long-term profit due to both higher revenue and greater customer retention.

And finally, while the transporter's investments and efforts did not grow the overall demand for polyethylene pellets for milk jug production, given the fixed market size, the trucking company was able to increase its market share versus the competition even while earning a premium over normal shipping revenues. The "magic" of more (and more durable) sales at a higher price came from the discovery of untapped explosive value in the channel.

Together, this suggests that explosive value can be created in all sorts of contexts, by any channel player. This is not a strategy that is limited to suppliers, retailers, or distributors. It is available to any channel member that understands that differentiation in *how customers want to buy* is a source of profitable sales, and that is willing to captain the channel system to satisfy that need.

Chapter 3: HOW DO CUSTOMERS WANT TO BUY?

In a core marketing class, you learn that consumers and customers vary in their valuations of product features. For example, when purchasing a car, some consumers may intensely value acceleration (i.e. going from 0 to 60 within a matter of seconds), while others value fuel efficiency more. Importantly, these differences in valuation translate into a higher willingness to pay, and *that* difference often forms the basis of customer segmentation. In a channels context, we generalize this same concept, except that channel strategists segment end-users on the basis of *how customers want to buy*. In other words, segmentation is not based on a customer's preferences for product attributes (*what* to buy), but instead on the value placed on ancillary benefits (*how* to buy).

Solve the Customer's Purchase Problem

Harper is a high school senior who lives in Portland, Oregon and will be starting school in August at Emory University in Atlanta, Georgia. In order to set up her dorm room, she needs to purchase many things: sheets, blankets, pillow, towels, a study lamp, rug, curtains, underbed storage boxes, a memo board, a shower tote, and health and beauty aid items, to name a few. She doesn't plan to bring a car, so it doesn't make sense for her to transport these things from Oregon. Besides, since she'll be arriving only a few days before classes start, it is critical that she be able to purchase all of these items in enough time for her to feel settled into her room before the first day of class.

Harper faces a complex purchasing problem. She must buy many products across a variety of product categories to accommodate a range of activities: sleeping, organizing, washing, eating, studying, relaxing. The long distance from Portland to Atlanta, combined with Harper's plan to forego a car at college, means that she prefers not having to transport the products to her dorm room herself. She also needs all of the items to arrive reliably before the start of class, and to spend little time getting her hands on them once in Atlanta, because the dorm move-in date is just five days before classes start. How does she solve this problem?

> *Understanding the intensity and variation in how customers want to buy is the right segmentation device for channel design.*

The channel strategist recognizes that the biggest issue Harper faces is not which lamp or soap dish is better, but a means by which to buy all of these things *conveniently* as she defines that. Retailer Bed Bath & Beyond ("BB&B") has created a solution that shows an understanding of her problem: a "Shop for College" webpage specifically for college students.[4] Their site offers decorating ideas and dorm kits, and distinguishes items for use in an apartment versus a dorm. BB&B

has also compiled information from various colleges on what items are allowed/prohibited (e.g. no halogen lamps, space heaters, hot plates, microwave ovens, or extension cords for Emory students).

Customers like Harper can choose from multiple shopping processes, including "Pack and Hold" (shop in store at home in Portland, pick up near campus), "Shop Now Ship Later" (shop now in Portland, ship when ready), "Appointment Scheduling" (meet with a BB&B college expert in Portland to facilitate shopping), or simply shopping online. BB&B's "Shop for College" site has thus created tremendous value for college students in terms of *how they want to buy*. By allowing students to shop at home, BB&B saves them scarce shopping, pick-up, and transport time once on campus.

Purchase risk is minimized, since BB&B can order and stock inventory to guarantee that the products ordered are in stock once they arrive on campus, and that they are not prohibited at the university they are attending. By organizing the picking and packing process for customers prior to their arrival, their shopping process near campus can be reduced from several hours to less than 30 minutes. The BB&B solution is elegant and easy, and solves the specific and particular problems facing the new college student setting off for campus. It resolves pre-purchase uncertainty by providing university-specific shopping list information; allows the student to shop at home before heading to campus, in a leisurely way; saves time and money for the family; and offers the complete array of products needed in a one-stop-shopping process.

Channel Benefits Defined

The very basis of all channel strategies lies in an understanding of the benefits that end-users desire in *how* they want to buy, above and beyond *what product* they desire. Knowledge of these benefits is an important strategic variable for both value creation and channel strategy. Like the cornerstone of a building, customer valuations for such benefits will ultimately form the basis on which all other strategic channel decisions are made. Those valuations also increase a customer's willingness to pay for the total channel offering (product + benefits).

Decades of research on channel management across a wide variety of industries, countries, and eras has shown that the most commonly valued channel benefits in both B2C and B2B contexts are those defined in Table 3-1:

Table 3-1:
Channel Benefits and Definitions

Benefit Sought	Definition
Package size/Amount	Preference for a specific quantity per unit (whether large or small)
Variety and Assortment	(a) Value placed on one-stop shopping ("variety" dimension) (b) Value placed on choice within a category ("assortment" dimension)
Waiting/ Delivery Time	(a) Value placed on timeliness to shop for product (b) Value placed on time to receive product, once bought
Distance	(a) Value placed on physical proximity of the channel outlet to consumer (b) Value placed on distance the buyer has to travel to reach the channel outlet
Customer service	Value placed on ancillary services such as: (a) Greeting when visit channel outlet (b) Sales clerk assistance in finding items on shopping list (c) Gift wrapping (d) Channel record-keeping of customer purchase history (e) Reminders/notifications re: time to restock, or re: desired item availability
Information and Education	(a) Pre-sale: value placed on information offered about brands, attributes of products, warranty provisions, return policies (b) Post-sale: value placed on installation and usage education, repair for damaged product, returnability (including restocking fees if any)

Clearly, this list is not exhaustive, but it does represent broad categories of benefit types that apply to most purchases. In practice, you should be very specific about the benefits that customers seek from a channel. For example, in the air travel industry, a benefits analysis might reveal that the right to board an aircraft first is a benefit that customers are willing to pay for. While this is specific to the airline industry, it is an example of the "short wait" benefit listed above. Although product attributes are likely to be fixed, a channel benefits focus allows the channel manager to leverage knowledge about *how*, not just *what*, the end-user wants to buy, thus affecting the end-user's value for the bundle of product plus channel benefits sought.

BB&B's Benefit Delivery

Let's now consider how BB&B created these valued channel benefits for Harper. Figure 3-2 highlights in bold the paths to explosive channel value created for the college student segment. Its investments in costly, but value-added, activities through the current channel, which attract new customers as well as generating incremental sales from existing customers, are notable on the demand side. These investments also help control costs elsewhere in BB&B's channel.

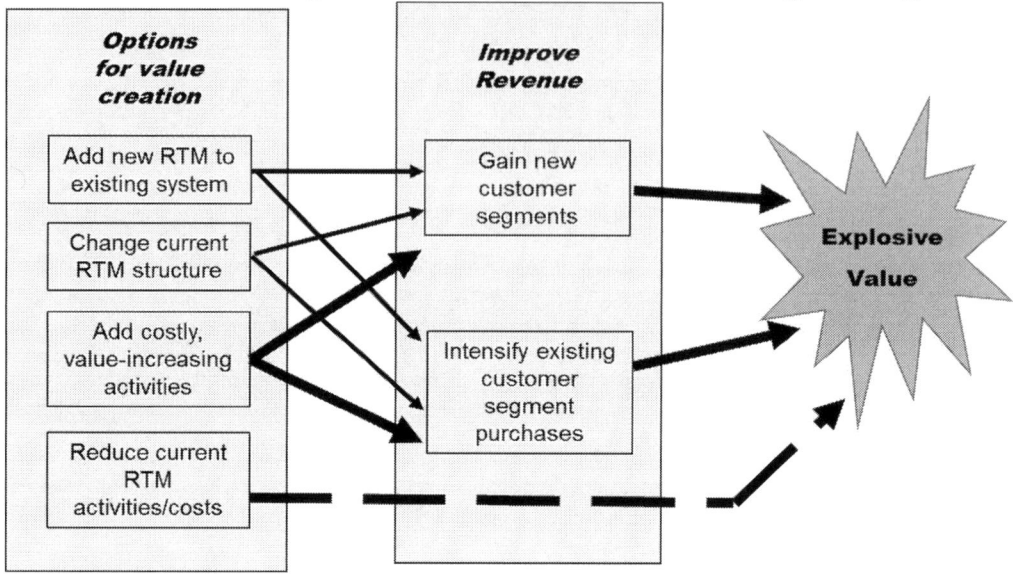

Importantly, while it is possible that consumers could source some of these products more cheaply from other retailers, lowest price is not always the main criterion. The value of buying the whole bundle in one place makes it worthwhile to pay more for the individual items in the bundle. In other words, customers are willing to pay for one-stop shopping (assortment) convenience.

Table 3-2 summarizes Harper's desired benefits, their definitions, and explains what the firm did to meet them.

Table 3-2:
BB&B's Value Creation Process

Benefit Sought	How BB&B Provides the Benefit	How to Assess or Measure the Benefit Creation
Package size/Amount	Offers what Harper wants, in the volumes she wants them	Difference between desired pack size and the pack size(s) on offer
Variety and Assortment	(a) Everything needed to move into Emory is carried at BB&B; thus, high variety benefit (b) Multiple brand/product options for given product categories; thus, high assortment benefit	(a) How much of desired "market basket" is available at this channel/retailer (b) How many product variants and/or quality tiers of specific product are on offer
Waiting/ Delivery Time	(a) Short time to reach local BB&B store: BB&B even offers a Google map to report travel time to closest store at home *and* at Emory (b) Shortened time to navigate the store, with offering of "Appointment Scheduling" (c) Exactly appropriate delivery speed – products arrive in time to move in to Emory dorm	(a) Time to reach this channel (e.g. travel time for physical store, or minutes elapsed to reach an e-commerce website) (b) Time to negotiate the "store," e.g. time to travel the aisles or pages, search time for product(s), or time needed for checkout, or time with a salesperson to accomplish purchase (c) Speed of delivery (number of days or hours), once product is purchased
Distance	(a) Short distance to reach local BB&B store: BB&B even offers a Google map to report distance to closest store at home *and* at Emory (b) Option to buy online offers a *zero* travel distance to use the BB&B "Shop for College" offering	(a) Miles from customer location to channel outlet (b) Physical distance to reach outlet (note: for e-commerce purchasing, this distance may be virtually zero)
Customer service	(a) Greeting is not the focus of "Shop for College" (b) "Appointment Scheduling" option offers sales clerk assistance in finding list items (c) Gift wrapping not offered (nor highly valued by Harper) (d) Loyalty program not the focus of "Shop for College" (e) Restocking reminder not offered as this is a one-time purchase bundle	(a) Is customer personally greeted when entering outlet? (b) Length of wait for assistance in finding desired items (c) Offer (or not) of gift-wrapping and costs (d) A loyalty program that tracks purchases; a database that is easily searched (e) Reminders re: seasonal/predictable/out-of-stock ordering times, and if so, with what information and offer of help? Auto-replenishment options
Information and Education	(a) Clerk in store gives valued pre-purchase information about products/brands to buy (b) Alternatively, online list of permitted/ prohibited items is available (c) Standard BB&B return policies apply (and are easy, given proximity of store to Emory campus)	(a) Presence (or not) of personal help before purchase (b) Presence (or not) of remote or online help before purchase (c) Presence (or not) of educational offer of post-sale installation and usage, repair provisions/policies, and ease of return

The last column of Table 3-2 illustrates how a channel captain might quantitatively assess *how and if the benefit was delivered*. This is vital information that allows it to verify a channel partner's activities and their provision of benefits.

The BB&B solution further shows a strategic focus on channel management through its combination of demand-side insights and corresponding channel supply-side actions:

- Deep insight into the consumer's demands, not just for *products*, but also for an array of *channel benefits* in the purchase process
- Investment in *technological* solutions to these problems, through its ability to allow the customer to shop at home, but pick up the order (or have it delivered) at the destination; this requires an information technology and inventory management channel system that shares purchase lists across geographic boundaries
- Investment in a broad bricks-and-mortar store (and warehouse) *network* to *fulfill* orders at a destination different from the shopping site

Together, these investments generate several profitable outcomes:

- *They increase sales per purchaser* because they provide the relevant information on exactly what should be bought and because BB&B therefore knows what to stock in its stores for college-bound buyers
- *They increase the number of purchasers*, because the BB&B total offer is superior to the alternative shopping possibilities
- *They reduce BB&B's inventory holding costs* because BB&B knows exactly what will be demanded, by store location, in advance of pick-up and thus can reduce its holdings of speculative in-store inventory.

In essence, BB&B's college shopping service turns what is otherwise a build-to-stock inventorying process into a "build-to-order" process, to use lean manufacturing analogical terms. Note too, that the BB&B solution does not involve creating an entirely new route to market; the existing retail stores and website retail option are used to solve the college freshman's problem. Nor does BB&B's solution involve changing the current channel structure. Rather, the solution invests in new activities that add costs, but clearly enhance value to their current customer, as well as new consumers who otherwise might not have used BB&B. And since BB&B has resolved consumer uncertainty about what to buy, its expected product return rate is much lower for this business than for its business overall, thus saving on the cost of handling product returns.

Channel Benefits at Lockheed Martin

The notion of channel benefits is not limited to individual consumer contexts; the concepts also generalize powerfully to business-to-business contexts. Consider Lockheed-Martin's aeronautics division, which manufactures numerous aircraft for the United States and foreign countries. Their largest program is the F-35 Joint Strike Fighter which is the largest defense program in the world with a total program lifetime value estimated at $1.5 trillion. In addition to providing new aircraft models, Lockheed also provides fleet sustainment in the form of spare parts and maintenance service.

One example of their main production aircraft is the C-130J, a four-engine propeller cargo plane used by the U.S. Air Force as well as in over 70 different countries worldwide. At a price of approximately $75 million per plane, the C-130J is targeted toward government/military customers who require a versatile cargo aircraft capable of operating on undeveloped air strips (taking off and landing on dirt runways and desert environments, for example).

The C-130J is targeted towards three segments of the U.S. Air Force: production, parts, and service. Each segment values essentially four channel benefits, albeit to different degrees:

- Field service – having a Lockheed trained service rep help with servicing issues
- Spare parts availability – Having parts available in the event of a parts breakdown
- LM expertise - having Lockheed consult on product usage
- Upgrade awareness – making the customer aware of potential upgrades and their benefits.

All of these benefits speak to the value created for the Air Force customer groups in terms of *how they want to buy*. These services enable target customers to fully leverage the equipment they purchase from Lockheed over the course of the product's life cycle, without having to develop in-house expertise for these aircraft alone. This is of critical importance to customers buying multimillion dollar planes.

Benefit weights matter and can vary by segments. Although these four benefits represent the majority of ways in which Lockheed's channel creates value for its end users, it's important to note that these four may not be equally valued or weighted similarly by all customer segments. And in fact, each of the three target segments weigh them quite differently. For example, the production group will weigh their expertise much more than spare part availability or field service. In contrast, even though the Air Force's service group might also value Lockheed expertise, they are likely to value Lockheed's field service substantially more as it is critical to the work that they perform. However, all of these benefits are critical for LM to provide and improve the customer's overall value by improving the process by which they purchase from Lockheed-Martin.

Channel Formats Create Different Benefits

Channel formats offer many different types of benefits in terms of how customers want to buy. Consider how cell phones and their accompanying subscription packages are purchased. Some customers place the greatest value on the education experience that comes from a Verizon store. They want to understand how to use the product and how information from their previous phone will be migrated onto the new device. Others care most about reassurance that their phone purchase was the best value for the price compared to competitive offerings. They might therefore prefer to purchase from a big box retailer like Best Buy in order to see and touch the variety of competitive phone styles. And others greatly value the convenience of not having to leave their house, preferring instead to purchase from a website and having the phone delivered the next day.

In this way, the relative value of the bundle of {product + channel benefits} is different for the three buyer types, and therefore the market can support three different channels to distribute exactly the same products. The corollary of this statement is that a consumer who finds herself at a "mismatched" outlet has *lower willingness to pay* for the same physical products than she would at a "matched" outlet – because the bundle available for purchase at a mismatched outlet provides too little of her most highly-valued channel service elements, and too many elements that convey no value to her at all. Thus, even if the Verizon store charged lower prices, the Best Buy-preferring customer might be unwilling to buy at this outlet, because the price isn't low enough to counterbalance the lack of competitive alternatives in their purchase process. This customer places the highest value on the assurance that her purchase is best for her across the entire cell phone competitive landscape.

> *A customer's willingness to pay for a given product can vary widely across two channels offering different channel benefits along with that product.*

In the channel realm as well as in basic product-based segmentation, therefore, it is unlikely that just one offering is ideal for all buyers. Instead, a well-conceived strategy that matches each target segment to a route that will delight the target justifies a multi-channel system when the firm wishes to target different - service-based segments. This is why we observe many suppliers taking their brands to market simultaneously across many different channel forms.

Price is Not a Channel Benefit

It's important to note that price, particularly a low price, is not a channel benefit. A product's price is what the consumer pays to consume the bundle of {product + channel benefits}. Although consumers may regularly trade off price in their willingness to pay for a channel benefit, it is nonetheless considered a product attribute (from the original 4Ps of marketing strategy). But it is not a channel benefit as we have defined them here.

Determining Channel Benefits

How does the firm determine the range of channel benefits that customers value? Managerial insight is one starting point; but market research can enhance the validity of those insights. Benefits can be identified from the use of focus groups, customer surveys, or observation studies of customers, whether in stores or during a sales representative's visit.

Once the range of valued channel benefits is identified, the channel strategist can investigate the extent to which customers are willing to *trade off* these benefits via the use of a conjoint analysis. A conjoint analysis is a quantitative marketing research technique that identifies not only how the various channel benefits are rank-ordered and valued by the customer, but also the degree to which each might be traded off vis-à-vis the other.

Strategic Implications

The above analysis implies (as you might expect) that customers will generally prefer more benefits to less. Even if the customer values information provision more than fast delivery, for example, any firm willing to provide the customer with more of both will be preferred over its competition. However, a key constraint is that channel benefits, while highly valued, are very costly to provide. This means that the channel strategist must determine which benefits are both highly-valued *and* cost-effective to provide. This implies that *not all channel benefits should be provided*: the channel manager needs to make a strategic choice about which benefits should be offered and which foregone.

When the channel manager does a good job of segmenting the market by channel benefits demanded, the result is positive on multiple fronts. First, consumers are willing to buy products that may be of only "parity" product quality (that is, that are not "best in class" on a pure product basis), but that offer a superior combination of product and channel benefits offered. This strategy validates the sellability of legacy products – not just new ones – in the company's line.[5] This is exactly the BB&B solution – their product offerings might not be the cheapest or highest quality, but the value from purchasing multiple items simultaneously in a convenient manner overrides whether a lamp or iron must be best in class.

Second, the consumer who is delighted with the channel benefits offered is one who does not "shop around" when buying again in this category. The combination of the two insights is that a well-understood consumer market gives the channel manager access to *loyal* consumers, who are in addition willing to pay more for the same product than otherwise.

How the customer wants to buy is a key source of explosive value.

This combination means that the channel manager benefits from a virtual "monopolist" position, even when there are pure-product competitors operating in the market. In short, understanding consumers' demands for channel benefits, above and beyond the value they place on the firm's products' features, is a source of explosive value to the savvy channel manager.

Chapter 4: HOW CAN I AUDIT MY CUSTOMERS' CHANNEL BENEFIT PREFERENCES?

In this chapter, we show you how to systematically record your best information about different customer segments' demands for channel benefits. The vehicle for doing this is a Channel Benefits Analysis that progresses through multiple stages, culminating in an overall assessment of customers' demands for benefits, and channels' abilities to offer them. This is designed to help you (a) segment your market in ways that matter for distribution design; (b) report on the segments' different demands for channel benefits; and (c) generate insights that improve your targeting and implementation.

You'll recall from Chapter 3 that a general list of channel benefits includes package size/amount, variety & assortment, waiting/delivery time, distance, customer service, and information/education. This list can be customized to precisely describe the demands facing your industry – for instance, if you sell durable products, your customers may have very different demands and (or) expectations for delivery speed for the product itself than for the delivery of post-sale service.

Steps in the Analysis

For clarity, we examine a single product, sold by a manufacturer through multiple routes to market. A Channel Benefit Analysis then includes the process outlined in Figure 4-1.

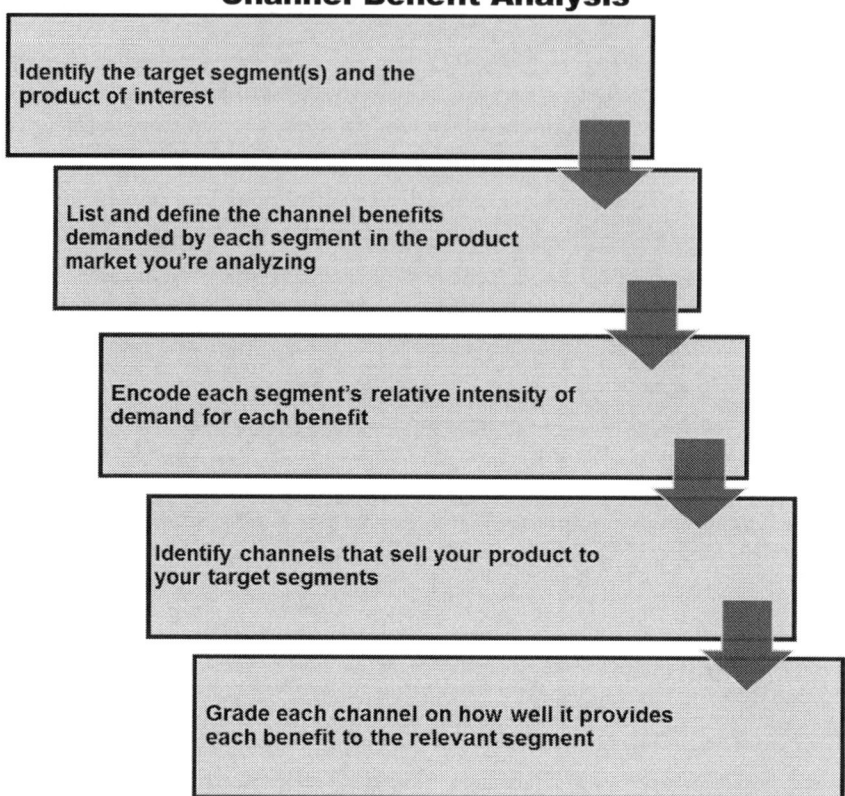

**Figure 4-1:
Channel Benefit Analysis**

How is this information gathered? Ideally, you will survey your customers to find out what channel benefits mean to them, how important each is, and how they rate your channels on provision of those benefits. That is, ideally you let the customer speak – after all, he or she is deciding whether to buy your product, and how. A sophisticated analysis would involve focus groups to identify relevant channel benefits, followed by quantitative research such as a conjoint analysis to evaluate the intensity of demand for those benefits. However, channel strategists may not have the luxury (of time or budget) to undertake a full marketing research study. Even so, combining existing market research information with managerial knowledge will still provide useful insights, especially when confirmed with channel partners closer to the buyer.

Application of the Analysis to Zappos.com and 6pm.com

Identify the Target Segment(s) and the Product of Interest

In this application, we'll extend our Zappos.com/6pm.com example from Chapter 2 and examine one purchase segment: a busy professional woman from Chicago who runs for exercise and relaxation and seeks to buy a new pair of running shoes.[6] She runs a moderate amount (no race running) and has heard that

New Balance shoes would be good for her; she is most interested in the New Balance "Fresh Foam Boracay" model.

List and Define the Channel Benefits Demanded by Each Target Segment

First, we'll use our general list of channel benefits to characterize *how* our "busy professional woman runner" segment wishes to buy a new pair of running shoes, by defining what each general benefit means in context.[7] In the running shoes example, we can codify the types of benefits demanded as follows:

Table 4-1:
Channel Benefit Names and Descriptions, Running Shoes

Channel Benefit Name	Channel Benefit Description
Volume bought (pack size)	Value associated with buying just one pair
Short distance	How near is the shopping "outlet" to me?
Variety/Assortment	How many shoe options are available to choose from?
Wait/Delivery Time	Once I know what I want to buy, how long will it be before I have the shoes at home?
Customer Service: information and help	How easy is it to shop this outlet / see and choose what to buy? Is there store or online help if I need it, and how available and friendly is it?
Customer Service: touch and feel	How much do I value touching the shoe materials, seeing color, physically trying on the shoe before purchase?
Customer Service: returns offered?	How hard is it to return a pair of shoes; do I have to pay extra to do this?

Table 4-1 illustrates how to make our general set of channel benefits concrete. First, a benefit may have multiple dimensions, as in the case of "customer service" (which includes information/help, touch/feel, and returns policies). Second, while each benefit description links to a particular channel benefit, the description reports the "voice of the customer" in words that make sense to that customer and conveys what could be valued about that benefit in each situation. Third, the descriptions lay the groundwork for an assessment of how well a particular route to market performs, because it identifies the value created by good performance on that benefit. And finally, no pre-judgment is made about the segment's intensity of demand for each benefit or perception of its value. The purpose of this step of the analysis is simply to identify and define channel benefits.

Encode the Relative Intensity of Demand for Each Channel Benefit

Although all channel benefits are good – and would be demanded at ever higher levels by our consumer segment if it were free to do so – they are costly for New Balance's (or any) channel to produce. We therefore ask our target segment buyer to place a *relative* worth on each benefit, allocating a fixed number of points (totaling 100) across all benefits according to their importance to her. She is thus forced to make trade-offs between what is more and less important to her, and this

47

is valuable to a channel manager seeking to satisfy buyers without wasting resources on low-valued benefits.

Market research reveals that the busy professional woman / recreational runner segment assigns the following relative weights to channel benefits:

Table 4-2:
Relative Valuation of Channel Benefits, Target Segment for Original Purchase of New Balance Running Shoes

Channel Benefit	Relative Valuation of Channel Benefit (points out of 100)
Volume bought (pack size)	5
Short distance	10
Variety/Assortment	25
Wait/Delivery Time	10
Customer Service: information and help	15
Customer Service: touch and feel	25
Customer Service: returns offered?	10
TOTAL	100

The analyst should provide commentary when reporting on these relative valuations. Comments on the set of valuations in Table 4-2 include:

- Buyers in this segment allocate very few (5) points to "pack size," because the expected norm is that one can always buy just one pair of shoes. This benefit is therefore not important to the buyer. However, if there were an outlet that only allowed a buyer to buy (say) five pairs of shoes at a time, the "pack size" benefit might be allocated a higher number of points.
- The most important benefits to this segment are variety/assortment and the touch/feel element of customer service (25 points each). This is because the buyer has never tried these shoes before, so values being able to assess several options, and to see, feel, and try on the shoes before buying them.
- Less important, but still valued, is the information/help element of customer service. This segment does not know how to extrapolate from the feeling of trying on a shoe to the ultimate feeling of actually running in the shoe over many miles and weeks – so the advice of an expert can help resolve pre-purchase uncertainty.
- Short distance, low waiting time to get the shoes, and the handling of returns are not *un*important to this consumer segment, but the constraint of 100 points forces the buyer to allocate just 10 points to each of them. This buyer enjoys running enough to be willing to trade

off some distance and waiting time for excellence in the more important benefits like variety/assortment and touch/feel.

In sum, this buyer segment values all the channel benefits listed here. A smaller number of points allocated to one benefit versus another signifies only the *relatively* lower weight placed on this element, and only in this specific transaction.

Identify Channels that Sell Your Product to Your Target Segments

Our focal buyer is considering purchasing her New Balance shoes either from Fleet Feet Sports, a very well known, high-end bricks-and-mortar sporting goods and runners' store in Chicago (hereafter abbreviated as "FFS"); from Zappos.com; or from 6pm.com. Her preferred Fresh Foam Boracay running shoe model is available at all three retailers, with the following prices[8]:

Table 4-3:
New Balance Boracay Running Shoe Prices

Store	Price
Fleet Feet Sports (FFS)	$120.00
Zappos.com	$119.95
6pm.com	$65.99 or $97.99, depending on color

Price is, of course, important to this buyer (as it would be to most buyers). However, recall that it is not itself a channel benefit, but rather what the buyer will pay for the right to consume both the product *and* its associated benefits via the channel from which she buys.

Report and Interpret Grades for Each Channel

The next step is to assess the buyer's perception of channel benefits at the three outlets. The buyer "grades" each outlet on the provision of each channel benefit, on an A/B/C/D/F scale (as in the U.S. school grading system, where "A" is excellent and "F" is failing). We then calculate a "grade point average" (GPA) using the weights and grades the buyer has provided.[9] The results from this analysis are presented in Table 4-4:

Table 4-4:
Weights, Grades and GPAs for Original Shoe Purchase at Fleet Feet Sports, Zappos.com, and 6pm.com

Target Segment: Time-Constrained Professional Woman, New Shoe Model Buyer		Grade on Benefit Provision		
Channel Benefit	Intensity Weight	Fleet Feet Sports	Zappos.com	6pm.com
Volume bought (pack size)	5	A	A	A
Short distance	10	C	A	A
Variety/Assortment	25	B	A	B
Wait/Delivery Time	10	A	A	D
Customer Service: information and help	15	A	B	D
Customer Service: touch and feel	25	A	F	F
Customer Service: returns offered?	10	A	A	C
GPA:		3.55	2.85	1.8
PRICE:		$120.00	$119.95	$97.99 or $65.99 (depending on color)

As with the explanation behind the intensity weights, it is important to note the reasons for the "grades" given for each benefit. Our target consumer explains her grades as follows:

- I can buy a single pair of shoes – my preferred "pack size" – at any of the three outlets, so I give each of them an "A" grade on this benefit.
- There is no shorter shopping distance than buying online, so Zappos.com and 6pm.com earn an "A" for the distance benefit. However, I have to travel to FFS, which lowers their grade to a "C" on this benefit.
- Zappos.com offers 95 New Balance women's running shoes; 6pm.com offers 56; and FFS offers 17. Zappos.com earns an "A" for their broad variety, but the relative value to me of a variety of 56 or 17 is not far behind (i.e. it is not linear in the number of SKUs), so I give them each a "B".
- I can go home with my pair of shoes today when I shop at FFS, earning them an "A" for low wait/delivery time. I am a "VIP" member at Zappos.com and thus get one-day shipping on anything I order; I am as happy with this as with delivery time at FFS, so Zappos.com also earns an "A". But 6pm.com offers me a 4-5 business day delivery lag with standard shipping, and for that I give them a "D".
- Information and help are superb at FFS, so they receive an "A" on this dimension. Zappos.com offers online chat support and the "Zappos Customer Loyalty Team" a phone number should I need help – worth

a "B" but not quite as good as FFS. 6pm.com offers email support but no phone support of any kind, so they receive a grade of "D" on this dimension.
- On the "touch/feel" customer service dimension, FFS (as the only bricks-and-mortar outlet) lets me literally touch and feel a pair of shoes before buying; this is impossible for any e-tailer to provide. I therefore give FFS an "A" and Zappos.com and 6pm.com an "F" on this dimension.
- FFS offers a "Happy Fit Guarantee" providing for a refund on returns within 60 days of purchase, whether for performance, looks, or fit reasons. Zappos.com offers free returns within 365 days of purchase and covers shipping fees for both purchases *and* returns. They both earn an "A" from me on returns. 6pm.com normally offers refunds within 30 days of purchase (60 days around the Christmas holiday), but I have to pay the return shipping, so this merits only a "C" from me.

The resulting GPAs for this purchase by our target segment are: 3.55 for FFS; 2.85 for Zappos.com; and a paltry 1.8 for 6pm.com. In other words, FFS is in the A-/B+ range of channel benefit performance, Zappos.com is in the B- range, and 6pm.com merits only a D+. Not only does FFS unambiguously "win" on channel benefit provision, but on the other end, 6pm.com is essentially on "academic probation" for channel benefits to this segment!

Some insights from this New Balance example are easily portable to other channel benefit applications in both the B2C and B2B worlds:

- Remember that the product is the same across all three channel outlets, so the buyer's purchase decision will weigh benefits against price.
- If price is not perceived to be significantly different across channels, then the highest GPA determines where this buyer wishes to shop – in this case, FFS.
- FFS wins on GPA because of its superior performance on benefits of maximum importance: the "touch and feel" aspect of customer service, as well as "information and help" and "variety/assortment."
- FFS is notably worse than Zappos.com or 6pm.com on "short distance" – but this doesn't hurt FFS's GPA much, because this buyer allocates only 10 points out of 100 to that benefit. Speaking generally, *you do not have to excel in the provision of **all** benefits; even relatively poor performance on unimportant ones can be easily counterbalanced by excellence on those benefits that are most important to the buyer.*
- Zappos.com and 6pm.com, as e-commerce platforms, are seriously hurt by their inability to offer "touch and feel."
- Zappos compensates for this to some extent with its "free shipping both ways" offer (not matched by 6pm.com), which encourages the consumer to "touch and feel" by buying many pairs and trying them on at home, then returning the unwanted ones for free.
- 6pm.com further suffers because of its slower delivery time than Zappos and its lower-quality provision of "information and help."

The ultimate question is whether FFS "wins" with this buyer segment. Remember that a combination of {product, price, channel benefit bundle} is what's being bought, and here the product is the same across outlets. In light of this, FFS most likely does beat Zappos.com, because the Boracay *product* is the same at FFS as at Zappos.com, and because the Zappos price is only 5 cents lower than the FFS price. The total utility value of the bundle at Zappos.com is thus lower than at FFS.

> *You do not have to excel in the provision of **all** benefits – even relatively poor performance on unimportant ones can be easily counterbalanced by excellence on the benefits that are most important to the buyer's purchase decision.*

6pm.com appears to be a seriously deficient outlet for these benefit preferences, but it is not obvious that FFS beats 6pm.com – because both price and benefits vary between the two. Which outlet is preferred depends on how sensitive these consumers are to limitations on shoe color, and how much incremental utility they get from saving 55 percent (about $54.00) on the purchase price of the shoes. The question is whether a 55 percent price savings on a $120.00 purchase is sufficient to compensate this consumer for a D+ channel benefit experience (a 1.8 GPA) – when she could have an A-/B+ channel benefit experience (3.55 GPA) at FFS.

In sum, a higher-"quality" outlet does not always win the sale; nor does the lowest-price outlet always win. The complex interplay between benefits and price can sway sales toward one or another channel competitor – always depending on the preferences of the buyer.

This analysis suggests some intriguing extensions to the baseline scenario involving a particular segment making the first-time purchase of a running shoe. We discuss the implications of relaxing these assumptions next.

What About Multi-Channel Shopping?

Multi-channel shopping (sometimes rather grandly called "omni-channel") occurs when a consumer patronizes more than one channel in shopping for a single product. While it can be tedious and time-consuming, visiting multiple channels can offer the buyer a wider set of benefits than shopping through just one.

Consider our busy professional woman runner. She places a high value (25 points) on the "touch and feel" customer service benefit component. Note that FFS earns an "A" at this, while Zappos.com and 6pm.com completely fails with an "F." Further, her 15-point weighting of "information and help" is also accompanied by great performance by FFS ("A"), with poorer performance again by Zappos.com ("B") and 6pm.com ("D").

A savvy consumer whose time cost is not too great might shop first at FFS in order to collect pre-purchase information and "touch" the shoes – neither of which is a benefit at the other outlets – without actually buying there. She may then visit Zappos.com and 6pm.com and discover that while Zappos.com's price is virtually equal to FFS's, the price is considerably lower at 6pm.com. The shopper stands to save either $22.00 or $54.00 (depending on color) on the Boracay shoe by buying at 6pm.com – which may well compensate her for the extra effort of shopping at two channels rather than one.

Note that FFS suffers under this shopping behavior because it provides valued pre-sale education, information, and touch/feel benefits (all of which are costly), yet garners no revenue from the ultimate sale of the shoe at 6pm.com. The problem here is that those valued customer service channel benefits are *alienable from* the purchase of the product itself. That is, these pre-sale channel benefits can be consumed by a prospective customer without actually purchasing the product. As long as this shopping behavior does not dominate FFS's store traffic, it might tolerate consumer "showrooming" (also called "free-riding"). But if showrooming grows too large as a proportion of all store traffic, FFS's enthusiasm to carry and promote New Balance running shoes is likely to wane, and it may even cut the line from its stores.

New Balance must therefore balance the benefit of multi-channel availability of its shoes (at different price points), against the potential loss of channel partner support and even shelf space for its products in high-service channels. Alternatively, it can encourage high-service retailers to give extra information and training *after* the sale to consumers who buy from them, thus making it harder for the consumer to engage in showrooming. For example, FFS offers post-sale community-building and training events including a "Good Form Running Clinic" and "Free Injury Screenings" at its stores. Such efforts help connect the consumption of valued channel benefits with the purchase of the products at FFS.

Repeat Purchase: Same Person, Different Channel Benefit Segment

Even if showrooming is not a threat, our focal shopper may love her Boracay shoes so much that she decides to buy an additional pair (or more than one) as replacement shoes. When this happens, she has joined a different channel benefit segment, because the values she places on benefits change as a result of already having bought and experienced the product. While the three channels' *grades* do not change, the consumer's *weights* do – and this can shift the relative attractiveness of FFS, Zappos.com, and 6pm.com. Let's see how, with the new channel benefit weights for replacement (as opposed to original) purchase, along with the three outlets' grades and resulting GPAs, in Table 4-5:

Table 4-5:
Benefit Weights, Grades and GPAs for Repeat Shoe Purchase at Fleet Feet Sports (FFS), Zappos.com, and 6pm.com

Channel Benefit	Intensity Weight	Grade on Channel Benefit Provision		
		Fleet Feet Sports	Zappos.com	6pm.com
Volume bought (pack size)	5	A	A	A
Short distance	35	C	A	A
Variety/Assortment	25	B	A	B
Wait/Delivery Time	10	A	A	D
Customer Service: information and help	10	A	B	D
Customer Service: touch and feel	5	A	F	F
Customer Service: returns offered?	10	A	A	C
GPA:		3.05	3.7	2.75
PRICE:		$120.00	$119.95	$97.99 or $65.99 (depending on color)

FFS's dominant GPA in the original-purchase situation has slipped behind Zappos.com's now-top rating (3.7) among the three outlets. 6pm.com's GPA is now uncomfortably close to FFS's as well (2.75 vs. 3.05). With price parity between FFS and Zappos.com, but a dominant GPA for Zappos.com, our shopper is predicted to buy her replacement shoes from Zappos.com rather than from Fleet Street Sports. She may even decide that the price difference between Zappos.com and 6pm.com is large enough to merit defecting to 6pm.com instead. Thus, FFS no longer clearly beats either competitor in the combined offer of {product, price, channel benefits}.

What happened here? The product, after all, has stayed the same, and the prices haven't changed either. Clearly, the remaining element of the purchase bundle – channel benefit valuation – flips the preferred buying location even though the product and price remain constant. Specifically, the two customer service elements (information/help and touch/feel) account jointly for 40 of the available 100 benefit points in the original purchase, but only 15 points in the replacement purchase. This consumer has already learned the Boracay's characteristics and benefits through her original purchase, and while short distance and variety/assortment were always important to her, they now play a *relatively* larger role for replacements than original shoes. Zappos.com's large variety and online no-travel shopping benefits now carry it to the preferred-retailer position.

The Channel Benefit Analysis reveals that FFS is in a precarious position if it can only rely on original product purchases to carry its business. These are the highest-cost sales to make because of the high expenditure on personal attention.

This issue should be of concern not only to FFS, but to New Balance – because without FFS's original sales efforts, later replacement sales at online retailers like Zappos.com or 6pm.com are unlikely to occur. That is, original shoe sales (generated through the costly but valuable provision of benefits by FFS) create positive conditions for FFS's retail competitors. Managing a multi-channel system therefore becomes an important part of the channel manager's strategy for brand management and providing lifetime value to the customer.

In addition to the types of in-store community building activities mentioned above that FFS offers to reduce showrooming, New Balance sometimes introduces new shoe models and stock-keeping numbers over time so that it is not always possible to purchase an exact replica of a prior purchase when looking for a replacement shoe. Further, New Balance does not offer all the models available at FFS to Zappos.com or 6pm.com,[10] thereby protecting FFS from head-to-head competition across its full New Balance product line. In effect, New Balance (like many other manufacturers) manages the available *assortment* of its products over time in an effort to support the special position of its highest-service retail channel partners by reducing competitors' ability to free-ride on the benefits offered during original product sales.

Some Insights from the Analysis

- The trade-off of benefits for price – holding the product constant that you, the manufacturer, distribute through various routes to market – is key to satisfying multiple target segments. True channel segment differentiation implies real differences in the valuation of benefits, as we found when contrasting an original running shoe purchaser with a replacement purchaser of the same shoe. An important implication of channel segmentation is that *any given channel will appear to be inferior to others – because it appears **not** to meet several segments' benefit demands*. However, its goal is not to delight all consumers, but rather the single segment whose benefit demands it can best meet.
- Consumers are typically willing to pay a higher price for a more attractive bundle of benefits, holding the product constant, so benefit analysis can enhance revenue and profit. Air Canada discovered, for example, that when it altered its aircanada.com website to offer multiple fare families with different bundles of added-value services, 45 percent of buyers bought a ticket with a price higher than the lowest, no-frills fare.
- Because the consumer buys a {product, price, channel benefit bundle} combination, a product that is only of parity quality with competitors can still win profitable sales – through research to discover those benefits that delight the target segment(s). Similarly, if a firm hopes for higher sales, lowering price is not the only tool available; analyzing benefit demands can allow a parity product to be sold at a "premium" price.
- Competitive threats are a function of how you rate on benefits versus your competitor *today*, and that's subject to change. A channel benefit

analysis can help you beat the competition tomorrow, even if your product is not noticeably superior to theirs.

Once filled in, this information can be put to several strategic uses:

- It can help you find out why sales tend to cluster in one segment to the exclusion of others. For example, if you have poor post-sale service and you sell computer equipment and peripherals, you may have a hard time selling to home and student buyers who are unable to service their own equipment.
- It can give you an idea for a new channel opportunity to build sales to an under-served segment (viz., Zappos.com's purchase of 6pm.com to appeal to the less benefit-sensitive but more price-sensitive buyer). By so doing, you open the possibility of locking out competition that otherwise would fight with you on the basis of price alone for these sales.
- It can alert you to commonalities among segments that you previously thought were totally distinct. Home and student computer/peripherals buyers may share enough similarities that you can serve both with only minor variations on a single channel theme.

Finally, the benefits *demanded* by your end-users are also *produced* jointly by you and your partners through the design and management of the channel. You cannot know what functions should be engaged in, and at what level, by you and your partners without first knowing what end-users expect from you in the way of benefits. The goal of the Channel Benefits Analysis is therefore to reveal how your current channels excel in serving certain segments, and fall short in serving others, on each specific benefit. This information can be used to modify just one or a few benefits for a channel serving a segment that is falling short; to make major changes in your channels' work flow; and even to analyze how your competitors are doing and the threats they may pose. The next chapter discusses the work of the channel and how to harness your and your partners' efforts to create a benefit bundle suitable for each target segment.

Chapter 5: WHAT FUNCTIONS AND COSTS ARE THE RESPONSIBILITY OF EACH CHANNEL MEMBER?

Darren, an area sales manager at a leading B2B flooring company, has just been told that he must convince his distributors to accept a new flooring product developed by his company and targeted at the existing B2B customer base. The good news is that the product is superior to the legacy product. The bad news is that Darren's company wants to recover its substantial R&D costs by raising distributor wholesale prices (thus increasing the manufacturer's gross margin) while requiring distributors to maintain their service levels and list price (thus decreasing distributors' gross margins). The company refuses to raise list prices, hoping to achieve fast penetration of the new product.

This situation is not uncommon to many channel settings. How should Darren go about convincing his distributors that it is in their best interest to enthusiastically adopt and sell the new product, and combatting the suspicion that Darren's company is just asking them to do more for less? This dilemma cannot be solved without an understanding of channel functions, which are the activities and processes that channel members engage in to create and deliver the desired channel benefits at the right place and time.

In this chapter, we will introduce you to the five most commonly valued channel functions and to a key concept we refer to as the Equity Rule, i.e. paying partners what they are worth. Then we'll demonstrate how these ideas must be incorporated into channel negotiations in order for Darren, or any other channel strategist, to induce partners to do the work required for successful sales.

What is the Work of the Channel?

We have already discussed how to diagnose channel benefit demands: *how, not just what,* customers want to buy. The next step is to organize channel activities to create and deliver these benefits, as discussed in Chapter 3. As an example, imagine wanting to drive a car to attend a concert, restaurant, or sporting event in a crowded city. The "product" the patron wants to buy is a parking space for their car for the evening. But not all parking spaces are valued equally. The most highly valued channel benefits for this occasion are likely to be proximity to the venue (near to versus far from the garage), customer service (supervision of the vehicle while parked and retrieval upon demand), and short wait (timeliness of access at the end of the evening). While the patron can use a public parking garage (a "do it yourself" channel), valet parking is often preferred because of these benefits.

The valet activity thus creates value, but it is costly for the restaurant or theater to provide. However, the channel strategist who can figure out how to cover these costs while providing valet parking benefits to customers at a price they are willing to pay increases the overall value of this entertainment option to patrons with many options from which to choose.

This simple example, providing a valued activity or service at an acceptable and profitable price, illustrates the job of the channel, and it is the heart of understanding channel functions. Concert venues, restaurants, or sports arenas may not want to become specialists in parking cars – this might require investments in multilevel garages and training of certified individuals to drive the cars. An intermediary that can create efficiencies in this activity and thus offer it to the venue operator at a lower cost will be able to participate profitably in this channel.

Many channel members are capable of providing a wide range of channel operations. Understanding the nature of these activities and their associated costs allows you to:
- Diagnose where the channel is falling short in creating customer channel benefit value, which lets you
- Begin to identify potential functional solutions in your channel strategy

The Necessary Functions: SIFCO

Channel members can contribute to the production of valued channel benefits through their specific operations and value-added activities, flows, or *functions*. Five generic functions describe the work that must be done to take a product to market: (i) Sales/Promotion, (ii) Inventory Holding/Transport, (iii) Financing, (iv) Contracting/Relationship Management, and (v) Ordering/Payment. We refer to these functions collectively by their acronym, SIFCO. In addition to these five channel functional categories, another type of cost pervades channel operations: *Risk*. Table 5-1 below defines these categories.

Table 5-1:
Channel Functions and Their Costs

Channel Function	Costly Activity	Costs Incurred
Sales/Promotion	Communication activities designed to increase awareness, educate, and build brand equity	Field sales and sales management, advertising, consumer and trade promotion, PR, trade shows
Inventory Holding/Transport	Storage of and transportation of goods between channel members; holding title to goods	Storage, delivery, and inventory carrying costs
Financing	Underwriting the costs of delayed payment, loans to channel partners and end-users, equipment/training financing	Credit terms, terms and conditions of sale
Contracting/ Relationship Management	Contract design, negotiation of terms of business, use of legal counsel, relationship management investments	Time and legal costs; personnel costs for skilled bidders and associated IT systems; account management costs
Ordering/Payment	Completion of purchase order and all arrangements for payment made by seller and buyer	Order-processing costs (accounts receivable/payable), investments in just-in-time information systems, late payment collections costs, bad debt costs
Risk	Uncertainty in any of the SIFCO functions, e.g. unpredictable sales response; inventory loss; bad debt write-offs; uncertain negotiation/bidding outcomes; stochastic payout on price guarantees, warranties, and insurance	Insurance costs (if insure against bad event) or self-insurance costs (if bad event occurs)

Importantly, each channel activity creates a cost, and these costs should inform the compensation of channel members who create the desired benefits, in order to preserve their motivation. Such costs can be measured through an activity-based costing process.

Sales/Promotion These are all activities that increase liking or attraction, education, and purchase intention toward the product(s) being sold. Thus, the cost of running a sales force (whether inside the manufacturer's firm or in a distributor or retailer) falls in this category, as do advertising, consumer/trade promotion, public relations, and trade shows. Note that most channels are easily able to distinguish sales force costs from advertising or consumer/trade promotion costs; indeed, these activities are frequently managed in different divisions or departments of the company and therefore operate under distinct budgets. When this distinction is observable, we suggest that the channel auditor separate out the functions into their sub-parts, in order to facilitate budget allocation and productivity assessments. Clearly, the sales/promotion function category is frequently shared among more than one channel partner: for example, franchisors often charge franchisees an advertising royalty but match the advertising budget dollar for dollar, implying a 50-50 split in bearing the cost of advertising.

> *Channel functions not only contribute to the production of valued channel benefits, but also carry an associated cost.*

Inventory Holding/Transport This is a collection of costly activities involved with holding and moving products. Warehouse costs to hold a finished product and trucking or rail costs to move it to a retailer's distribution center are classic examples of this category.

Even in the sale of services there are inventory holding costs, such as the cost in the insurance industry to collect, curate, and maintain current data on each insured customer, their level of insurance coverage, claims, payments, and resulting adjustments in premiums. If the insurer sells through a set of independent insurance agents, this curation and maintenance of the database (a key element of running the business) typically resides with the insurer, although each agent may hold separate information on his or her clients. Further, the channel member that holds *title* to the goods (or information) bears a cost in the inventory holding/transport category, namely the opportunity cost of the money tied up in the inventory which could otherwise be put to other productive use. Note that ownership/title need not travel through the channel with the physical movement of product; *consignment selling* means that the upstream provider (e.g. manufacturer) retains title to a product even as it moves through the channel to downstream partners such as retailers. In such selling situations, title passes hands only when the product is ultimately sold to an end-user.

Financing These are any channel costs incurred when one member allows another to delay paying for a benefit or product received. For example, a manufacturer that allows its wholesalers 30 days to pay an invoice is financing those wholesalers, who can invest the money for a full month after acquiring the manufacturer's goods. Retailers like Wal-Mart are known for their ability to make money on financing terms from upstream suppliers, because they are so adept at demand forecasting that they turn their inventory faster than the payment terms.

Because financing (like other channel functions) is costly, upstream sellers often offer early-payment discounts to encourage shifting the financing function onto the buyer's shoulders. For example, a 3 percent discount for payment within 10 days (rather than the maximum 30 days) is known as a "3-10 net 30" offer. The manufacturer is not the only channel member that can perform this type of financing; specialist intermediaries like credit card companies or PayPal do so in the online channel world, and without their financing services, e-commerce could not flow as freely as it does today.

Contracting/Relationship Management These costs refer to legal and negotiation fees incurred in the course of doing business. For example, some B2B sales are made through a "Request For Proposal" (RFP) process, where the buyer (e.g. a government) solicits sellers to bid to provide services or products. Companies seeking this business generally employ specialists who are expert in bidding, proposal preparation, and post-proposal negotiation to close the deal; the cost of these experts' services falls under contracting/relationship management.

Other costs in this category include those that help maintain good channel relationships, such as the costs of key account managers (KAMs)[11] who may work with channel intermediaries when serving a multi-regional customer.

Ordering/Payment This comprises all expenses incurred in consummating a sale, once the customer has stated the intention to buy. While this may seem a pedestrian channel function, investments in information technology have greatly automated the ordering and payment functions so that payment can be received when a truck delivers a shipment to a consignee's warehouse – instead of after a paper invoice is generated, mailed to the buyer, then processed through accounts payable.

Third-party companies may facilitate these processes. For example, Paymode is an independent company facilitating payments between payers and vendors. Payers benefit from adopting Paymode through increased efficiency of accounts payable activities, increased payment security, lowered fraud risk, reduction in paper billing, and increased control over payment timing. Vendors benefit from accepting payments this way due to greater security and speed in payment, availability of reports on all payments made in the past as well as the present, and easy enrollment through a Web portal.[12]

Finally, *Risk* includes channel costs owing to imperfect predictability. It is not possible to perfectly predict the success of a sales initiative; to be sure whether or when product will be subject to theft, fire, or other loss out of inventory; to know ahead of time what proportion of products sold into the channel will be returned for a manufacturer refund; to predict when renegotiation of sales terms will be necessary; or to know which buyers will be late in making payments or ultimately fail to pay. The cost of these risks can be estimated by pricing out an insurance policy to protect against such bad events, with the insurance premium being a measure of the cost of risk.

As an alternative to buying insurance against these potential events, some channel managers choose to "self-insure," that is to invest in technologies and processes to reduce the risk of engaging in channel activities that could result in bad events. For example, sales tracking and demand forecasting models can improve predictions of seasonalized unit sales and returns, thus improving the management of inventory holding costs. Channel managers can assess the benefits and costs of outsourcing the risk management function to an insurance company versus seeking to manage channel risks on their own.

Autotrader: Monetizing Function Bundles

Functions are so critical to building effective routes to market that their effects can be seen in firms' market valuations. As an example, what do you think the market valuation would be for a firm that simply executed the functions of sales/promotion, ordering, payment, and negotiations? The answer is $7 billion, and the name of the firm is Autotrader, a key intermediary in the used car industry. Used cars represent a $363 billion industry in the U.S. – representing 68% of all vehicles sold annually. This enormous number of transactions must be executed cost-effectively by an intermediary like Autotrader, given that neither used car and fleet sellers nor retail outlets are interested in managing these functions.

Understanding the role and need for channel functions is critical to any firm's go-to-market strategy. Some of the best-known and best-capitalized intermediary firms are able to capture substantial market shares simply by providing valued channel functions: online travel agent Priceline's market capitalization, for example, has exceeded $60 billion.

> *Understanding the role and need for channel functions is critical to any firm's go to market strategy. Some of the best-known and best-capitalized intermediary firms are able to capture substantial market shares simply by providing valued channel functions.*

Solving Darren's Dilemma

Let's now return to Darren's distribution dilemma. The first things Darren needs to understand are (1) what function costs distributors would bear with the new B2B flooring product, (2) how they compare to function costs for the legacy product, and (3) how the overall distributor profit from handling the new product could exceed profit on the legacy product. At the same time, Darren must not lose sight of linkages between functional performance and the generation of benefits to prospective customers. The two channel functions Darren focuses on are those whose performance diverges most widely from those in the legacy channel, as they will be critical in the customer's perceived value of the new product and will directly impact product launch.

Sales/promotion – Since the new product will be superior to the legacy product, it is important for these benefits to be communicated through education and messaging; this could be accomplished by the sales force as well as through additional communication efforts such as trade shows, advertising, etc.

Risk – The new product will essentially replace the legacy product. For intermediaries who have relied on the legacy product as a source of revenue, that profit stream will be eliminated altogether. The inability to provide a comparable or better product to downstream customers, or to round out a product line, represents a serious financial risk to intermediaries.

Beyond these functions, Darren understands that his distributors will be concerned about *inventory holding* to the extent that they will need to dispose of the legacy product as the new product takes hold; *contracting* issues as they pertain to agreements not just about wholesale and list prices, but about who will do what parts of the work of the channel; and, as always in the normal course of business, *ordering and payment* for the new product (although this should be analogous to practices for the legacy product).

Darren's company's short-term focus on recovering R&D costs while aggressively pushing the new product to its B2B customers is not uncommon in many such situations. However, given the company's reliance on independent distributors, a longer-term financial performance focus may lead to better channel support and long-term results. Although this could require the company to reallocate some of its proposed "distributor margin squeeze," it helps to preserve their incentives to continue participating in key channel functions in the future.

Additionally, if the benefits of this new product are superior to those of competitors, flooring demand and product volumes for Darren's company should increase. With the possibility of larger sales, Darren can communicate the possibility of higher *overall* revenue and profit from selling the new product over time (even if unit margins are lower). Further, a truly superior new product will drive out older and weaker versions of Darren's as well as competitors' products. Darren needs to convince his distributors that the true benchmark in agreeing to distribute the new product is the new norm that will prevail in the market – not today's sales, market share, and profits.

For Darren, it is critical to estimate the loss that will be incurred if distributors do nothing or lose the legacy revenue streams; this is the correct benchmark against which the new product's attractiveness should be assessed. By understanding the channel functions and costs incurred by distributors, Darren also communicates his company's commitment to their welfare, not just to his own, and rationalizes how benefits and margins are currently allocated between his company and downstream intermediaries.

Additionally, if sales/promotion costs are likely to increase (at least during the launch phase), Darren can increase acceptance of the new product among his distributors by clearly communicating the types and amounts of promotional costs that the manufacturer will take on. For example, Darren's company plans on covering all trade show promotional costs, and has developed extensive training materials and promotional brochures to facilitate distributor sales reps' abilities to promote the new product. Communicating these commitments will convey a strong (and costly) commitment to the distributors and to the new product launch.

In sum, by reorienting the distribution channel's mindset from short- to long-term and conducting a function analysis that accounts for the manufacturer's and intermediaries' costs and value creation, channel members can understand why taking less in the short-run can be outweighed by the long-term benefits of a channel captain's new-product launch strategy.

By reorienting the distribution channel's mindset from short- to long-term and conducting a function analysis that accounts for the manufacturer's and intermediaries' costs and value creation, channel members can understand why taking less in the short-run can be outweighed by the long-term benefits of a channel captains new-product launch strategy.

As it turns out, Darren's distributors were not aware of the costs associated with the various functions that they or Darren performed, nor did they fully allocate overhead costs over time. When they understood Darren's company's costs associated with training workshops and with advertising and trade shows accompanying the product's launch, distributors were better able to appreciate the manufacturer's role in supporting the channel.

Darren worked with his distributors to better understand the information they received on customers, and together they were able to develop market share estimates of the impact of this new product on competitors, as well as their possible reactions. In fact, distributors offered Darren more and better data to help sharpen his estimates. This type of buy-in would be impossible without an analysis and understanding of the role of channel functions and costs incurred by all members.

Functions and Strategic Channel Design

Three important rules apply to the concept of channel functions:

1. Anyone can supply a function – functions may be performed either by one channel member (a specialist) or by multiple members (in tandem or in sequence). No one split of functions is always right; the channel strategist must assess how many channel members, and which ones, should be involved in the performance of each function.
2. Functions can be disaggregated and dispersed – channel members may specialize in performing one or more functions and may not participate at all in the performance of others. Thus, these activities and processes may reside among multiple members at multiple levels of the channel.
3. Channel functions are necessary for the creation of channel value – while it may be tempting to remove a particular partner from the channel because it implies reclaiming a financial margin, one must remember that the activities cannot be eliminated, unless they are already provided by other members… or unless those activities are wasteful. This implies an Equity Rule: it is worthwhile to pay a channel member for the worth and value it creates through performance of any costly, but valued, channel function.

When the cost of SIFCO functions of sales/promotion and risk are properly assessed, the channel manager can make better decisions about how to allocate activities among channel members; how to properly reward members for taking responsibility for the performance of costly functions; when to reduce one or more functions; and when to add a new member to an existing channel in order to improve function at a reduced cost. The analysis is not trivial, because it ideally involves the equivalent of an activity-based costing (ABC) analysis *across all channel members* (much more difficult than an ABC within a factory!). However, even an imperfect assessment of channel function performance by all partners can enable the manager to improve productivity and efficiency, while maintaining (or improving) customer satisfaction. Channel function costs can be estimated from analogous activities in your own firm or industry, e.g. the cost of transport or storage. Be willing to share information with your channel partners so that they understand the value of the work you do and the cost of the functions you perform.

> *Comparing a current vs. a zero-based channel structure identifies what flows need improvement, and what the optimal channel structure should be.*

Finally, because of the cost associated with performing channel flows, it is important not to perform *unnecessarily* high levels of any of them. Knowing what channel benefits are demanded by target end-users, and at what level of intensity, helps the manager control the total cost of running the channel, using only those functions that create valued benefits.

The Zero-Based Channel Structure

A channel function analysis is a necessary step in identifying the "zero-based channel structure," which is the route to market with the minimal cost for meeting customer demands for channel benefits. This is the nirvana of channel design – a route to market that efficiently performs needed functions, creating channel benefits at the right place and time and at the lowest possible cost. Who could ask for more?

Chapter 6: HOW TO AUDIT THE WORK OF THE CHANNEL?

This chapter uses the information on channel functions from Chapter 5 to outline a process to audit the work you and your partners do in each channel on the way to market. We discuss the purpose of such an audit and then delve into the process. The case of Darren, seeking to sell a new flooring product, is continued to show how you can use an audit in your own design and negotiation processes.

Elements and Purpose of a Function Audit

Chapter 5 discussed channel functions, the costly activities undertaken by you and your partners that result in channel benefits. The generic list of such functions can (and should) be customized to your particular situation when you conduct an audit. Note that any given function may be performed by just one channel member or shared by more than one – there is no one-to-one mapping from a function to a member's responsibility.

Auditing the work of your channels will help you discover and encode:

- Who is doing what function(s) in the channel
- The share of the combined cost and value for which each member is responsible
- Whether each channel member is being fairly compensated for their performance.

Your audit will result in:

- A clearer, analysis-based allocation of profits among channel members (rather than an *ad hoc* set of arguments)
- Recommendations regarding any alteration of the profit split
- Recommendations regarding future emphasis on the performance of particular functions.

A separate audit should be completed for each channel in your go-to-market system (e.g. independent distributors for some accounts and an employee sales force for others constitute two different channels and should be analyzed separately).

Steps in Your Function Audit

An audit of the work of your channel should proceed as follows:

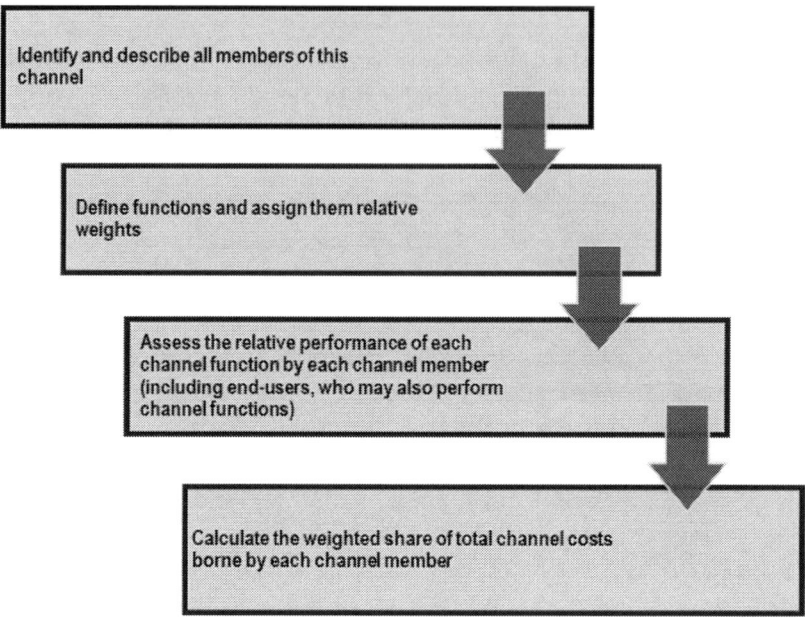

**Figure 6-1:
Channel Function Audit Process**

Identify and Describe Channel Members

The list of all channel members in a specific channel includes all entities that perform costly channel functions that (presumably) contribute to the creation of valued benefits for end-users. The manufacturer, distributors, wholesalers, sales rep firms, brokers, and retailers are obvious candidates for this list, depending on the product or service sold.

Less obvious perhaps are entities like banks or other financing agencies such as PayPal; web-hosting entities like Amazon, Etsy, or eBay; social media platforms like Facebook; enterprise cloud storage providers (*e.g.* HP, Microsoft, IBM, Amazon, or Google); and influential individuals in social media networks (e.g. Ariana Huffington of the *Huffington Post*). Although such entities may not store or move physical inventory in a standard way, and may not even identify themselves as active partners, without their work and the costs they bear other channel members would have to step in and provide those functions. The success and survival of such entities suggests that channel managers have concluded it is less costly or more effective to outsource the financing, data storage, promotion, ordering/payment, and risk management functions to partners than to perform the functions themselves.

When identifying players in the channel, it is therefore useful not only to list them, but also to provide a description and brief commentary on their roles.

Define Functions and Assign Them Relative Weights

The generic list of channel functions (*sales/promotion, inventory holding/transport, financing, contracting/relationship management, ordering/payment* –

SIFCO – plus *Risk*) defined in Chapter 5 should all be accounted for in an audit of the work of your channel. Still, you should customize the list to fit your company and market.

For example, a company selling consumer durables like white goods (washing machines, dryers, and the like) may wish to consider separately the inventory holding costs for the machines themselves versus the holding costs for machine parts used in after-sales service. In this situation, the channel analyst would want to represent *two* types of inventory holding cost functions: one for the original equipment and one for the parts. Further, the analyst might represent the transportation costs for each of these elements as two separate channel functions.

Similarly, it is common to split the *sales/promotion* function into (a) employee sales force costs; (b) distributor or other independent sales force costs; (c) advertising costs; (d) trade promotion costs; (e) end-user [consumer or B2B customer] promotion costs; and (f) trade show costs. One of the reasons the function is so frequently split this way is the financial measurability of the component costs: we have yet to encounter a firm whose finance and accounting data do not distinguish, for instance, between sales force compensation costs and advertising budgets/costs. The general principle, therefore, is to split out measurable costs when you can easily do so, and to tolerate higher levels of cost aggregation when the data are less reliable.

> *The general principle in auditing channel functions is to split out measurable costs when you can easily do so, and to tolerate higher levels of cost aggregation when the data are less reliable.*

Once you define your channel's functions, you can assess the proportion of total channel costs accounted for by each, using a 100-point scale. Thus, inventory holding and transport may account for 30 points out of 100 in a distribution channel moving physical products like grocery or consumable office supplies through one or two intermediary levels, with a turn rate of two or three weeks. Meanwhile, this function's costs when selling a less tangible product such as software apps or video games may account for a much lower proportion of total channel costs.

These proportions cannot always be precisely known, nor is there a database of "usual" proportions across different industries. Indeed, this is one reason we advocate working with a 100-point scale rather than estimating the exact dollar cost of each function across the whole channel. We have found that the 100-point allocation is understandable and easily permits sensitivity analyses. Other scaling mechanisms are of course also possible, for instance assessing each function's proportion of overall channel costs as "Low," "Medium," or "High," then creating a metric to translate these intuitive ratings to quantitative proportions.[13] The importance of either method lies in its estimate of proportion shares for each function's performance, across all members of the channel.

Assess Performance of Channel Functions by Each Member

Ask yourself what proportion of each function's work is borne by each channel member. Again, it is convenient to allocate 100 points. For example, consider a channel consisting of a manufacturer using an independent sales rep to reach small retail accounts for its line of specialty gift products. The independent sales rep acts as the manufacturer's "feet on the street" or sales force – but the rep does not carry inventory, own it, or take responsibility for stocking it in the stores. This means that allocating 100 points among the manufacturer, rep firm, and retailer according to their proportionate shares of the cost of inventory holding/transport will give the rep firm *zero points*, splitting the 100 available points between the manufacturer and retailer according to the days in inventory held by both and the shipping costs borne by each. Note that it is not only permissible to allocate zero points to a channel member in the performance of a given function – it is extremely common to do so.

Further, the consumer or end-user can be considered a channel member for the purpose of performance of channel functions. B2B sales in which the buyer pays earlier than the allowed 30-day payment period, or consumer sales in which the buyer pays with a credit card for items to be shipped in two weeks from an e-tailer, are both examples of the end-user taking on some of the financing function in the channel.

In short, this part of the audit produces a function-by-function assessment of the proportionate shares of work done by each channel member.

Calculate the Share of Total Costs Borne by Each Channel Member

At this point in the audit, the analyst has enumerated the set of relevant channel members; identified the set of functions that comprise the work of this channel; estimated the proportion of channel costs attributable to each function; and estimated the share of each function's cost borne by each member. These data are sufficient to calculate a *weighted average channel cost borne by each channel member*, by multiplying each functional weight by the proportional cost borne, and adding up over the functions for each member.

The sum of all channel members' weighted cost shares will equal 100. What do these numbers signify?

One important criterion for allocating *channel profit shares* is the extent to which each partner shares in bearing channel function costs. On an Equity Rule basis, then, the weighted cost shares calculated in your audit suggest what proportion of channel profits (equal to total channel revenues minus the cost of goods sold minus the costs of all functions) each channel member *should* get – that is, each partner's expected profit share given the current channel structure. To get a good idea of the allocation of profits among channel members, you need to do a sophisticated analysis on the order of activity-based costing.

> One important criterion for allocating channel profit shares is the extent to which each partner shares in bearing channel function costs.

Note that the *normative* profit share may or may not equal the member's *actual* profit share. And when these two numbers are not equal, you need to ask why. Inequality between normative and actual profit shares can arise because:

- Profits are misallocated in the channel and should be recalculated
- Competitive conditions force a channel member to take a lower profit share than its normative performance would indicate; its "economic rents" were essentially competed away in the market
- External constraints such as government regulation confer economic rents on a member, above and beyond its performance of channel functions.

A Function Audit of Darren's Flooring Distribution Channel

Darren's channel challenge is to convince distributors to carry his company's new, lower-gross-margin industrial flooring product. How he analyzes and solves the problem illustrates the importance of the audit process.

Darren's Baseline Situation and What He Knows

You'll recall from Chapter 5 that Darren is an area sales manager at a leading B2B flooring company that has just commercialized a new flooring product superior to the company's legacy product. However, the company has decreed that the wholesale price for the new product will be higher than for the legacy product, while keeping list prices constant. Darren faces a classic challenge: to convince distributors to adopt and support the new product, despite its lower gross margin vis-à-vis the legacy product.

Darren knows certain facts about the situation:

- His distributors are not "finance-savvy"; he has discovered that they do not fully allocate overhead costs, viewing these as overhead but not attributable to any product
- Distributors are uninformed about the volume potential for the new product: will it simply cannibalize Darren's company's legacy product, or will it grab additional market share from competitors?
- Distributors' benchmark when considering new opportunities is the current situation (today), so any new proposal typically has to be viewed as superior to the current market situation to be appealing
- Darren's distributors are unaware of the channel function costs borne by Darren's company on the legacy product
- The distributors are also unaware of the incremental channel costs that Darren's company plans to bear in conjunction with the launch of the new product – namely, increased advertising and trade-show activity and increased training of its own and distributors' sales forces.

Darren realizes that convincing distributors to carry the new product will hinge on understanding the distribution channel costs they will bear for the new product (versus those for the legacy product), the value-adding costs his company will bear, and the ultimate profit a distributor will reap (taking volume, not just margin, into account) from adopting the new product.

Darren's Analysis

The first task in Darren's audit of his channel is to identify its members. Darren's company goes to market through only one channel – using independent distributors to reach the B2B flooring customer, who typically owns or operates an industrial warehouse. This is shown in Table 6-1 below:

Table 6-1:
Channel Member Identification:
Darren's Industrial Flooring Example

Channel Member Name	Description of Member
Manufacturer	Darren's industrial flooring company; Darren is an Area Sales Manager
Independent Distributor	Darren focuses first on a "beta test site" top distributor
B2B Flooring Customer	Industrial warehouse owner/operator

Darren chooses to focus his efforts first on one of his best distributor partners, a top seller he thinks of as his "beta test site" for communications efforts. Notice that the end-user – here, the flooring customer – is a channel member for the purposes of auditing costs in Darren's channel. You can add as many rows as necessary to include all such functional partners in another analysis.

Next, Darren needs to define the costly functions in his channel and allocate weights to them, to apportion out the total cost of distribution. He is not certain of all the costs the distributor bears, but with a little investigation he has come across an industry association report on distributor productivity that gives him some basis from which to add his distributor's activity costs to his own. The result is presented in Table 6-2:

Table 6-2:
Proportionate Function Costs:
Darren's Industrial Flooring Example

Channel Function	Cost Represented	% of Total Cost Accounted for by this Function
S/ Sales force effort	Sales calls, sales support & overhead costs	25
S/ Trade Shows	Booth, personnel costs	10
S/ Training	Train salespeople, installers	15
I/ Inventory mgt.	Inventory holding costs, transport to distributors and customers	25
F/ Financing	Offering of payment terms	5
C/ Negotiation	Price setting and negotiation of terms	5
O/ Ordering and payment	Usual ordering/payment activities	10
R/ Risk	(Probable) costs of pilferage, loss of inventory, risk of installation failures, etc.	5
TOTAL		100

Darren separates the sales/promotion function into three components: sales force costs (both his and his distributor's); trade show costs; and training costs. He estimates that these jointly account for 50 percent of distribution costs, and that when inventory management is added on, a full 75 percent of distribution channel costs are accounted for. Other functions tend to be routine and relatively low-cost.

Darren then assesses the proportion of each function's cost borne by each channel member (Darren's company, the distributor, and the B2B flooring customer). Note that both sets – the channel members and functions – must match what has already been noted, in order for the audit to be coherent. Table 6-3 reports Darren's assessments:

Table 6-3:
Relative Cost of Each Function Borne by Each Member:
Darren's Industrial Flooring Example

Function	Manufacturer (Darren's company)	Distributor	B2B Flooring Customer	TOTAL
S/ Sales force effort	30	70	0	100
S/ Trade Shows	100	0	0	100
S/ Training	100	0	0	100
I/ Inventory mgt.	50	50	0	100
F/ Financing	50	50	0	100
C/ Negotiation	25	50	25	100
O/ Ordering and payment	16	42	42	100
R/ Risk	20	80	0	100

Darren determines that the distributor is responsible for the lion's share (70 percent) of all sales force effort in the channel, as well as being a majority (80 percent) risk-bearer. Darren's company bears all costs of trade shows and sales force training. Darren estimates that he and his distributor equally share the costs of inventory management, given that both carry about the same number of days' worth of inventory at any given time. He estimates equal shares for financing costs as well, because Darren provides financing terms to his distributor, who in turn provides similar terms to its B2B customers. The distributor, he estimates, carries twice the costs of negotiation because of its two-sided negotiation tasks. Finally, ordering and payment costs are equal for the distributor and customer, since each has to order from the upstream channel member, while Darren's company's share of this function is much smaller.

Now Darren has all the necessary data to calculate the weighted share of total channel costs borne by his firm, his distributor, and the B2B flooring customer. He combines the information from Tables 6-1, 6-2, and 6-3 into Table 6-4 as follows:

Table 6-4:
Channel Functions / Cost Borne, Summary:
Darren's Industrial Flooring Example

Function	% Total Costs Accounted for by this Function	Manufacturer (Darren's company)	Distributor	B2B Flooring Customer
S/ Sales force effort	25	30	70	0
S/ Trade Shows	10	100	0	0
S/ Training	15	100	0	0
I/ Inventory mgt.	25	50	50	0
F/ Financing	5	50	50	0
C/ Negotiation	5	25	50	25
O/ Ordering and payment	10	16	42	42
R/ Risk	5	20	80	0
TOTAL WEIGHTED COST SHARE BORNE:		51.35%	43.20%	5.45%

The total weighted cost share borne by Darren's company is calculated to be 51.35 percent; for the distributor, 43.2 percent; and for the B2B flooring customer, 5.45 percent. Each percentage is the weighted average of the function cost weight, multiplied by the channel member's proportionate cost-bearing in that function.[14] This analysis shows that while Darren's company bears a bit more than half the total cost of channel functions, the distributor is a very strong partner with responsibility for over 40 percent of channel costs.

Darren's Insights from the Function Audit

Darren's audit provides immediate information for him to share with his distributor about the work that his company will be doing to support the launch of the new flooring product, and how costly that work will be. Darren can point out that any incremental distributor sales/promotion costs during product launch will coincide with Darren's company's promotional launch costs. For example, Darren's company plans to cover all trade show promotional costs, and has developed extensive training materials and promotional brochures to facilitate distributor sales reps' abilities to promote the new product. These activities constitute a credible and costly commitment to the channel and to the new product launch. Sharing this information with his distributors makes clear that it is not only they, but also Darren's company, that are asked to bear the costs of the launch.[15]

This analysis is also a good opportunity for Darren to communicate the financial realities of channel efforts to his distributors. They may not be "finance-savvy," but seeing an analysis of the work of the channel and its concomitant costs can help a distributor understand how to manage these costs better – and how to assess a vendor partner like Darren against other vendors.

Beyond the pure analysis here, Darren needs to convince his distributors that a smaller gross margin per square foot of flooring is actually reasonable. After all, the new product will essentially replace the legacy product, eliminating its revenue and profit stream for distributors. Darren's proposal thus imposes an apparently serious financial risk to his distributors. Darren must therefore move beyond the percentage-focused analysis presented here to a total-volume analysis.

> *This analysis is a good opportunity for Darren to communicate the financial realities of channel efforts to his distributors.*

Darren's company has tested its new product against both its own legacy product and the products of competitors, and has established the new product's superiority. Once this is understood in the market, flooring demand and product volumes for Darren's company are predicted to increase. Darren therefore can make the argument to his distributors that while the gross margin per unit will decrease, total volume of Darren's company's products will increase – both from earlier replacement purchases by customers attracted to its superior performance, and from acquisition of new customers who have previously bought from a competitor. In short, the superior new product is expected to drive out others currently commanding sales in the market.

The corollary of this insight is that *the proper benchmark is not "today" but rather the "tomorrow" that a distributor will experience if it does **not** adopt Darren's new product*. It is the new norm, not current sales, market share, or profits, which distributors must recognize as the appropriate benchmark against which to weigh Darren's offer.

By understanding the channel functions and costs incurred by distributors, Darren also communicates his company's commitment to the welfare of his distributors, not just of his company alone, and rationalizes the way benefits and margins are currently allocated between his company and downstream intermediaries.

The distributor's positive reaction to Darren's message noted in Chapter 5 stems from two main sources. First, the beta-test distributor is impressed that Darren's company would care enough about the financial health of a distributor to even attempt this sort of channel functional cost analysis on its behalf. And second, the distributor understands in objective terms – rather than from an emotional, non-quantitative and possibly coercive approach – the implication of the offer for his distributorship. Changing the distributor's point of view by changing his benchmark calculation makes it clear to the distributor that staying in the present is not a realistic option; rather, adopting the superior product, even with lower gross margins, is the best option given future volume increases and cost-sharing from the manufacturer.

In sum, by altering the distribution channel's focus from short- to long-term and providing a function analysis that accounts for both the manufacturer's and intermediaries' costs and value creation, Darren helps channel members better understand why taking less in the short-run can offer long-term benefits.

Summary: What Can We Learn From a Function Audit?

This audit of the work of the channel lets the channel manager consider several structural channel questions more objectively and quantitatively than would be possible without such an analysis:

- Which channel member is doing most of the work of the channel? If that is not us but another channel member, should we be concerned about over-dependence on their performance to get our product to market?
- How many and which functions are characterized by specialization, in the sense that only one channel member performs this function? If this channel member fails to carry out their designated functions, what backstop must we have in place to avert disaster in our go-to-market strategy?
- Are the weighted cost shares borne by channel members consistent with the relative channel profits earned by each? That is, does the Equity Rule hold, and is each channel member paid what they're worth? If not, why not?
- What changes in allocation of work among our current partners should we consider that would decrease overall channel costs and/or increase benefit levels offered to buyers?
- What changes in channel structure (i.e. in the identities of channel partners) could we consider that would lead to these same benefits?

Importantly, even if the information used for the audit is not perfect, the analysis is still worthwhile. Perfect data about all channel costs is an ideal but not a reality in nearly all real-world situations. The channel audit provides a baseline from which to consider alternative scenarios. It also fosters further analysis that can fine-tune initial estimates with better data, as in the example of Darren's distributor. And it makes explicit to all channel members what the work of the channel is, which elements of that work each of them participates in (and to what extent), and the costs involved.

> *Importantly, even if the information used for the function audit is not perfect, the analysis is still worthwhile.*

The discussion thus far has centered on auditing the work of your current channel. You can also analyze the *zero-based channel*, which is the channel that meets end-users' demands for benefits at minimum cost (i.e., the optimal channel design). The zero-based analysis may exhibit several differences in appearance from the current channel's analysis, viz.:

- The function weights may not be the same in both analyses. You may conclude that an optimally-designed channel involves running warehouses more efficiently; thus, the cost-based weight on inventory holding will drop in the zero-based analysis as compared to the current analysis.
- The ratings in the two analyses may also differ. If more efficient warehousing means that your distributor (who specializes in state-of-the-art warehouse management) takes over inventory holding, the inventory holding function percentages will shift toward the distributor and away from the manufacturer.
- The column headings themselves may be different in the two analyses. If you decide, for instance, that more efficient inventory handling can only be accomplished by bringing a logistics expert into your channel, the zero-based analysis will have one more channel member than the current analysis.

It can be a very insightful exercise to analyze both a zero-based channel and your current one. The contrast can serve as a roadmap for you in planning how to improve the internal workings of your marketing channel, in effect closing misalignments in the design and performance of key channel functions.

Ultimately, auditing the work of the channel can be a good catalyst for conversation across channel members, as we see with Darren and his distributor (which offered to improve the analysis with its own data on distributor activities). An audit can move the conversation about changing margins, functions, and responsibilities away from the emotional and toward the rational.

Chapter 7: HOW CAN YOU ALIGN CHANNEL ACTIVITIES AND BENEFITS?

Up to now, we have developed a tool set for identifying and understanding (1) the channel benefits that customers demand and (2) the channel functions that must be supplied in order for value to be created. These are the critical first steps. The next step is an *alignment analysis*, to systematically evaluate where, when, and how those benefits and functions are improperly matched.

In short, channel value creation rests on the *resolution of the differences* between the benefits demanded and those supplied through the channel's costly functional activities. Identifying and aligning the appropriate functions and benefits is the necessary first step toward developing a *zero-based channel strategy* (involving the minimum cost incurred to meet customer demands) – in other words, the optimal channel offering.

A channel alignment analysis will lead you to ask the following key questions of your current strategy:

- *Where are the redundancies?* Are there likely to be any redundant activities? Which of them could be eliminated to result in the lowest cost for the entire system, without compromising the delivery of valued benefits? E.g., could good transportation make it possible to eliminate some inventory holding depots in the system, without slowing down delivery time?
- *Where is reorganization needed?* Is there a way to eliminate, redefine, reallocate, or combine certain tasks in order to minimize the steps in a sale or reduce its cycle time? E.g., can customer information be centralized so that all channel members can find it in one comprehensive system
- *Where can we cut or modify costs?* Is it possible to automate certain activities in a way that reduces the unit cost of getting products to market, even if this increases fixed costs? E.g., are there opportunities to modify information systems to reduce the costs of prospecting, order entry, or quote generation activities?[16]

Aligning the Channel

Channel alignment occurs when the benefits that buyers demand are efficiently supplied by the channel. Recall that a benefit is *produced* by the costly efforts of one or more members of a channel. Producing a given benefit can require more than one function, and conversely, performing a particular function can affect more than one benefit. Producing or modifying a particular benefit may also involve reallocating responsibilities across members or adding or subtracting members. Thus, aligning benefits with functions can involve multiple partners engaged jointly in multiple functions. That said, the general concept of "Supply = Demand" is still applicable in assessing the degree of channel alignment, as the following discussion of demand- and supply-side (mis)alignment will demonstrate.

Demand-Side (Mis)Alignment: Drugstore.com

Let's consider the demand for benefit "W" (low waiting time) in the shipment of a purchase from drugstore.com. Drugstore.com offers the e-buyer three different wait times, at different prices[17]: (i) 7-day shipping for $5.99; (ii) 2-day shipping for $12.99; or (iii) 1-day shipping for $19.99. Demand-side alignment for W is said to exist if a consumer who chooses 7-day delivery is just willing to pay $5.99 for it; if a consumer who chooses 2-day delivery is just willing to pay $12.99 for it; and if a consumer who chooses 1-day delivery is just willing to pay $19.99 for it.

> *Being able to identify and properly align the appropriate functions so as to create or support the desired benefits is the necessary first step toward developing a zero-based channel strategy.*

Figure 7-1 below illustrates a scenario with three distinct buyer segments. Segment A's willingness to pay is $19.99 for delivery/wait time of up to one day, and zero for any longer delivery/wait time. Segment C's willingness to pay is $5.99 for any delivery/wait time up to 7 days, and zero for any longer wait time. Segment B's willingness to pay is $14.00 for up to 2-day delivery; $5.00 for delivery in more than 2 days but no more than 8-days; and zero for longer delivery/wait times. We could thus think of A as an "urgent" buyer segment; C as a "patient" buyer segment; and B as an "intermediate" buyer segment.

Let's assume that drugstore.com uses state-of-the-art shipping technologies and covers its shipping costs at the fee schedule described above, so that supply-side misalignments are absent. Then the question is whether its shipping fee schedule aligns the channel on the demand side: are consumers willing to buy and do they pay up to their maximum willingness to pay for shipping?

Segments A and C are indeed aligned. Segment A pays $19.99, opts for 1-day shipping, and has no willingness to pay for any other shipping speed – so this shipping fee schedule offers segment A exactly the level of delivery speed its members are happy to buy for the price charged. Similarly, members of segment C are indifferent between 1-day, 2-day, and 7-day shipping – as long as their shipping fees are all no greater than $5.99. Offering 1-day shipping for only $5.99, however, would be inefficient because all segment-A would then also be charged less than their willingness to pay for 1-day shipping (because it is impossible to segregate segment-A from segment-C buyers). Offering 2-day shipping at $5.99 would similarly be inefficient because then segment-B members would opt for it, gaining positive consumer surplus, which would be economically inefficient for drugstore.com. Instead, offering 7-day shipping at $5.99 leaves segment-C members equally happy, charges them what they are willing to pay for this delivery speed, and does not "leave money on the table" that drugstore.com could charge other buyer segments for faster shipping speeds.

The story is a bit different for segment B. Clearly these consumers are not willing to pay the 1-day delivery fee of $19.99 (their willingness to pay for 1-day delivery is only $14.00); they are also not willing to pay the 7-day fee of $5.99 (their willingness to pay for 7-day delivery is only $5.00). They are happy to opt for 2-day delivery at the quoted $12.99 fee. However, this is not an aligned shipping fee because it *undercharges* relative to segment B's $14.00 willingness to pay. A segment-specific demand-side gap in delivery speed is evident: money is left on the table for this segment.[18]

Figure 7-1:
(Mis)Alignment in drugstore.com's Delivery Offering in the e-Channel

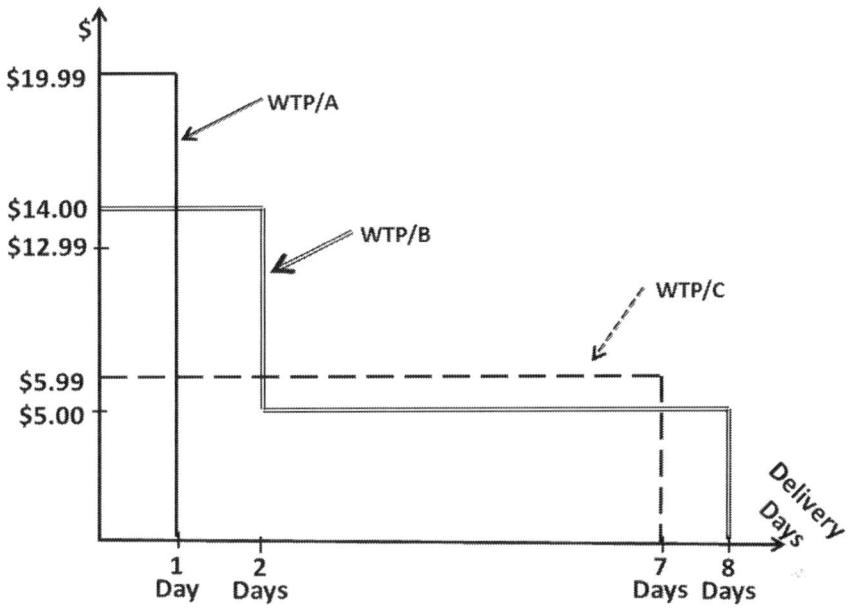

Now, imagine that drugstore.com drops the 2-day delivery option and offers only 1-day delivery or 7-day delivery, still at fees of $19.99 and $5.99, respectively. How is demand-side channel alignment on the provision of this channel benefit affected by such a change? Segments A and C are unaffected, because 2-day delivery was not a preferred option in our first scenario. But segment B consumers are now left with *no* delivery option for which they are willing to pay, leaving drugstore.com with a new and different demand-side misalignment on the delivery/wait time channel benefit dimension. Segment-B consumers who find themselves in this position may value attractive delivery speed highly enough that they turn to competitive sellers rather than buy from drugstore.com. Thus, misaligned channel benefit levels can not only leave buyers dissatisfied with a seller, but can lead to lost sales.

Demand-side misalignments should be carefully attributed to the *correct channel benefit*, as well as to the *specific channel segment affected*. The channel value proposition that is right for one target segment need not be right for all – for example, not all drugstore.com shoppers are "urgent" buyers like those in segment

A, so offering 1-day delivery to all consumers would simply introduce a supply-side misalignment due to over-provision of delivery speed to buyers in segments B and C. Further, if drugstore.com also offered too narrow an assortment of products for the tastes of segment-A consumers, perfection in the provision of delivery speed at an acceptable price would not fully align the channel because a different key channel benefit would be under-supplied. Thus, correct identification of demand-side misalignments requires a matrix approach as in Table 7-1 below:

Table 7-1:
Encoding Demand-Side Misalignments by
{Segment x Channel Benefit}

Identify Segment names and specific Channel Benefits. Then, enter degree of alignment of each benefit for each segment below, where "over"=over-provision; "under"=under-provision; "aligned"=no misalignment			
Benefit:	Segment A	Segment B	Segment C
1			
2			
3			
4			
5			

Supply-Side (Mis)Alignment

Our drugstore.com example demonstrates that channel alignment is achieved on the demand side when buyers are willing to pay for the benefit level provided and when the charge for this benefit does not leave money on the table. Beyond these demand-side insights, when the channel's functional performance produces the benefits demanded at *minimum cost,* then there are also no supply-side misalignments. We then say that the channel is *zero-based*.

However, real-world channels tend to over-supply (or under-price) some key functions and benefits, while under-supplying (or over-pricing) others, because alignment requires good information on segmented demands for channel benefits and a match with the costs of providing them – research data that many firms and channels do not invest in.

Over-supply can imply that the costs of offering a particular channel benefit are higher than they have to be or that the channel benefit offer is under-priced (or both), which often means that at least some members are not receiving a level of profit that adequately compensates them. Over-supply is not generally accompanied by a great enough increase in consumer satisfaction to be worth the cost incurred or the revenue foregone.

When over-supply or under-pricing characterizes multiple functions in the channel, the *total cost* of performing all needed functions jointly is generally higher than a proper demand-side analysis would indicate. However, if one function is performed at an unusually high cost, the channel is not necessarily misaligned – as long as this higher single-function cost minimizes the total cost of performing all functions *jointly*. For instance, apparent over-stocking of sporadically-demanded inventory (e.g., spare parts) in many geographically-dispersed warehouses implies too high a cost of inventory holding in the channel system. It may nevertheless improve *systemwide* alignment if customers highly value quick delivery and close proximity of these parts due to the cost of factory downtime. Minimizing inventory holding costs in this type of market would lead the channel to much higher costs of express shipping spare parts when needed, which could overcome the benefit of reduced cost of inventory in warehouses.

> *Over-supply is not generally accompanied by a great enough increase in consumer satisfaction to be worth the cost incurred or the revenue foregone.*

Coordinating a too-high cost of one function with appropriately lower costs of other functions is most easily achieved when the relevant set of (costly) functions are all performed by the same channel member. In contrast, if a higher-than-minimum cost for one member is counterbalanced by a lower cost for a function performed by a *different* member, close coordination and cooperation between the channel members is necessary to prevent one member from "free riding" on the other. The optimal solution is unlikely to occur unless the two channel members make an explicit arrangement to share the total costs and benefits fairly.

Conversely, under-supply can result when the channel seeks cost containment through reduced performance of some or even many channel functions, without sufficient information about demand (i.e. willingness to pay) for various levels of resultant benefits. Under-supply may also be accompanied by over-pricing for the benefit levels offered. Under-supply does not cause the channel to risk lower profit *margins* but rather lower profits in general, due to buyer dissatisfaction and lost sales. Even when an attractive product is offered for sale in this channel, competitors may benefit from the channel's misalignment as buyers defect.

> *Under-supply may also be accompanied by over-pricing for the benefit levels offered.*

Supply-side misalignments are correctly categorized across three dimensions: by channel, by function, and by channel member performing the function. Implicit in this is the assessment of over- or under-provision *for a specific target segment*, since more than one type of buyer may use a given channel. For example, a manufacturer of women's makeup may distribute through channels including drugstore.com, department stores, and the bricks-and-mortar retailer Sephora. If a distributor in the Sephora channel inefficiently performs the ordering/payment function, this misalignment increases cost only in that channel – not in the drugstore.com or department store channels. Thus, a series of tables like Table 7-2, one for each channel, can be used to analyze supply-side misalignments:

Table 7-2:
Encoding Supply-Side Misalignments by
{Channel Member x Function}
(replicate for other channels in the channel system)

Identify the channel you are analyzing; the names of members in columns; and relevant functions performed in rows. Enter alignment information for each function for each member below, where: "costly"=cost-inefficient; "low"=too little of this function is done; "OK"=no misalignment; "N/A"=member does not perform this function.				
Function:	**Member A**	**Member B**	**Member C**	**Member D**
1				
2				
3				
4				
5				
6				
7				

Table 7-2 allows you to encode *non-performance* of a channel function by a particular channel member, as well as encoding either alignment or misalignment. Misalignment could occur because the cost of that channel member performing the function is too high, even though the function is accomplished (e.g., enough inventory is held, but without a state-of-the-art IT system to inform the channel what is available where and in what quantities). Or, misalignment could occur because too little of the function has been achieved for the benefits demanded (e.g., insufficient inventory holding leads to frequent stock-outs, which is incompatible with the target segment's high demand for quick delivery). The possible entries in a given cell are therefore: "N/A"; "OK"; "costly"; "low"; or both {"costly", "low"}. Understanding how supply-side misalignments occur – by channel, by channel partner, and by channel function – allows the channel manager to fix the problems that do occur, without engendering new misalignments by "fixing what isn't broken."

Implications

A mistake on either the demand or supply side results in lost profit opportunities, either by unnecessarily increasing channel costs and/or prices, or by skimping on channel benefits for which the target market would be willing to pay a premium. Incorrectly identifying a demand- or supply-side misalignment inflicts a double cost on the channel: first, the real misalignment has not been identified and hence not fixed; and second, the attempted "fix" typically introduces a new misalignment where none existed before.

Correct diagnosis of channel misalignments requires a focus on both the demand and supply sides of the channel. It is possible to have supply-side misalignments without any demand-side misalignments, for example if the channel delights the end-user but incurs high costs to do so because of inefficient channel management practices. Conversely, the supply-side may be quite efficient, but demand-side misalignment can still arise from under-provision of desired channel benefits in the pursuit of cost-cutting. Frequently, though, a supply-side misalignment does give rise to one on the demand side, so verifying channel benefit demands by segment is a cornerstone of misalignment analysis on either side.

> *Incorrectly identifying a demand- or supply-side misalignment inflicts a double cost on the channel: first, the real misalignment has not been identified and not fixed, and second, the attempted "fix" typically introduces a new misalignment where none existed before.*

Alignment analysis is a multi-dimensional activity, and supply-side misalignments are not expected to be the same across the whole system. After all, different channels within one system do not include the same roster of channel partners, so it would be unreasonable to expect supply-side (mis)alignments to be the same throughout the system. Similarly, on the demand side, the channel manager must consider differences in channel benefit valuations across segments.

It should also be noted that our shipping speed demand-side example permitted us to examine the *fee* for shipping explicitly along with the channel benefit (speed) delivered. In many cases, the incremental price paid by the buyer to consume more channel benefits is not made explicit – think for example about the incremental price you might pay to choose from a broader variety of goods; to be able to get product and usage information from a salesperson or B2B service rep; or to be able to choose to buy a small amount of product rather than buying in bulk. Some of these price increments are rather easily seen (the bulk-buying versus bulk-broken per-unit price, for example), but others are implicit in the overall price charged by the channel for the combination of the product and the bundle of all channel benefits offered. It is the combination of {product, channel benefit bundle, overall price} that the buyer will compare across competitors and channels. It is sometimes possible in these situations to delight the buyer sufficiently on some elements of the overall purchase so that they are willing to tolerate less-than-ideal levels of some other channel benefit; insight into the relative importance of various channel benefits is fundamental to the success of such an offer.

Solutions for Misalignment

When the channel value proposition involves under-supply of valued channel benefits, there are three main methods for realignment: (1) expand the level of benefits provided, so as to better match the target's true preference for each benefit; (2) offer multiple, tiered service levels to appeal to different segments while retaining the overall channel structure; or (3) alter the list of segments targeted so as to avoid serving consumers whose demands the channel is simply not equipped to meet.

When supply-side misalignments arise from cost-inefficient execution on channel functions, solutions for achieving alignment include: (1) changing the roles of current channel members to allocate functions to those who are best at them; (2) investing in new distribution technologies to reduce cost throughout the channel; or (3) bringing in new distribution function specialists.

> *Functional realignment is not trivial to implement, and therefore should be carefully weighed in order to choose a productive but feasible solution to the misalignment problem.*

These realignment actions are not trivial to implement, and therefore should be carefully weighed in order to choose a productive but feasible solution to the misalignment problem.

Alignment Constraints

Since channel misalignment hinders productivity, growth, and profit, it's fair to ask why we observe so much misalignment in channels. That is, why would channel managers not quickly move to realign under-performing channel structures? The main reason is *constraints* upon imposing any aligned channel structure, specifically of the legal, environmental, and managerial types.

Legal constraints can vary from market to market and differentially constrain the alignment between supply and demand. For example, some government contracts specify that a certain percentage of the vendors chosen must be small businesses, or must be run by minority owners. This can shape how a bidder allies with other partners to submit a winning bid, leading to the choice to partner with a channel member of otherwise lower channel execution skills.

The physical and *infrastructural environment* can also place constraints on a company's route to market. For example, selling goods in rural towns in emerging-market countries requires a different go-to-market solution than selling in big cities because of the differences in business infrastructure, such as the lack of roads, refrigeration, and banking access.

Both legal and environmental constraints occur outside the companies directly involved, and prevent members from establishing a zero-based channel either due to an inability to offer an appropriate level of benefits or because the constraints impose unduly high costs on channel members.

Managerial constraints or strategies may prevent alignment of channel design due to the orientation, culture, or rule set of specific channel members. Management may lack knowledge of what levels of investment or channel activity are necessary and appropriate to achieve the benefits desired. For example, a firm may enforce "no e-mail Fridays" in an attempt to get people out of their offices or off their computers and talking to each other, but in doing so unintentionally hamper communication with channel partners outside the company. Alternatively, management may choose *not* to align the channel activities in favor of a greater common good. For example, fulfilling an e-order in multiple shipments may seem like an overly costly way to ship product to e-consumers, but may make overall cost-management sense when an e-tailer has optimally organized multiple warehouses with different pick-and-pack processes.

These factors are important to keep in mind when you conduct your channel alignment analysis, as they can profoundly affect your ability to achieve a zero-based design as well as your channel's performance on either the demand or the supply side.

The interesting question is whether a channel manager can go even further and challenge the underlying constraints that facilitate misalignment. Some constraints (particularly of the legal or environmental types) simply cannot be relaxed completely, making it impossible to achieve a true first-best design. It is virtually impossible, for example, to quickly transform the physical infrastructure of a rural emerging market environment. However, many of the managerial constraints are routinely challenged, particularly if a "champion" can explain the benefits of changing rules and policies to the channel as a whole.

A Final Word

When attacking channel misalignments, it is useful to think about *where you invest your marketing dollars*. You can invest them not only in new product design, branding, and promotional activities, but also in changing the ground rules of engagement in the market in such a way that permits you to put together a channel structure much closer to the zero-based model. It is very costly to realign necessary functions with the benefits that customers demand, which is why it is important to develop a judicious understanding of the ways to achieve that key outcome.

The process of channel alignment analysis is never finished. Not only can environmental and managerial constraints change, but so do buyers' demands and distribution technologies. The inevitability of change creates a constant opportunity for channel design innovation, pursuing the moving target of a zero-based channel for each targeted segment in the market.[19]

PART 2: HOW DO I EXECUTE?

Chapter 8: BECOME A STRATEGIC SKEPTIC!

Up to now, we have discussed the key principles of channel design and the need for coordinating functions supplied with channel benefits demanded. In the remaining chapters, our focus will be on *how to make your great channel design work.* This is easier said than done. In fact, the greatest challenge of channel strategy is to get all of the members on board and acting in a manner beneficial to the overall system and structure (versus benefitting themselves individually). Ultimately, the goal of any channel strategist is to achieve *coordination;* this occurs when all members act in harmony so that their joint productivity is maximized. Put differently, the team must win, not just individual players. Note that we use active verbs like *work, acting,* and *win,* because channel coordination can only be achieved through the coherent and collaborative actions of all channel members.

> *The channel team must win, not the individual members.*

Let's consider an example that shows how easy it is for a system to become dysfunctional, and highlight the types of conflict that can drive your partners to shirk or even sabotage your channel efforts. We will also see how channel power, the array of assets that give you leverage and influence with your channel partners, can be used to implement your initiatives. Ultimately, a healthy dose of skepticism is advised in assessing whether conflict and poor implementation are brewing – and if so, what to do about it.

Flanders Wallcovering Inc.

Chelsea Cavanaugh was redecorating her dining room and was impressed with the recent "comeback" of wallpaper in recent discussions on her Houzz.com app. She didn't know the names, designs, or reputations of any wallpaper brands, so after ordering the room's furniture, Chelsea planned a trip to Flanders Paint & Wallpaper,[20] her local store in Austin, Texas.

The standard shopping method was to peruse a set of wallpaper books at a store to see what colors, patterns, and materials seemed most appealing. Each book was published by a manufacturer and consisted of a series of 16" x 24" sheets of actual wallpaper. These books contained the branded product line, with different books focusing on particular designs: florals, stripes, metallic, modern abstract patterns, children's patterns. The shopper would borrow the books containing her favorite patterns, taking them home to look at the samples in the room to be decorated. Store employees might help obtain measurements and calculate the number of rolls to order, then place the order for store pick-up.

Chelsea arrived at Flanders, greeted the clerk and asked where the wallpaper books were kept. She was surprised when the clerk sharply responded, "Well, I certainly hope you intend on *buying* your wallpaper here if you're going to use our books… You're not going to buy from one of those pirates, are you?"

Chelsea had no idea what a wallpaper "pirate" was, or why the store clerk was attacking her rather than welcoming her and helping her shop. Without realizing it, Chelsea has stepped into the crossfire of *channel conflict*.

A few days later, she found Flanders' website and came across a page labeled "Wallpaper Pirates":

> "Wall covering pirates are a *nice* name given in our industry for those companies that sell wall coverings online with no local store or catalog. These companies tell you to go into your local wall covering store and use that dealer's books (which the dealer paid for) and the dealer's help (which the dealer also pays dearly for). These pirates then tell you to get pattern numbers of the wallpaper you want and call them. The pirates will guarantee to sell those rolls of wallpaper to you cheaper. Of course, they will! They didn't have to buy books, rent store space, pay sales help or be there if a problem comes up. They just throw wallpaper in a box and ship it... (That is....they ship it "*IF* you are lucky...)."

With heightened curiosity, Chelsea looked up "online wallpaper store" and found several e-tailer (or "pirate") listings. She clicked on www.wallpaperdirect.com and found a striped wallpaper pattern that looked promising. It was made by Ashford – a brand she was not familiar with. The website offered a sample of the wallpaper for $9.95, with full rolls priced at $33.59 per roll. She called Flanders and found that they charged $47.99 per roll for the same wallpaper. She estimated that she would need 16 rolls for her dining room, so she could save 30 percent – $230.40 plus tax – by buying online rather than at Flanders, where the bill would run almost $800.00. However, Wallpaperdirect.com charged a 20 percent restocking fee if Chelsea decided to return the wallpaper after buying it; Flanders did not charge restocking fees to their retail customers.

Paradise Lost... And a Possible Map

The Flanders Wallcovering example illustrates a classic case of channel conflict, which occurs when a lack of common vision among channel members impairs the harmony of their actions, and with it their productivity. Conflict is found in almost all distribution channels because of the way in which a channel strategist chooses partners. Manufacturers sell through retailers like Flanders because of their expertise in providing key functions such as customer service, location benefits, and assortment and variety of offerings, and for their cost-side transactional efficiencies. If a manufacturer could perform these functions at least as well as Flanders could, it would not want to give away valuable profits to the retailer. The very fact of these partners' different competencies naturally leads even reasonably congenial partners to disagree on what is "best for the channel."

Different competencies naturally lead even reasonably congenial partners to disagree on what is "best for the channel."

How does a channel get to the point at which a retailer behaves like the clerk at Flanders? Several factors give rise to conflict, any one of which may be driving the problems in your channel: free-riding, opportunism, and self-interest, as well as differing goals, timelines, expectations, and perceptions. Conflict-ridden channels can be a mess to face and even messier to solve.

The key to channel strategy success is to ensure that valued interests and outcomes – revenue growth, value creation, and successful coordination – are *safeguarded* for you and your partners. There are many ways to safeguard channel value, all of which involve the use of some sources of power, such as the use of contracts, incentives, and pricing policies. Building and managing your arsenal of channel power sources provides you with the influence and leverage to safeguard the effectiveness of your efforts.

> *The key to channel strategy success is to insure that valued outcomes – revenue growth, value creation, success coordination – are safeguarded, to insure their achievement.*

Channel Conflict

The first type of conflict between Ashford and Flanders is *goal conflict*. Ashford wants to maximize its sales volume and share, which requires maximizing its distribution breadth, given the lack of consumer brand awareness. In contrast, Flanders cannot reach its sales and profit goals because consumers are showrooming them – using their costly sample books and services to discover their preferred wallpaper choice, then buying from lower-priced online retailers. Wallpaperdirect.com can hold its costs (and prices) down because it free-rides on the valued channel benefits provided by Flanders. Thus, although each of these companies wants to maximize its profits, their goals are very different, leading to actions that prevent the other partner from achieving its goals.

Chelsea also found the following webpage on Flanders' website, which further increases the conflict:

> "Some local wall covering dealers … fight back by coding their books. They mix up the pattern numbers so that when you choose a wallpaper pattern of pretty pink flowers for little Susie's room, the wall covering store might put the pattern number on the sample that will give you big ORANGE cars if you order it from the pirates. So my advice is this. Stay away from those online stores. Then *if* you have a problem the dealer will be around to help you resolve your problem. You are dealing honestly with merchants who have made a huge investment in making certain that you have a place to come and choose those pretty patterns. An added advantage is that they will be there the next time you want to order some more pretty patterns."

This underscores Flanders' irritation at bearing the costs that create valued channel benefits, including inventorying sample wallpaper books for customers' use and providing in-store help (both promotional functions that improve consumers' awareness of the Ashford product line) and running a brick-and-mortar store (channel benefits of customer service, information provision, variety, and locational convenience). This could be an efficient and realistic channel functional allocation, and Flanders would not be so irritated if its cost-bearing was rewarded with ownership of the customer – that is, if the costs and benefits were better matched. At this point, though, neither Ashford nor Wallpaperdirect.com appears to share this view. The mismatch gives rise to *domain conflict* in the wallcoverings channel.

Finally, *perceptual* differences create conflict as well. Ashford is likely unaware of how irritated Flanders is about the "piracy" of e-tailers, or of their strike-back response in the webpage threatening to attack "pirates" on its website and in face-to-face customer interactions. This is a very dangerous form of conflict, because you cannot fix something if you're unaware of its existence. If Ashford knew about the issue, it could teach Flanders to differentiate itself by stressing the channel benefits and services that it provides (and that e-tailers fail to provide), rather than viewing e-tailers as competition stealing their customers.

Channel Power

Can either the retailer or the manufacturer restore the channel to a productive and non-confrontational status if faced with such conflicts? The answer lies in their abilities to apply sources of channel power – that is, to exert leverage over other partners to improve channel performance. We focus here on Ashford and Flanders, because an online wallpaper retailer is unlikely to act as the channel captain in this instance.

Ashford might be expected to exhibit some channel leadership – after all, it cannot make sales without retail presence, and to the extent that consumers value seeing a sample of wallpaper before buying, brick/mortar retailers serve an important role. And indeed, Ashford does have some channel power assets that benefit Flanders:

- It has *expertise* in the design of a broad assortment of quality wallpaper in patterns that match popular tastes, so that Flanders can be confident that consumers won't complain about Ashford product quality if they buy through Flanders
- It has *expertise* in production and inventory management so that orders are correctly fulfilled and promptly delivered – allowing Flanders to offer quick delivery and good customer service to its consumers
- Its wallpaper books *promote* all of its wallpaper designs, thus assisting Flanders by taking on some of the promotional burden
- It *rewards* Flanders by offering a profit level at parity with other wallpaper manufacturers.

Is this enough to make Flanders willing to subsidize online retailers by providing free pre-sales service without earning the sale as well? Evidently not, given Flanders' current actions to sabotage wallpaper model numbers! It's also worth noting that Ashford does *not* possess or wield some key elements of channel power that might have induced Flanders to be more cooperative:

- Ashford's product line is not substantially *differentiated* from competing manufacturers, all of whom offer similar arrays of designs for various rooms, styles, and architectural spaces
- Ashford has not invested in building *brand equity and preference* that would make it a preferred or "must-have" in Flanders' store; it is just one of many similarly unknown brand names in the marketplace
- Ashford's lack of brand power means it cannot coerce Flanders into promoting its brand over the competition or dropping competitive brands from its retail offering
- Ashford cannot afford to *reward* Flanders by pulling out of online retailing (which would restore Flanders' ability to "own the customer" to whom they provide pre-sales service), because doing so would reduce Ashford's market presence (its best available substitute for true brand equity).

In short, Ashford has painted itself (no pun intended) into a corner with its unbranded channel strategy. It has unwittingly set the stage for conflict and competition among all of its retailers. It is unable to reduce the domain conflict Flanders is experiencing; its goals are indelibly different from Flanders'; and worst of all, it is likely unaware of Flanders' website or store shopping experience.

Could Flanders be a possible channel leader? Let's consider the sources and strengths of channel power on Flanders' side that Ashford would value:

- Flanders is a local store with local patronage, and thus has some *local retail brand equity* in the eyes of consumers
- Flanders has the ability to show wallpaper sheets through its offering of Ashford's books, allowing the consumer to *touch* the sample, *see* true colors and see *how they will look* in the home
- Flanders' staff has *expertise* and knowledge about how to pick wallpaper and who might be able to hang the wallpaper a consumer buys
- Flanders has the *coercive* ability to sabotage Ashford in the hopes of inducing it to change its ways in Flanders' favor; conversely, it can also *reward* Ashford by promoting its brand over the competition.

Indeed, Flanders has taken action already, sabotaging model numbers on wallpaper brands sold by "pirates." The question is whether this coercive "play" from Flanders' roster of possible sources of power gets the job done. Probably not, for the following reasons:

- Flanders is only one small, *undifferentiated* retailer, and any retaliatory behavior on its part has only a small influence on Ashford
- Ashford is likely unaware of Flanders' actions, so they cannot cause Ashford to change its behavior

- Flanders is likely facing the same problem from other manufacturers, so it does not have a "safe haven" of manufacturers whose brands it can promote with the confidence that consumers will buy from them
- Flanders' actions, sadly, harm the *consumer* more than Ashford – exactly the wrong outcome if Flanders is trying to change the way manufacturers like Ashford act.

In short, Flanders' lack of importance to Ashford – in terms of its sales of Ashford products – severely hampers its ability to turn the tide of broad distribution by Ashford. Ashford's lack of awareness of Flanders' sabotage makes such efforts unproductive (even if the revenge is satisfying). No channel partner in this situation is poised to *make this channel work*. The worst news is that consumers who do engage in showrooming with Flanders, and get the "big orange cars" instead of the "pink flowers" they thought they had ordered, will finally become permanently aware of the Ashford brand name – but for all the wrong reasons. They are unlikely ever to buy the Ashford brand again, after suffering the high restocking fees it charges. Some may even choose never to buy wallpaper again, when they can paint their walls instead, and this would eventually decrease the overall size of the wallpaper market, harming all of its channel members.

The Strategic Skeptic

The example of Flanders and Ashford illustrates several broader channel coordination challenges that can result in a range of conflict situations. These challenges are embedded fundamentally in any context in which two organizations transact. Every channel strategist must be aware that these factors are constantly present and systematically color the views (and resulting actions) of each partner. This is why Ashford and Flanders each needs to be a "strategic skeptic." A skeptic is one who often questions or doubts the claims and statements of another. Channel partners need to do the same – not in an offensive or openly suspicious manner (this will lead to more conflict), but in a strategic manner, recognizing the common pitfalls associated with working in coordination with valued channel partners. We recommend asking the following four checklist questions, as a means by which you can regularly assess how you are transacting with a partner and all the channel assets that must be safeguarded.

> *Every channel strategist must be aware that these factors are constantly operative and systematically color the views (and resulting actions) of each partner member.*

1. What do they need to know? This question reflects the common reality that most channel members do not understand the value proposition – i.e. why joint coordination of all members will make the channel system and its respective players better off as a whole over the long run. Sometimes long-run profits are only achievable with short-run forbearance. Like compound interest, the regular deposit or performance of channel activities over time can result in higher profits than one or two high-margin deals in the short-term. However, most channel members fail to see or understand these possibilities. This is an information problem, and the solution is to educate channel partners in the full channel value proposition.

2. What's in it for them? The dominant tendency at work here is that channel members are self-interested – they always seek to maximize their own benefit first, typically without regard to the implications for the broader channel system. Recognizing this fundamental tendency allows the channel manager to consider rewards and penalties that can steer partners toward more collaborative behavior.

3. Can my partner do less than it should? One challenge in working with any other firm is that their actions are difficult to observe. For example, the manufacturer typically cannot see whether the wholesaler is promoting its product as promised (or as the wholesaler is paid to do). Similarly, a retailer cannot observe whether a manufacturer has actually put into the product the quality ingredients that it has said it would. This inability to observe a partner's actions has been dubbed "the moral hazard problem," which refers to your partner's ability to shirk in its efforts because of your inability to observe them.

4. Can they take advantage of me or of other channel partners? The fundamental issue behind this question is the free-riding problem, which may in fact be observable (i.e. not a moral hazard). As you'll recall from Chapter 4, free-riding is the act of taking gains (such as revenue, sales, or other benefits) while others bear the associated costs.

We summarize below the fundamental incentive problems that arise whenever transactions are executed between two channel partners:

Table 8-1:
Fundamental Incentive Problems

The Observed Problem	The Underlying Issue	Question to Ask	What do I Need to Do?
They don't understand the value proposition	Incomplete information	What do they need to know?	Share information with partners re: channel opportunity
They do not behave collaboratively or invest in channel-wide productivity	Self-interest seeking	What's in it for them?	Alter prices and/or incentives to make their self-interest coincide with yours Co-invest in channel relationship to increase the cost of poor behavior
Their actions can't be observed	Moral hazard risk	How might they do less than they should?	Co-invest in a stronger channel relationship to change incentive to shirk Invest in monitoring and enforcement efforts to deter would-be shirkers
They free-ride on others' efforts	The free-riding problem	How might they take advantage of me or of other channel partners?	Use reward and pricing mechanisms to compensate partners whose cost-bearing creates positive external benefits for other channel partners

Research on each of these problems has identified a variety of possible solutions for each. The key for you, as a channel strategist, is to know which best applies to your context.

What Do They Need to Know?

Incomplete information is the norm amongst channel partners, not the exception. Any channel participant – including the channel manager – likely lacks information about the true costs borne by channel partners, or about payoffs from adopting new channel technologies and initiatives, or about consumers' preferences in channel benefits. This leads to missed opportunities to improve coordination.

> *When one party has more or less access to information, this creates the potential for exploitation or dishonest gain. Even more important than hiding bad behavior is the missed opportunity from not understanding what might be gained as a result of cooperating.*

A particularly vexing form of incomplete information is information *asymmetry*: the situation where one channel member has more or better information than another. It is also possible in such situations that partners are unaware of the information that other members know. Either creates the potential for exploitation or dishonest gain by the member with superior information. This was exemplified by Flanders' attempt to sabotage online sellers by mis-identifying wallpaper patterns to showrooming consumers.

Often, simply sharing information is the best way to reduce the risk that arises with information asymmetry. As an example, Flanders may not realize the negative brand impact to its suppliers created by the hostile language on their website. They see e-tailers as the enemy, but their reaction may harm customer demand for all wallcoverings more generally.

Ashford's first job would be to recognize Flanders' irritation, and then to share its information on the effect of such postings on customer attitudes and satisfaction. Flanders may not have realized that by targeting their "enemies," they were in fact shooting themselves in the foot.

Another way that wallcovering suppliers like Ashford can help their physical retail channel partners is to identify cases in which such retailers have managed to stay successful *despite* the presence of competitive e-tailers. It may be that understanding how to be successful in this new world would assist stores like Flanders to better adjust and compete, without damaging category demand or brand equity. Manufacturers might need to be willing to retrain physical retailers in best practices for selling against e-tailers and capturing and keeping their customers, or in better understanding and defining their target segment (e.g., those who value their consultative services but are less price-sensitive).

The answer to the question "What do they need to know?" is only available to a channel manager insightful enough to dig into the true attitudes and market-level behaviors of its channel partners.

What's In It for Them?

An economic actor's fundamental tendency is to maximize its self-interest. Every firm and individual seeks to maximize its profit or welfare; this is the general goal of business. The difficulty in a channel of distribution is that one member's self-interest seeking often generates *externalities*, which are ancillary effects experienced by other actors around them. When these effects are *negative* (e.g. lack of investment in a common asset like service provision because of a lack of private gain), the result is a failure to create a common benefit that could have accrued to the channel at large. In short, self-interested channel behavior can result in underinvestment in collaborative channel assets because costs accrue to one channel partner, but benefits accrue to all; this is widely known as the *tragedy of the commons*.

> *When each channel member receives only part of the overall margin resulting from performing costly channel functions, there is an incentive to shirk and underprovide them. This is because costs may accrue to one channel partner, but benefits accrue to all.*

The solution to this quandary is to create reward structures that *internalize the externality*, that is, to reward the channel member for investment in a common asset whose total benefit is enjoyed by other channel members as well as internally. In the Flanders example, Ashford could compensate Flanders for some of the costs it bears to promote the Ashford brand in-store, such as subsidizing the cost of wallpaper books. Ashford could also invest in its own brand equity, which would relieve some of Flanders' promotional burden, increase Ashford's demand-pull, and increase its share vis-à-vis less well-known brands. Note, however, that advertising is expensive, and although it could increase demand and channel traffic, the benefits are not exclusive to a single channel partner, so no channel partner has an incentive to foot this cost in its entirety. Many brand manufacturers therefore use *cooperative advertising* where they offer to pay a portion of retail advertising costs to subsidize this expense. Savvy manufacturers consider the costs of generating customer brand awareness, and the resulting margins each channel member can earn, and can arrive at an advertising subsidy that shares these costs in a way that incentivizes the retailer to run local ads.

Flanders also faces the problem of price competition from online retailers, which reduces its ability to compete in the marketplace. In these cases, the manufacturer can set a manufacturer's suggested retail price, or MSRP. MSRPs discourage an intermediary from setting its prices too high, since pricing above an MSRP printed on the product package makes the retailer look as if it is price-gouging consumers. Many consumer packaged goods companies – from Frito-Lay to Sara Lee – use the MSRP tool to reduce channel partners' incentives to set their prices too high.

Slotting allowances (manufacturer payments to a retailer in return for placing its product on the store shelf) are yet another incentive reward mechanism offered by many consumer product manufacturers to major retailers such as Wal-Mart and Target to encourage retailers to provide shelf space for new product introductions. Ashford could consider offering analogous service subsidies for Flanders to provide customers with customized information, matching services and in-store support.

These statements implicitly assume that your channel partner perceives the actual value of fulfilling its designated channel functions – in which case the main issue is really *willingness* to collaborate as a true channel partner. But sometimes, the problem is even more fundamental: your channel partner may simply be *unaware* of the benefits it can reap from behaving cooperatively. Michaels Craft Stores found itself in this position when it sought to upgrade its suppliers' use of computerized bar coding, proper shipping labels, consistent UPC coding, and shipping into centralized distribution centers rather than directly to individual stores. Supplier benefits from complying included faster payments and re-orders, greater sales volume, and better information for future production planning. These seemed so obvious that initially Michaels sought simply to impose these "good" retail behaviors on its suppliers – with very poor results. It turned out that 90 percent of suppliers' volume went through small "mom 'n' pop" retail craft stores, which did not impose these rules and could never offer the volume and profit that Michaels could; so the suppliers never dreamed of the potential benefits. Once Michaels realized the problem of suppliers' incomplete information about true retail potential, it successfully mounted an educational and training campaign to show suppliers the benefits, which led eventually to complete compliance with its policies.[21]

All of these suggestions require a fundamental understanding of your partner's desired benefits from participating in your channel, recognition of the externalities their activities provide for the rest of the channel, and use of your *reward power* to restore their incentive to perform the desired activities.

Can They Do Less Than They Should?

A chief difficulty between Ashford and Flanders is their mutual inability to observe each other's actions. Ashford cannot observe whether the reason why customers don't buy from Flanders is because Flanders never shared their sample books, or if Flanders is receiving promotional money from an alternative supplier and therefore promoting the competition, or whether Flanders is actively demarketing the Ashford brand. Similarly, Flanders may not be able to observe whether a product being offered to them as "exclusive" by Ashford truly is one-of-a-kind in all of Ashford's markets worldwide. This raises the possibility that Flanders may shirk in its promotion of the Ashford brand, or that Ashford may shirk in supporting Flanders' competitive retail position, both examples of moral hazard.

The most obvious solution to moral hazard is to monitor the channel partner: Ashford can send secret shoppers into Flanders stores to observe the extent to which Flanders sales personnel promote their products versus those of competitors. Beyond this, Ashford could blunt Flanders' incentive to shirk by offering a proprietary inventory management system or agreeing to make investments in updating Flanders' information system in return for more visibility into customer purchase patterns.

> *Moral hazard is a real and ongoing risk whenever transactions are occurring.*

In a similar vein, a menu of rewards can be developed to incentivize Flanders to specifically push Ashford products to customers; these incentives are most effective when Ashford can combine them with monitoring to observe Flanders' effort, or when it uses customer surveys and focus group evidence to verify the value Flanders is adding and thus the level and nature of rewards that Flanders merits. Conversely, channel members who fail to promote Ashford can receive punishments or penalties, either financial or in regard to access to inventory (e.g. they may have to wait to receive the company's newest products). The key in reducing moral hazard in channel relationships is to identify observable activities such as cooperative advertising expenditures and promotions for the purpose of inferring inputs, i.e. effort. Discounts or payments might be made for key channel functions such as purchase volumes transacted, timely deliveries, or the acquisition of customers with high lifetime values.

Can They Take Advantage of Me or Other Channel Partners?

Flanders is a great illustration of the showrooming problem, also known as *free-riding*. E-tailers are taking advantage of Flanders because more savvy buyers (and Chelsea may join the ranks of that segment!) learn how to free-ride on Flanders' in-store service, and then go online to buy wallpaper at a 30 percent lower price. This also shows what happens when showrooming is allowed to persist without any support given to the benefit-providing retailer: that retailer will figure out ways to protect itself. Flanders' protection mechanism – sabotaging pattern numbers for showrooming consumers – will almost certainly negatively impact not just Wallpaperdirect.com, but also the manufacturer, Ashford. This is because Chelsea was not aware of the Ashford brand name before, and therefore had a neutral attitude, implying willingness to try and buy the brand. But if Chelsea orders and gets the wrong wallpaper because she relied on Flanders' incorrect pattern numbers, she will have to pay a 20 percent restocking fee to return that wallpaper. She'll now know the brand name Ashford, certainly, but it will have a strongly negative association as she will believe it to be an unreliable manufacturer. Ashford therefore also suffers from the free-riding problem.

What can Flanders and/or Ashford do to solve this problem? The first option is the development of "branded variants," or exclusives. The two firms might come up with a numbering system that is exclusive to Flanders, which makes it difficult for customers to find the exact same wallpaper pattern elsewhere. Ashford could even offer to support a price-matching guarantee offer by Flanders, under which Flanders could offer to match lower prices at other Ashford retail outlets. Such price-matching guarantees are sometimes viewed by consumers as a signal that the retailer's offer is fair and that their commitment to value pricing is strong. Ashford might also pay for the sample books that Flanders loses to customers who do not return them, in order to mitigate the e-tailer's free-riding impact on Flanders.

Another common solution is to go beyond model-number differentiation to create or dedicate a product or product lines as exclusive to Flanders. This would mean that Ashford would have to restrict distribution of some products to the Flanders channel or to members in markets that do not compete directly with Flanders. The downstream channel partner can then market its exclusivity as a key value point with customers. The fashion industry commonly uses this tactic, where brand such as Ralph Lauren or Tina Turk may limit some styles or product lines to a specific retailer such as Macy's or Bloomingdale's. This offer is of course most attractive to Flanders if Ashford also promotes the brand and model number to create awareness and desirability for the exclusive item; otherwise no customer is aware of the exclusivity or indeed of the existence of the item at Flanders.

If not mitigated through one of the above mechanisms, one consequence of showrooming is that the intermediary (here, Flanders) might respond by lowering its price points to approximate the pricing at Wallpaperdirect.com. Two clear downsides of this response are that lower prices can dilute Ashford's brand equity and cheapen its image; and that a lower price leaves less margin for Flanders and thus reduces its incentive to provide service and promotion on Ashford's products. One way to avoid this is for Ashford to implement a minimum advertised price policy (known as a MAP policy) across all of its channels. Compliance with such policies is often linked to rewards: for example, retailers may receive advertising allowances if they comply by setting the MAP price. MAP is an example of the broader concept of *resale price maintenance* (RPM), which refers to any policy aimed at maintaining prices in pre-specified ranges. A minimum resale price maintenance policy establishes a price floor, while a maximum resale price maintenance policy establishes a price ceiling.

The key to making resale price maintenance policies work is consistent enforcement. If a channel member fails to comply (or the manufacturer fails to monitor), a *gray market* can result, in which goods are acquired in lower-priced markets and then resold in higher-priced markets. Gray markets are common in the sale and distribution of designer goods that are sold in countries with weak currencies and then resold in countries with stronger currencies.

> *The key to making resale price maintenance policies work is consistent enforcement. If a channel member fails to comply (or the manufacturer fails to monitor), a gray market may result.*

In this manner, resale price maintenance policies can be useful in preventing the downstream channel from competing too fiercely on price, which could drive down profits for themselves and the manufacturer. Some have criticized RPM because it can increase the manufacturer's profitability. However, it can also be viewed as effective at ensuring that distributors who invest in promoting a manufacturer's products are able to recoup their promotional costs, thus minimizing free-riding and increasing the incentive to invest in channel-wide valued service provision.

The Vertical Integration Solution

Despite a channel member's best efforts, there is no way to fully eradicate these four fundamental incentive problems in a route to market. The best that you can do is to attempt to mitigate information incompleteness, self-interested behaviors, moral hazard, and opportunistic free-riding in other channel members. The only way to completely resolve these problems is for the channel captain to *vertically integrate*, or own the distribution channel outright. In a vertically integrated firm, the optimal margin levels for achieving channel coordination can be set, the removal of goal conflict helps overcome informational incompleteness, and complete monitoring allows for the minimization of free-riding tendencies and moral hazard.

If the answer is this obvious, why don't more firms vertically integrate and bullet-proof their channels from these fundamental incentive problems? There are many reasons, ranging from the fact that acquiring companies can be extraordinarily expensive, and that in-house expertise to effectively manage the performance of important channel functions is frequently lacking. As an example, Ashford may need transportation and logistics services in order for products to reach their end consumers; however, Ashford's expertise is in manufacturing wallpaper in bulk quantities. A completely different set of competencies and experience is required in order to reach effective scale economies in the provision of transportation services. This can be an expensive endeavor that Ashford would rather not manage on its own; in contrast, there may be channel intermediaries who excel at providing these necessary functions at much lower costs.

The difficulty of vertically integrating means that most firms must work with other intermediaries in bringing their products to end-user markets. Having a brilliant channel design is not enough – the challenge now is to make it all work. In practice, one solution will not cover all problems. Thus, the challenge for the channel strategist is to develop an appropriate and effective portfolio of approaches and assets.

The difficulty of vertically integrating means that most firms must work with other intermediaries in bringing their products to markets of end users. Having a brilliant channel design is not enough!

The Strategic Skeptic's Kit

Ashford's and Flanders' implementation challenges show how important it is to recognize potential and actual conflicts, manage and use channel power assets, and set rules, rewards, and channel pricing strategies to incentivize collaborative channel behavior. The rest of the chapters in this part of the book delve more deeply into each of these issues.

Chapter 9 asks "How do I govern my channel to minimize opportunism?" This chapter discusses how a channel strategist determines how to work together with channel partners, which requires the promulgation of rules of conduct, penalties for violations, investments in monitoring partner behavior, and most importantly the consistent enforcement of rules, expectations, and work norms.

Chapter 10 deals with the question of "How to thrive with a powerful channel partner?" This is one of the most common questions we are asked, and the answer lies in viewing power as a strategic channel asset that can be systematically leveraged and invested in over time. In this chapter, we make the important point that everyone, even the most dependent partner in a transaction or channel relationship, has some form of leverage. We also discuss how power is most valuable when used for the greater good, and so we introduce the idea of benevolent dictators as effective channel captains.

The following two chapters consider the strategic use and application of organizational relationships, which are widely seen as an important means of mitigating conflict and minimizing opportunism. We ask in Chapter 11 the question "Why do I need a channel relationship?" and in Chapter 12 "When should I take the leap to strategic partnering?" A variety of relationship types can be used to facilitate channel coordination; the key is to understand their differences and the circumstances under which they work best. Relationships are also dynamic, and the strategies for managing them therefore need to be regularly evaluated and monitored. Chapter 12 deals specifically with the decision to form close strategic partnerships, which are costly investments whose success is not always guaranteed. However, the discussion provides guidance to maximize your chances of success.

CHAPTER 9: HOW CAN I REDUCE OR PREVENT OPPORTUNISM?

What Could Go Awry – And How To Keep It From Happening?

Your channel relationships and strategic partnerships may be sufficiently strong for you to avoid having to face a partner that misrepresents your products or customers or simply doesn't execute on your design. But not all channels are set up with strong enough commitment levels for this to work, and not all strategists are prescient in their design decisions. Your great design may run into roadblocks because you've assigned functional responsibilities to your partners that they just don't want to perform. Or you may have a channel that works very well – with just a few bad apples that threaten to ruin the overall balance and equilibrium. Or your partners may have goals and horizons that don't match yours. In short, conflict pervades even the best-designed channels.

It is important to recognize this fact and plan for it, just as you plan for other elements of your business. A strategic skeptic not only seeks a good design, but also imagines what could nevertheless go wrong – before the worst happens. This is why you will need a governance plan to warn you of possible partner malfeasance. A governance plan defines how channel members will work together, what is expected of each, and the consequences for falling short of these expectations. Your communication of this plan to your partners can help deter bad behavior by them. Good governance processes can therefore be thought of as preventive efforts to safeguard an effective design and support relationship-building.

> *A true channel skeptic not only seeks a good channel design,*
> *but also imagines what could nevertheless go wrong.*

Where do we see examples of effective governance strategies? One channel structure that is typically characterized by strong governance plans as an inherent part of its go-to-market strategy is direct selling. Direct selling is a distribution form used to sell myriad consumer products including household cleaning supplies, cosmetics, vitamins and supplements, jewelry, candles and scents, clothing, energy services, legal services, and insurance. Direct selling retail sales were over $36 billion in the United States in 2015.[22] Some of the best-known and largest direct sellers worldwide include companies like AdvoCare, Amway, Arbonne, Herbalife, Isagenix, LegalShield, Mary Kay, Melaleuca, and Nu Skin, among many others.[23] Well-established firms have hundreds of thousands or millions of distributors worldwide and generate billions of dollars of sales per year. Table 9-1 shows a common structure for many direct selling firms and their channels:

Table 9-1:
Characteristics of the Direct Selling Channel Structure

Characteristic	Direct Selling Specifics
Products	Generally researched and developed by the direct-selling firm itself and thus often patented, proprietary and branded to the firm
Target Segments	Product-guided, but targets consumer valuing customer service (pre- and post-sale), education, and locational convenience channel benefits
Channel Structure	Includes the firm itself and a set of independent distributors who register with the firm as independent contractors and who have the right to retail the firm's products as well as to recruit and mentor other individual distributors who wish to do the same
Function Allocation	Direct selling firm: product line development; logistics, inventory management, shipping; IT systems for ordering, payment, distributor compensation; little or no advertising; no direct recruitment of new distributors Distributors: sales effort; recruiting new distributors; training and developing downline distributors; product and rules knowledge
Compensation	No salary; access to wholesale discounts on personally consumed products; retail markup on units sold to consumers; commissions and bonuses above threshold level on sales of downline recruited distributors; compensation typically accounts for 25 – 40% of the firm's sales revenue

Given the extensive set of functions allocated to distributors – not only sales generation but the finding, recruitment, mentoring and development of *other* distributors – the firm is strongly dependent on distributors' performance. Because distributors are the face of the firm, they are the purveyors of its brand equity (in products and in distributor business opportunity) to the market. As a result, a governance process defined by the establishment, communication, monitoring, and enforcement of appropriate *rules of conduct* and associated *consequences* for the distributor force (defined in Table 9-2 below) must be carefully crafted to protect brand equity and the firm's (and other distributors') investments in the business. An effective governance strategy contains the following elements:

Table 9-2:
Essential Elements of a Governance Strategy

Strategy Element	Definition
1. Establish channel "rules of conduct"	Encode what is expected of each member – including the channel captain
2. Clearly communicate consequences of violating the rules	Communicate rules and consequences to each partner
3. Monitor activities/behaviors of partners	Invest in verification of partners' performance of allocated functions
4. Enforce consequences when violation is found	Implement a (possibly multi-step) process that equitably applies penalties when warranted

All direct-selling companies offer broad guidance to their distributors about how to join, how to run their businesses, how to promote products, how to recruit and mentor downline distributors, and how to communicate with others about the firm's products and business opportunity. The establishment of a set of "rules of conduct" defines what is expected of each member, including the channel captain itself – so that all are well aware of how their performance contributes to the overall success of the channel effort. This should already be in place if you have done a good job in the design and allocation of functions (discussed in Chapters 5 and 6). An audit of the work of the channel combined with an analysis of supply-side misalignments (discussed in Chapter 7) is a natural input to this step of the governance strategy.

Clear communication to all partners of the *consequences* of violating the rules of conduct makes all partners aware not only of the benefits of opportunism and shirking, but the expected costs of engaging in bad behavior.

> **It is best to invest the most monitoring efforts against the most severe rule violations.**

The creation of a process for *monitoring* the activities and behaviors of partners, and making concrete investments to make such monitoring possible, is necessary to be able to verify that each is in fact doing what the channel design dictates. Making monitoring visible also sends a convincing signal to partners that compliance with the rules is not secret, but rather is known to the channel strategist, thus deterring some non-compliance.

Last but certainly not least, the consistent *enforcement* of the stated consequences when violations of the rules of conduct are discovered is the linchpin on which your whole governance strategy rests. Without such consistency in enforcement, partners will not believe that rules have "teeth," and shirking and other forms of non-compliance can be expected to rise.

Just as no channel is entirely devoid of conflict, even the most carefully-crafted governance strategy cannot be expected to perfectly control all non-compliant partner behavior. A successful strategy therefore balances the value of incrementally better compliance against the monitoring and enforcement costs of achieving better compliance. The economics literature on optimal monitoring and compliance shows that perfect monitoring is generally too costly to be efficient.[24] Nevertheless, failing to set up rules and monitor partners' compliance is another economically inefficient path. Between these two extremes, it is best to invest in monitoring efforts against, and assess steeper penalties for, the most severe rules violations. Further, investing in education that improves the target's understanding of why compliance is good for the system can be more productive than penalizing non-compliance after the fact.

> **Invest in education that improves understanding of the benefits from compliance.**

Rodan + Fields: How Some Key Rules of Conduct Govern Distributor Performance in Direct-Selling Channels

Let's now consider more closely an example of how one company, Rodan + Fields, structures its governance strategy. Rodan + Fields[25] (R+F) is a direct seller of skin care products whose Policies and Procedures document illustrates the setting of rules that protect and thus foster investments in the value of the business both for the company and for its distributors (called Consultants). Table 9-3 summarizes some of their rules and how adherence to them helps protect its investments in and overall value of its channel:

Table 9-3:
Rodan + Fields Rules and Their Protection of Channel Investments and Equity

Function	Rule	Key Statement
Promotion of R+F products	Product Claims	"Consultants shall not make any claims or representations regarding the R+F Products other than those found in the R+F Marketing Materials."
Promotion of the R+F business opportunity	Adherence to the Program	"Consultants shall present the Program in a truthful and accurate manner consistent with the Consultant Agreement and the R+F Marketing Materials."
Promotion of the R+F business opportunity	Income Claims Prohibited	"Consultants shall not make claims or representations of potential or guaranteed income or profits in connection with the Program. Any amounts that Consultants earn through the Program are based only on the sale of R+F Products and not on the mere act of sponsoring other Consultants."
Promotion and *Sales Manager* functions, *Monitoring/Training* downline Consultants to improve rules compliance	Sponsoring Responsibilities	"Sponsors are responsible for assisting, motivating and training their downlines.... [they must] train... their downlines to ensure that [they] do not make improper product or income claims, engage in illegal or inappropriate conduct or otherwise violate the Consultant Agreement."
Financing, Risk Mitigation, Inventory: value creation through function cost control	No Inventory Requirements	"Consultants are neither required to purchase nor required to carry any amount of inventory of the R+F Products; it is possible to maintain an active status and earn Commissions and Performance Bonuses without carrying any inventory at all."
Contracting/Relationship Management: R+F's ownership of this information allows it to provide assurance of reliable support to Consultants to run their businesses	Protection of R+F's Proprietary Information	R+F provides "access to R+F's sensitive, confidential and proprietary information and trade secrets.... A Consultant shall not disclose to any third party Confidential Information, [including] Performance Reports (Downline Activity) and all information contained in such reports, all Customer Data, and R+F's Product development plans, pricing, problem reports and performance information, marketing and financial plans and data, Customer e-mails, consultant e-mails, contact information and training materials."
Contracting/Relationship Management: protection of the future value of a sponsor's time/effort investments in mentoring downlines	Prohibition on Switching Sponsors	"A consultant is not permitted to encourage, offer or assist any other consultant to change Sponsors or Uplines. Under no circumstances shall any Consultant offer or provide any financial or other consideration or incentive to another Consultant.... Once a Consultant is sponsored, R+F requires that the relationship between the Consultant and her or his Sponsor be maintained and protected."
Contracting/Relationship Management, Promotion: Protects and encourages promotion efforts and investments.	Non-Solicitation and Non-Compete Provisions	While a Consultant and for six months afterward, "Consultant will not solicit any R+F Consultant or any R+F employee for engagement as an employee, or as an independent consultant, contractor or distributor of any direct selling company"; "Consultant will not promote, market or sell the products, services or programs offered by any competitive business"

Promoting R+F Products and Business Opportunity

R+F sets rules about how its products and its Consultant business opportunity may be presented, both of which are parts of governing the *promotion* function. Its rules on Product Claims and Adherence to the Program require Consultants to follow the company's marketing materials when promoting the products to consumers and when recruiting new Consultants. They foster consistency in the representation of R+F's assets to the marketplace, which benefits R+F directly through protection of its brand equity, and also benefits Consultants through the assurance that the company's brand and business opportunity are consistently positioned.

R+F further governs how promotion of the Consultant business opportunity may be communicated to prospects through its Income Claims rule. This rule requires sponsoring Consultants to accurately and truthfully represent the income opportunity to a prospect, and to emphasize that product sales (not just recruiting) are the source of income to a Consultant – protecting prospects from being misinformed about the opportunity and joining under false pretenses.[26] These outcomes also protect the overall equity of R+F's brand and channel, and thereby protect the investments made by Consultants in building and maintaining their R+F businesses.

A Consultant who is successful in sponsoring one or more downline Consultants is required by the Sponsoring Responsibilities rule to perform various promotional and development functions to improve downlines' productivity. The provisions of this rule enhance Consultants' *promotion* productivity; designate the sponsoring Consultant as a *sales manager* vis-à-vis her/his downline Consultants; and require the sponsor to teach downlines to comply with the Product Claims and Income Claims rules. The sponsor is thus not only expected to improve function performance, but also to *monitor* and train downlines in compliance with the rules in order to protect the value of R+F's and all Consultants' investments in the channel.

Managing Channel Function Costs in the R+F Channel

R+F's No Inventory guidance is designed to promote more efficient (lower-cost) performance of the *financing*, *inventory holding*, and *risk bearing* functions. Given the direct-selling practice of welcoming most or all applicants, such a rule serves a teaching purpose to increase the financial attractiveness of Consultantships to prospects who might otherwise incur high inventory holding costs. Because R+F's Consultant compensation plan includes incentive payments based on sales and purchases by downline Consultants, there is a possibility that an opportunistic sponsoring Consultant might encourage her downlines to over-order inventory beyond the quantities they could reasonably be expected to sell, thus increasing her own commission earnings – but to the detriment of channel-wide inventory-holding costs. Left unmanaged, such behavior can result in lower retention of Consultants as those who have over-ordered are now "stuck" with inventory holding costs and slow movement of product – and decide to abandon their business as a result. This rule makes explicit both to sponsors and to their downlines that such inventory holding is unnecessary and is not a requirement of being a Consultant. This fosters lower system-wide inventory holding costs, which also reduces financing costs and the risk of uncertain inventory turnover rates.

Contracting and Relationship Management Rules in the R+F Channel

R+F's designation of its information database and product investments as proprietary trade secrets, owned by R+F (and not by its Consultants), is important to the protection of the value of all Consultants' investments in building their retailing and downline Consultant businesses. It therefore enhances the *relationship management* effectiveness of the R+F channel. R+F's ownership of these informational assets allows it to reliably provide support to Consultants to run their businesses, including the assurance that their sales and recruiting efforts will be protected from the possibility of poaching by other Consultants or outside companies' distributors. Consultants incur current costs in performing these functions, but reap the financial benefits only in the future. Without this protection, Consultants would be likely to exert less effort to find consumers and recruit prospects because they could not reliably expect to reap a return later for current investments in these costly functions.

Conversely, if R+F did not protect the confidentiality of Consultant performance and contact information, Consultants other than one's sponsor might access the information and seek to use it to improve their own businesses, thus harming the sponsor who invested in building retail and recruiting results. These same assets could also be poached by outside firms.

Similarly, R+F's "Line Switching" prohibition and its non-solicit and non-compete rules protect Consultants' investments in the productivity of their downlines from being poached by others in the R+F network. If these were not in place, an opportunistic Consultant would be able to recruit away the most productive downline Consultants from an upline and bring them into her/his own downline network. Such behavior would strip away the benefits the original sponsor expects from working to find and mentor productive downlines, and dampen all Consultants' incentives to engage in these activities to begin with. As with the proprietary information rule, then, these two rules also protect the value of R+F's investments in the channel.

R+F's Rules Improve Channel Protection for Both Consultants and Itself

These rules exemplify how a channel captain such as R+F can set appropriate boundaries on its partners' behaviors that simultaneously control the harm inflicted on some partners by other, opportunistic, partners. Investments in governance processes thus help ensure the integrity of partners' investments in channel performance and help prevent the few opportunistic players from reducing value for all. When all members realize that malfeasance does not go undetected or unpunished, their incentives to invest in the channel are increased, and total productivity can correspondingly increase.

Of course, simply setting rules does not guarantee that they are obeyed! Communicating the consequences for non-compliance is the next step in building a coherent governance strategy.

Communicating the Consequences

The clearest communication of the consequences for non-compliance with rules occurs in the document outlining the rules themselves or in a companion document. A firm's policies and procedures document generally reports the rules as well as noting penalties for violating the rules.

Violation of any Consultant rules in the Rodan + Fields network can result in one or more of a series of "remedial actions" at the discretion of R+F, including these escalating possibilities [27]:

- Coaching e-mail or phone call
- Issuance of a written warning letter
- Requiring that the Consultant take immediate remedial measures as directed
- Withholding R+F payments to the Consultant during the investigation period
- Suspension of the Consultant's compensation and eligibility for incentive program awards for one or more compensation periods
- Permanent termination of the Consultant
- Instituting legal proceedings against the Consultant.

> *Optimal monitoring investments typically do not detect all violations.*

While any of these actions can be taken when the Consultant violates rules or engages in deceptive or unethical business conduct, the implication of this escalating set of actions is that the "penalty will fit the crime" – both in pursuit of an equitable solution and in order to convey integrity in the imposition of consequences. In cases of severe rules violations, terminating a Consultant deprives her of future rights, compensation, and awards from her R+F business, including commissions on downlines' sales or the right to sell R+F products.

Another direct selling firm, USANA,[28] discusses similar consequences for violating rules of conduct in its Annual Report:

> "Infractions of the policies and procedures are reported to our compliance group, who determine what disciplinary action is warranted in each case. More serious infractions are reported to our Compliance Committee, which includes USANA executives. If we determine that an Associate has violated any of our policies and procedures, we may take a number of disciplinary actions, such as warnings, fines or probation. We may also withdraw or deny awards, suspend privileges, withhold commissions until specific conditions are satisfied, or take other appropriate actions in our discretion,

including termination of the Associate's purchase and distribution rights."[29]

Monitoring Activities in a Direct Selling Channel

The economic theory of rules monitoring and enforcement balances the costs and benefits of enforcement to maximize social value. Two important implications are that expenditures on monitoring activities will typically not be large enough to detect all violations, and that lower-cost enforcement technologies lead to greater enforcement and thus a lower violation rate.[30]

For example, Mannatech, a direct seller of nutritional supplements and related products, describes its monitoring by the company's legal/compliance department,[31] but explicitly notes limitations on its ability to detect all violations: "We actively monitor our independent associates' sales of our products and the promotion of certain business opportunities by requiring our independent associates to abide by our policies and procedures. However, we have limited control over the actions of our independent associates."

Direct selling firms seek to control the costs of monitoring in multiple ways. One tactic is to encourage distributors to provide information about possible violations, rather than relying only on the firm's own enforcement efforts. Doing so increases the efficiency (i.e. lowers the cost) and effectiveness (i.e. leads to the uncovering of more violations) of overall monitoring and enforcement efforts, because distributors interact with each other and with consumers on a daily basis and may thus face a lower cost of monitoring and discovering rules violations than if the firm bore the entire burden of monitoring. Distributors or consumers can thus offer a lower-cost monitoring "technology" than internal monitoring efforts by the manufacturer itself. For example, direct seller Mannatech encourages its Associates to report violations with an appeal to the interdependence of all Associates and the company itself:

> "The Company is committed to complying with all legal requirements. It is essential for all Associates to comply as well. We all depend on one another. The non-compliance of one may result in problems for everyone else. Accordingly, to enable the Company to ensure that its operations at every level comply with legal requirements, you are requested to report any violations of Company Policies & Procedures that come to your attention."[32]

The thoughtful channel strategist recognizes the potential for rules violations and seeks governance mechanisms that help prevent them in the future – rather than only reacting when a violation has already occurred. Consistent with the idea that "an ounce of prevention is worth a pound of cure," the cost of monitoring and enforcement of rules can be reduced through education of partners about the regulations, rules and norms by which the channel is expected to operate. After all, your partners cannot comply with rules of which they are not aware! Training can *deter* future rules violations because distributors understand better what is expected of them (thus resolving *perceptual conflict*), as well as rehabilitate a violating distributor who may then go on to productively sell and mentor other distributors, to the benefit of the direct selling firm and the distributor network as well. The Direct Selling Association's Code of Ethics encourages this attitude in its requirement that member firms "provide adequate training to enable independent salespeople to operate ethically."[33] This investment in distributor education is not costless. However, educating partners from the beginning of their relationship with the channel strategist, and reinforcing that education in multiple venues and at multiple times, serves a preventative purpose, as those who are educated are not likely to violate these regulations simply through ignorance.

> *An ounce of prevention (educating your partners) is worth a pound of cure (enforcement).*

Direct selling companies also hire outside firms with superior monitoring technologies, effectively adding a partner participating in the governance strategy at a more effective and efficient level. For example, big-data analytics firms can help direct selling firms identify abnormally high order volumes from individual distributors' per-period purchase behavior, a useful input to monitoring for inventory-loading behavior. Similarly, legal firm Vorys[34] offers services to firms to track and combat unauthorized online sales of their products, a growing concern with the rise of unauthorized sellers of products on sites such as eBay and Amazon.

Lower-cost monitoring and detection technologies permit greater detection of malfeasance to take place. In turn, when partners like direct-selling distributors are made aware of the extent of monitoring and enforcement practices by the channel captain, they are less likely to seek to violate the channel's regulations, rules, and norms of behavior, because of the greater likelihood of being discovered. The extent of the captain's investments, the company's interest in discovering better monitoring/detection technologies, and the extent to which it welcomes inputs from partners or consumers themselves are all consistent with a strong channel governance strategy.

Enforcement of Penalties

For a governance strategy to be effective, the firm must be willing to enforce the stated penalties for non-compliance with rules. Research suggests that more serious infringements carry greater penalties, while minor rules infractions may not be detected and punished – or may only carry a minor penalty in a well-managed governance strategy. A first-time or minor rules violation may also trigger rehabilitative training to improve the violating member's understanding of the rules of the channel.

Applied to the direct-selling rules enforcement context, this logic suggests that punishments for at least the more moderate rules infractions should fall short of termination of the offending distributor under the best-managed policy – because termination not only reduces network productivity through the removal of the distributor and his direct productivity, but also inflicts indirect costs on others in the network who rely on this distributor for training and mentoring.

> *Greater penalties are warranted for more serious infringements.*

When they are financially feasible, research also recommends fines over termination as a penalty to a violating direct-selling distributor. One possible meaning of financial feasibility (though not necessarily the only one) would be limiting a fine to no more than the financial gain enjoyed through violation of the relevant Rule. The option of suspending a Consultant's compensation for a defined time period is an example of such a fine in R+F's system.

Imperfect Governance is the Norm: Monitoring and Enforcement Efforts in Other Contexts

Incomplete detection and enforcement are common behaviors in many situations, not just in direct selling distribution, because the economic costs of very extensive preventive actions are so high as to swamp the marginal benefits of increased detection of malfeasance or imperfect performance. The example of the purposeful holding of safety stock inventory that either overshoots or undershoots actual demand illustrate these points.

Some level of "failure" is not only tolerated in inventory management processes, but sought as the best compromise between cost and effectiveness. Operations management models of optimal inventory holding (where "optimal" balances the profitability impact of being in-stock against the cost of holding high inventory levels to achieve in-stock status) show that under uncertainty in either demand or delivery speed (or both), the inventory level that maximizes expected profits entails a positive expected occurrence of out-of-stocks.[35] That is, it is not profitable to hold so much inventory that there is never a stockout; the cost of foregone sales from a disappointed customer who cannot find his/her desired product is counterbalanced by the cost savings in inventory holding costs. Further, overstocks – the situation where more inventory is held than current demand requests – are also expected to occur in the optimal stocking solution, due to uncertainties on the demand and supply sides.

A related concept is *safety inventory* or *safety stock*. In some inventorying situations, the objective of the stocking firm (be it a manufacturer, distributor, or retailer) is to never exceed some $x\%$ out-of-stock percentage. Optimizing safety stocks then involves holding enough stock at all times to guarantee that stockouts will occur no more than x percent of the time (or for no more than x percent of orders, or for no more than x percent of SKUs).

Whether the channel captain's inventory management problem is to choose the most profitable stockout rate, given informational and marketplace conditions, or to choose inventory holding levels given a target stockout rate, the outcome that maximizes overall system performance (on the demand and supply sides jointly) only imperfectly meets all customer demands for products. Thus, imperfect performance is in fact the optimal outcome of a profit-maximizing inventory process in a well-managed channel structure.

From "What Could Go Awry?" to "How to Keep It from Happening"

Even the best-laid design plans are subject to implementation challenges. You therefore need a governance process that "verifies," not just "trusts," when managing your strategy. A good governance process includes the key elements of the establishment of rules of conduct, the clear communication of those rules to all partners, investments in monitoring your channel to assure its smooth operation, and an enforcement plan to assess consequences for malfeasance and to signal your seriousness about cooperation and performance. Table 9-4 summarizes the mechanisms to make these elements work in your governance strategy:

Table 9-4:
Mechanisms for Effective Channel Governance

Strategy Element	Definition	Mechanism
1. Establish channel "rules of conduct"	Encode what is expected of each member – including the channel captain	Audit of desired function allocations to each partner; Share your "rules of conduct" with partners for clear communications of expectations for performance; Assess misalignments in current execution
2. Clearly communicate consequences of violating the rules	Communicate rules and consequences to each partner	Include consequences for violations in your "rules of conduct" document
3. Monitor activities/behaviors of partners	Invest in verification of partners' performance of allocated functions	Identify metrics to flag possible malfeasance; Encode an investigation process, shared with all partners; Invite partners to flag suspicious behavior; Allow for partner feedback during an investigation
4. Enforce consequences when violation is found	Implement a (possibly multi-step) process that equitably applies penalties when warranted	Use an escalating scale of penalties for increasingly severe rules violations – not an immediate-termination clause; Assess penalties fairly; Seek to "rehabilitate" moderate offenders; Communicate with all members that you are enforcing the rules

At each stage of the process, communication with your partners and their involvement in making the process work are both important. Most of your partners want the channel to work properly because it promotes consistency in the market and protects the upfront investments made by you and your partners – which typically bear fruit not only when they are made, but in the future. Without the reasonable guarantee of a "lifetime value" of those investments, your channel performance will suffer because your partners will expect a lower payback from costly upfront investments. With good governance in place, however, you set the stage for strong investments with long-term payoffs to all partners.

Chapter 10: HOW TO THRIVE WITH A POWERFUL CHANNEL PARTNER?

One of the most common questions we are asked is, "How do we work with a channel partner when we have no power over them?" Our short answer is that every firm has *some* form(s) of power; the key is to identify and exploit them. Whether you are an equally powerful or less powerful partner, many strategies are possible. In this chapter, we'll consider both. We'll begin with the situation of asymmetry – one partner has more or less power than the other – and use the example of Cinnabon and Pillsbury to illustrate how to manage events. Then we will consider "dancing with equals": how powerful partners can actively manage their powerful partners, and how to diagnose various sources of power and systematically manage conflicts.

Asymmetric Power, or How to Dance with Elephants

Let's learn from the example of one small company that successfully "danced with an elephant." Cinnabon was founded in 1985 and its cinnamon rolls are sold through 1100+ corporate and franchised bakeries (most commonly found in shopping malls) across 47 states and 56 countries.[36] Cinnabon is one of several brands, along with Auntie Anne's, Carvel, Schlotzky's, and Moe's, that belong to Focus Brands. In 2006, Cinnabon began to license its recipes and proprietary cinnamon flavoring in a distribution agreement with Pillsbury, the category leader in refrigerated dough, which dominated virtually all retail routes to end customers. Pillsbury's products were rolled into a cylinder and sold through every major supermarket in America. Cinnabon's signature cinnamon flavor was first included in the Pillsbury Grands! product. Initially, the branding on this package was predominantly Pillsbury, with a smaller space devoted to Cinnabon's branding. However, this joint effort was so successful that by 2010 Pillsbury had added Cinnabon's cinnamon to its heritage / core line of sweet rolls and Cinnabon's branding grew in prominence relative to the Pillsbury branding on product packages, as illustrated in Figure 10-1.

Figure 10-1:
Evolution of the Cinnabon Pillsbury Product Packaging

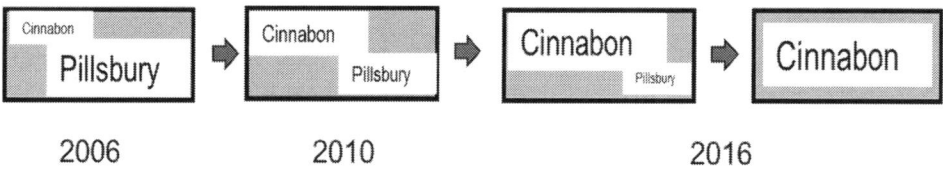

Sales continued to increase until now all of Pillsbury's sweet dough products are made with Cinnabon cinnamon and branded as such. Moreover, some

Cinnabon products, such as Cinnabon Mini Pull-Aparts, are made by Pillsbury, but the Pillsbury branding no longer appears on the packaging.

This example illustrates two powerful insights about the nature of power in channel relationships. The first is that the apparently less powerful (more dependent) partner, Cinnabon, can in fact thrive with an extremely powerful partner, Pillsbury. In other words, *even in asymmetric power situations, there still exists some form of leverage.* Firms are not always disadvantaged simply because they are smaller or have lower market shares or revenues than their partner. In this chapter, we will explain why this is the case and what the channel strategist can do in such a situation.

The second key insight is that *the judicious use of power plays a key role in improving and achieving channel coordination.* Powerful partners, acting as benevolent dictators, can drive a tremendous amount of channel value to all members in the channel structure in a long-term and sustainable manner.

> *Channel power is the ability of one channel member to get another channel member to do something it otherwise would not have done.*

"Power" is an emotionally charged term, often with negative connotations. Of course, power can be misused or abused, and this can cause significant harm to the channel's short-term performance and longer-term viability. As an example, one supply partner of Sears Roebuck famously said "I hate Sears, but they made me a wealthy man." However, this view that power always corrupts, and corrupts completely, does not have to be confirmed when power asymmetries exist in a channel. In fact, we would contend that this should not occur in a well-managed channel.

Channel power is neither uniformly to be praised nor condemned. Rather, it is a tool for effecting change. Because channel members typically do not have the same end goals in mind (for example, maximizing the profits of the whole channel does not usually lead to the maximization of profits for every single channel member), it is not likely that a channel will reach its optimal performance if each member is left to its own devices. Power can be a change agent not just for the enrichment of the channel captain, but of all channel members.

Invest to Build and Leverage Power

How Small Players Can Have Big Power

Why would a large and powerful firm work with a small one? Because the smaller firm typically has a resource or capability that the more powerful firm does not have or can't easily develop itself. Cinnabon has two proprietary resources, its cinnamon ingredient and a developed brand equity and market position, which can help differentiate Pillsbury dough. Cinnabon's ingredient and positioning resources are therefore *scarce*, and it has *expertise* in cinnamon flavor development that is not only widely acknowledged by consumers at large, but valued. This expertise also represents a form of *referent* power in that it makes the Cinnabon brand a valued asset for Pillsbury. As Pillsbury's utility for these resources increases, so does its dependency on Cinnabon. Put differently, Cinnabon has some power over Pillsbury despite its much smaller size.

There are several aspects to note here before moving on. The first is that Cinnabon's value or utility is *specific* to Pillsbury. This same value – Cinnabon's unique ingredients, market positioning, and expertise – may not be equally valued by other partners. Cinnabon has had a wide array of partners, ranging from snack bars, mass merchandisers, grocers, warehouse clubs,[37] coffee drink and beverage makers, to other ingredient product makers such as Oreos; it has even been placed in a television series.[38] Given this variety, it's not difficult to imagine that these partners likely valued a partnership with Cinnabon differently, with some partnerships not working out as well as the one with Pillsbury.

The scarcity of a resource and a channel member's acknowledged expertise (its referent power) is not limited to large firms with majority market shares and hundreds of employees. These elements are available to firms of *any* size and position and can form the basis of that channel member's power over its partner. This is critical to remember, as it helps to level the playing field of power sources.

Every channel member has one or more bases of power, and it is up to that firm to determine not only what their current and future source(s) of power may be, but how best to use them. Although Cinnabon did not have the channel pull power or marketing resources of Pillsbury, Cinnabon's basis of power was the brand equity that it had created with customers. When the United Parcel Service (UPS) considers its route to market through various retailers, the question they ask each is "What's your currency?" In other words, what power basis does the partner bring to bear on the exchange, or what skills and resources should UPS be valuing in this retail partner?

> *Every channel member has bases of power and it is up to that firm to determine not only what sources of power they will invest in, but also how best to use them.*

Note that lack of power need not imply that a channel member must be unhappy in the channel relationship. When the channel's profits are deemed to be fairly distributed, even a small-share channel partner may be very satisfied, so long as channel members believe that distributive justice has been served. In short, the lower-power partner does not expect the lion's share of channel profits – just its fair share.

Building Power

Like trust, power is a resource that is built slowly over time, but it can have substantial impact on the performance of a channel relationship. Bathwater in a tub is an apt metaphor for trust – the water levels in a tub build slowly, but can be quickly drained. Power operates in a similar manner. It is often built incrementally by consistent action, but if abused or not strategically exercised, it can be quickly lost.

Research has shown that there are benefits to being the lower-power partner.[39] Lower-power partners typically try to predict the needs of their powerful partners and are concerned with making a favorable impression during negotiations. As a result, they tend to ask more diagnostic questions. This pays off for the lower-power partner in that it results in more accuracy and creates favorable impressions during the negotiation. This attention to detail and search for opportunities that are congruent with the powerful partner's goals is one means by which power is built. In contrast, powerful partners have a tendency to feel overconfident and are typically less motivated to engage in careful information processing; put differently, they tend to search less for information about a less powerful partner.[40] This suggests that the less powerful partner is more likely to be the one that identifies opportunities for joint pie expansion and may in fact be an effective, if not outstanding, driver of the partnership.

From the perspective of the more powerful party, this approach from the lower-power partner aids in the building of trust, particularly when the powerful partner is more socially, or "we" oriented – i.e. they value mutually beneficial outcomes.[41] Such partners are more likely to be empathetic toward the lower partner's negotiation efforts. Together, these aspects underscore the importance of careful partner selection.

> *This suggests that the less powerful partner is more likely to be the one that identifies opportunities for joint pie expansion and may in fact, be an effective, if not outstanding, driver of the partnership.*

Cinnabon's strategy in its relationship with Pillsbury should therefore be to continue investing in and build its power base. This means that apart from Pillsbury, it continues to invest in marketing communications that strengthen and build its brand awareness. It may mean that it targets foreign countries in order to grow its brand presence. It could also mean that it continues to build its capability as a partner by working with alternative partners, thus developing its own strategies for building and maintaining successful partnerships. As a firm becomes better at learning how to manage partnerships, its facility in entering and exiting future partnerships increases. Moreover, it gains a market reputation as a good partner to work with. In this manner, less powerful parties can expand on and strengthen their sources of power vis-à-vis their powerful partners.

In sum, the strategy of both partners, but particularly that of the less powerful partner, should be to view their sources of power as *strategic assets* that are worthy of investment. In the same way that firms invest in and maintain their capital equipment and machinery, they should be investing in their reputations, key capabilities, and sources of differentiation that could be valued by potential partners.

The Benevolent Dictator

How is power best used? Recall that Pillsbury was the largest supplier of refrigerator dough to supermarkets and literally owned that category and all access to grocery and retail channels. It could easily have extorted or abused Cinnabon's brand equity as the price of its access to supermarket shelves. However, instead of exploiting its power and taking advantage of Cinnabon, it held its power in check and instead used its production capabilities and vast access to distribution resources to create a unique product for its customers that would not have been possible on its own. This suggests that powerful partners can create and drive a great deal of the joint partnership value. By acting as a "benevolent dictator," i.e. identifying and implementing an effective plan that creates value for itself *and* the less powerful partner, the firm ensures that both are better off than they would have been alone. Cinnabon's sales increase through expanded distribution and brand communication efforts, while Pillsbury acquires a valuable and differentiating attribute that increases demand for its refrigerated dough products.

It's important to realize that when we use the term "benevolence," we are not equating it to altruism. There is nothing altruistic about how Pillsbury works with Cinnabon – it is not giving anything away. Instead, it is in Pillsbury's *best long-term interests* to engage with Cinnabon in this manner. This is what creates the explosive channel value and returns that these two parties have generated.

However, "benevolence" does describe the perception of the less powerful party. Cinnabon realizes that Pillsbury can easily walk away from the deal at any point with minimal costs and it could probably pressure Cinnabon to take smaller margins for the value that it brings to the table. Pillsbury does not exploit this opportunity, which makes it appear benevolent in Cinnabon's eyes.

The benevolent dictator – a powerful partner acting in the best interests of both partners – can not only be a tremendous force for good, but can lead to the creation of substantial profits and productivity. Part of the reason for this is that the more powerful partner is often able to centralize resources and bring not just additive, but synergistic, investments to the table. Pillsbury's immense distribution structure is powerful, but when it is combined with the differentiated product offerings made possible by Cinnabon's participation, sales through this structure are enhanced.

> *The benevolent dictator – a powerful partner acting in the best interests of both partners – can be not only a tremendous force for good, it can also lead to the creation of substantial profits and productivity.*

The Nature of Power

Power is not innately destructive, but it is strongly influenced by an array of psychological processes, and these can result in either functional or dysfunctional consequences; as with most things, *it just depends*.

Power leads to a focus on the powerful party's goals and motivates that party to behave in a way that accomplishes its goals. Put differently, high-power parties are oriented toward what they want and how to obtain it; they view others through the lens of their current goals, as an instrumental means to an end. The powerful party thus views any firms that can enable it to reach its goal – a specific growth percentage of sales, a greater speed of innovation, or increased market share, for example – as its partners. Your partners may assist in achieving these goals by offering you expanded market access, differential ingredients, or unique competencies that would take time to build and develop on your own. The powerful party that is able to identify these linkages has taken the first step toward being an effective benevolent dictator.

Research has shown that power tends to make the good things about individuals better and the bad things worse. As an example, individuals with a more communal orientation – those who tend to think in terms of "we" rather than "me" – are more likely to behave generously when given power.[42] In contrast, individuals who are more exchange-oriented – focused on the *quid pro quo* – are more likely to act selfishly when given power. As an extreme example, social psychologists have found that men with a predisposition toward sexual harassment engage in more harassment when primed with power than men who do not (Bargh et al 1995). Importantly, the harassing behavior only surfaced among men who were predisposed to do so in the first place. Similarly, in the channels context power makes good partners better and bad partners worse. Those predisposed to work together for the common good are more likely to become benevolent dictators, while those that are self-oriented are more likely to use their power to force their position. Partners that are high in empathy are more likely to be generous when given power than partners that are low in empathy to begin with.[43]

This suggests that if exercised appropriately, power can be a strong force for good, benefiting the power holder and its associated partners. When *both partners* cooperate – i.e. the one with more power acts and the one with less follows – then both parties will benefit from the association. However, if this unravels, for example if a partner cheats or acts opportunistically, then the partnership becomes unstable and will likely disintegrate. The less powerful partner may begin to act against the status quo, while the more powerful tries to pull it closer. A common behavior among powerful leaders is to "keep their enemies close" when they perceive their power to be threatened. This might occur through increased monitoring activity, a demand for greater transparency, or the development of more contractual controls as a means to keep an eye on the less powerful partner. They seek this increased closeness in order to protect against the risk of losing power.[44]

> *When both partners cooperate – i.e. the one with power acts and the one with less follows – then both parties will benefit from the association.*

Researchers have found that when the more powerful party feels unqualified for its position, faces power instability, or no longer feels legitimate, it will worry about the level of respect that others have for it and might act aggressively and in a demeaning manner. This is typically done in an attempt to restore one's power.[45] When the powerful party feels insecure, it will also withhold valuable information from the partnership and try to reduce the influence of the less powerful party.

All of this implies that power is a key resource that can be leveraged for the good of the channel and its associated parties. However, its effects depend greatly on how that power is conceived, acquired, and exercised. Powerful partners that understand that their role is to lead and are willing to do so in a manner that is cooperative and prosocial are more likely to realize the fruits of their efforts. Less powerful partners that feel that they are treated fairly and reciprocate by following their lead create an interdependency between the parties that can be not only efficient, but lucrative. Power is a key resource or asset, and like any other the firm possesses, it must be managed *strategically*.

Balanced Power and Dancing with Equals

One of the most common channel scenarios occurs when a channel captain feels that its route to market isn't working and considers whether to augment its channels, in the process disintermediating (that is, going around) its existing partners. This was a particularly popular topic during the Internet boom years of the late 1990s. Many manufacturers and suppliers wanted to "do a Dell" – go straight to customers while bypassing an existing (working, but mostly inefficient) distribution channel. Unsurprisingly, this can be a huge source of conflict with legacy channel partners. The struggle to change your channel structure can result in a bloodbath, particularly if your partners are just as powerful as you are, or have sources of power complementary to yours. Let's examine how John Deere handled exactly this situation.

Targeting Homeowners at John Deere

Around 2003, Deere became aware that its residential products were not showing the sales and market share results of its farm equipment lines. Research revealed that brand recognition and reputation were strong, but in the residential side of the business these assets did not translate into strong purchase intentions. Further, four-fifths of residential purchases were influenced and/or made by a woman, and the woman was often the primary user as well (i.e. she mowed the lawn or did the snow blowing).

Deere dealerships were believed to contribute to the sales problem. These dealers originally sold agricultural products to farmers, but suburban creep caused many to be located near, or even in, suburbia instead. Although this afforded dealers a locational benefit vis-à-vis the suburban buyer, the emerging buyer segment was not technically knowledgeable about the products; did not view a riding lawnmower or snow blower purchase as core to their business or home lives; and appeared to care about accessories like cup holders as much as about functional lawn-mowing capabilities. Further, in many cases consumers did not even know where to find a Deere dealer in their locality. Those who did visit a Deere dealership found them unwelcoming and unappealing. Compounding the problem, dealers were unexcited about catering to a suburban homeowner who shared little in common with (what they viewed as) their core agricultural customer base. Yet Deere management recognized that these buyers were "the market of the future, the large property owner with two or three acres to mow."[46]

Given these problems, Deere management considered, but rejected, the idea of severing ties with its farm-focused dealers and building a new, consumer-focused channel network. The challenge of matching consumers' demands with the channel system's capabilities and interests therefore had to be dealt with if Deere was to increase its penetration of this attractive segment.

While considering this, Deere was approached by Home Depot with an offer to sell Deere-branded lawn tractors in Home Depot stores. Figure 10-1 indicates the current route to market through dealers and the proposed addition of Home Depot with a dashed line.

**Figure 10-1:
Proposed Channel Structure**

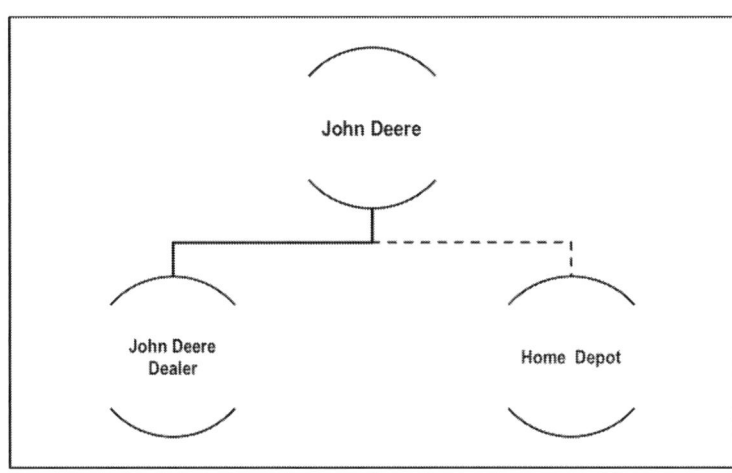

Prior to this, Deere had sold a brand of lawn tractors called Scotts through Home Depot, but the Home Depot offer would replace Scotts with Deere-branded products. The proposal would also expose dealers to a perceived risk of cannibalization from Home Depot, a much bigger competitor. In the face of this lucrative and high-volume offer, Deere management pondered how to coordinate a broader system including both the dealer channel and Home Depot.

Diagnosing Power Sources

John Deere management foresaw potentially serious conflict arising from accepting Home Depot's offer. After all, Home Depot offered to *sell* but not to *prep* or *service* the lawn tractors sold, two key functions that distributors offered. Without a strong dealer network to support customer service on *all* of its vehicles, Deere knew few consumers would buy or, just as importantly, form long-term brand preference for Deere residential products that could fuel future sales and a strong lifetime customer value model. Management therefore undertook an examination of its own sources of channel leverage and power, as well as of types and severity of potential conflicts, which could arise from accepting Home Depot's offer, and organized its expanding channel system accordingly.

The first step was an audit of power sources in the potential broader multi-channel system. An overview is provided in Table 10-1.

Table 10-1:
Power Forms

POWER OF	OVER:		
	John Deere	Dealer	Home Depot
John Deere	→	Moderate coercive/reward power Moderate legitimate power Strong expertise Strong referent	Much less power to influence Low to moderate scarcity Some reward power Moderate referent power Some legitimate power
Dealer	Strong scarcity power Strong expertise Moderate coercive/reward	↔	NONE
Home Depot	Strong scarcity power Strong reward power Strong referent power	NONE	←

John Deere recognized that its power position was stronger vis-à-vis independent dealers than it was with Home Depot, a retailing behemoth for which lawn tractors were a very small part of overall sales. Deere had moderate/coercive reward power over the dealers because of the strong sales Deere products generated, but the dealers carried competitive brands. Deere had the right to name authorized dealers and exclude others, which gave it moderate legitimate power in the channel. It also had strong expertise stemming from its products, engineering knowledge, consumer research, and consulting capabilities as well as strong referent power due to its brand name and market awareness.

Relative to the dealers, John Deere exercised considerably less power to influence Home Depot. Deere had some scarcity power because of its position as a reliable, exclusive supplier of high quality lawn tractors. It also had some reward power through its sales promise (although this was admittedly small, relative to Home Depot's size). Deere had reasonable referent power through its brand name and a legitimate power to grant or not grant the right to Home Depot to resell its lawn tractors.

While the dealers had limited influence over Home Depot (and vice versa), an analysis revealed their strong power position over Deere, largely arising from their unique provision of service on the lawn tractors, which was crucial to maintaining sales over time and thus creating a scarcity advantage. The dealers had moderate coercive/reward power in their ability to cut off service, and in their current status as the sole source of John Deere's ultimate sales to end-users.

Meanwhile, Home Depot exerted considerable scarcity power over Deere, centered on its superior ability to reach the desirable women demographic and new markets currently not accessible via the dealer channel. Home Depot also possessed strong reward power, due to the sheer number of unit sales it could promise and the lifetime value of these new customers. Home Depot also had strong referent power because women trusted the Home Depot brand and routinely shopped at their stores for lawn mowers and tractors.

Assessing Potential Conflict

Collectively, these counterbalancing power sources implied a need to carefully examine possible conflicts that could upset the balance in a channel system between new sales generated by Home Depot and strong legacy sales through dealerships. Deere's conflict analysis is encapsulated in Table 10-2.

Table 10-2:
Potential Conflict

AND:	POTENTIAL CONFLICT BETWEEN:	
	John Deere	**Dealer**
Dealer	High goal conflict High domain conflict High perceptual conflict	⬇
Home Depot	Moderate goal conflict Minimal domain conflict Low to no perceptual conflict	High goal conflict Very high domain conflict Very high perceptual conflict

The move to expand the distribution channel would likely create extreme conflict with Deere's existing dealer base. Goal conflict was high: although both parties wanted to maximize their profits, Deere wanted to accomplish this by including the new women-buyer segment, while the dealer had shown no inclination to help expand market reach to first-time buyers or women homeowner buyers. Additionally, Deere and the dealer experienced domain conflict over who was responsible for profit generation, with the dealer claiming it generated *all* profits from *all* sales of *all* Deere products in its market area, but Deere seeing dealers as unable to reach the female homeowner segment. Additionally, cost-based domain conflict was likely to arise over who should carry the costs associated with reaching this new segment. Why would dealers want to invest in selling to them if they didn't gain the profits from these sales? Finally, there would likely be high perceptual conflict between Deere and its dealers. Without some intervention, the dealer would perceive the sales expansion through Home Depot as cannibalizing and therefore injurious, while John Deere viewed the revised channel structure as market-expanding.

Between John Deere and Home Depot, conflict could be expected to be lower and of a different nature. The potential for goal conflict was moderate because Deere's goal was to maximize its profits by targeting the new women segment, while Home Depot was solely interested in maximizing its own profit. They showed little inclination to invest in the total channel's image/impact by providing post-sale service or much in-store customer service, and they made no commitment to provide Deere products top priority, shelf space, and stocking. Potential domain conflict was minimal: Home Depot saw its domain of benefits not as stealing dealers' sales but rather as profiting from sales of any Deere products in its stores, as well as from add-on sales due to shoppers coming in to buy a lawn tractor – thus, Home Depot's benefit domain spanned its whole store network, as well as non-Deere products. Conflict was possible in the domain of costs, as Home Depot did not want to bear the cost of high in-store customer service or post-sale ongoing maintenance. However, this did not guarantee meaningful domain conflict if Deere could craft a strategy to piggyback on the dealer's service provision. Finally, there was no obvious perception of reality conflict between Deere and Home Depot.

Between the dealers and Home Depot, potential goal conflict was very high: the dealer wanted to maximize its own profit from sales to all end-users (even the new women segment), while Home Depot's goal was maximizing its own profit across its full channel system, with little concern for dealers' profit protection. The potential for domain conflict was very high as well: the dealer saw its domain of benefits as all profits from all John Deere sales in its market area, while Home Depot presumably believed it was entitled to the profit from sales in its own stores. This carried the risk of generating its own possible conflict in the cost domain, as dealers would not want to continue to exert effort to build overall demand without gaining all of the associated profits. Finally, there was a real risk of potential perceptual conflict; without some intervention, dealers would likely perceive an expansion of sales through Home Depot as cannibalizing and injurious while Home Depot would perceive market expansion instead.

Collectively, Table 10-2 shows moderate to very high conflict potential for every pair of channel members in the potential expanded channel system. Goal conflicts were to be expected, but domain conflict was a potential sticking point for dealers, given the costs associated with servicing sales and growing demand. Further, perceptual conflict was strong and dangerous: John Deere saw Home Depot as a source of new customers and hence of new sources for customer lifetime value.[47] But dealers failed to see how many new sales Home Depot would produce, and instead worried about cannibalization of their business by a mass merchandiser selling at lower prices.

These conflicts could spell disaster for John Deere, given its core reliance on its dealer base. Fortunately, Deere management took this analysis to heart and conceived of a plan to simultaneously benefit from the increased market access offered by Home Depot and minimize the threat of conflict from any perceived or actual competition for dealers' business.

The Solution

Deere's solution involved embracing Home Depot's offer to sell Deere-branded lawn tractors, but necessitated efforts on multiple fronts to coordinate its new, multi-channel system. It walked this tightrope with a multi-pronged channel strategy:

- *Limited product line.* It offered Home Depot only a limited line of entry-level lawn tractors, not the full line.
- *Dealer consultations.* It consulted with its dealer advisory council about this development, rather than simply springing it on them as a *fait accompli*. Although reluctant, dealers accepted the idea, but asked to carry the same model line as Home Depot's, in addition to their current broader assortment of Deere products.
- *Training and store redesign.* Deere instituted dealer training and store redesign programs to help dealers reinvent themselves to appeal to the female homeowner customer segment.
- *Dealer education.* Deere sponsored dealer clinics specifically aimed at women, with positive dealer sales results.
- *Compensate dealers.* Because Home Depot refused to invest in post-sales technical service such as prepping a sold machine for use by the consumer, or doing periodic maintenance and repairs, Deere specified a dealer's mechanic to inspect and prep every sold vehicle before it was taken home. This led to two positive outcomes: first, the number of returns was very low, and second, dealers were paid for their activities and thus made some money even on Home Depot sales.
- *Direct service revenue streams to dealers.* Dealers were also told to affix a plate to every vehicle they prepped, listing the dealer name and contact information on every Home Depot-sold model. This effectively promised the lifetime value of service revenue streams to that dealer, rather than to Home Depot – another financial win for the dealer.

These actions illustrate Deere's judicious use of its channel power sources to effect valuable change in the channel – change with a real "win-win-win" implication not only for Deere itself, but for Home Depot and even dealers as well. Deere Chairman and CEO Robert W. Lane said, "We believe this agreement is unique by offering a new line of quality John Deere lawn tractors in the mass channel with the renowned service and support capability of John Deere dealers."[48]

The consumer who brought her lawn tractor to the John Deere dealership for yearly maintenance would further see all the accoutrements she could buy there to "trick it out" – including cup holders, fans, wineglass holders, canopies, and even air conditioning. Even more enticing was the entire line of higher-end tractors on display at the Deere dealership (but not at Home Depot!), which led to many follow-on sales and opportunities for cross-selling and selling-up.

Final Thoughts

The purpose of the frameworks above is to encourage you to at least *consider* a conflict resolution strategy – centered on the application of your sources of power and leverage – for every type of conflict you identify. However, in reality it may be difficult to reach a resolution for every conflict source. For example, note the lack of resolution of goal conflicts in Deere's strategy. It can be reasonable to decide *not* to seek to mitigate some conflicts, such as the innate goal conflicts here – either because they are relatively unimportant, because the offended channel partner is unlikely to take retaliatory action, or because it is too costly to do so.

Adding a mass-market retail presence to a pre-existing high-performing dealer channel usually generates bitter conflict in the legacy channel. Because of Deere's long-standing prior relationships – and thus the trust it had accumulated over time with its dealers – Deere management was able to *pre-emptively* design and implement a channel solution that convinced dealers to accept Home Depot's sales of the lower end of Deere's line and to build a win-win-win solution (that is, wins for Deere, Home Depot, *and* dealers) that actually rewarded dealers for Home Depot sales, rather than punishing them with pure cannibalization.

John Deere's sales rose by 10 percent in the first quarter they offered entry-level lawn tractors through Home Depot, and it added more than 100,000 new mid-level customers who previously considered Sears a primary outlet.[49] Since Deere's move to sell some models through Home Depot, it decided to also supply Lowe's (a Home Depot competitor) with the same entry-level models in 2006.[50] Deere continues to protect its dealers by reserving higher-level models for them rather than supplying the full line to all retailers, a classic channel practice that rewards high-end, service-providing channel partners by giving them sole access to more lucrative parts of the line.

However, the practice of common branding ("Deere" for all products sold through dealers, Home Depot, and Lowe's), yet segregating high-end products only in the high-end dealer channel, does create confusion around the brand's quality. One article stated in its headline, "John Deere Denies Big Store Items Are Inferior."[51] Both Home Depot and John Deere spokespeople countered that Deere's L118 model sold at Home Depot was the same as, and in fact was made in the same Tennessee factory as, the same model sold in dealerships. However, the columnist noted that Home Depot did not sell the same high-end products available at a John Deere dealership, which fostered the impression that product quality is lower at Home Depot. The same message is evident today, with a *Consumer Reports* headline, "Nothing runs like a Deere you buy at the dealer" – playing on the long-standing tag line for the company. It points out that Home Depot and Lowe's sell the "D100" class of tractors, which are also carried at dealers that service Home Depot and Lowe's customers. But dealers *also* carry the higher-rated (but more expensive) Select Series X-class products, as well as a broader array of accessories. These continuing promotional and image challenges suggest that a consistent educational effort is required to balance branding and channel-breadth imperatives in a multi-channel system.

Summary Insights

Your hard work on designing an efficient channel that responds to target end-users' demands can be useless without incentives for your channel partners to comply with the design, and indeed to enthusiastically represent your products. The power and conflict analysis reveals how much leverage you have in effecting change in the channel and in controlling nascent or explicit conflict. It also reminds you to explicitly strategize your conflict resolution actions so that you prevent conflict from destroying an otherwise promising marketing strategy.

Some key takeaways follow from this discussion:

- Identify your and your partners' power sources so that you are prepared to institute change, or to deal with incipient or erupted conflict.
- Analyze both current and potential sources of conflict. It is good to combat the conflict you see in your channel. But it is brilliant to predict the conflict that could erupt, and to pre-empt it through judicious use of power sources to encourage a coordinated outcome instead.
- Conflict resolution involves using one or more of your power sources. Thus, you should know what sources of power are available to you in which channels, partner by partner, because your power is not the same in all channels or in relationship with all partners.
- Zero conflict is neither the goal of an analysis of power and conflict, nor a realistic expectation of a channel manager.

Finally, remember that because distribution channels are purposely set up to share activities in a way that makes each channel partner dependent on other members, power is a universal asset in managing their ongoing performance. Power is typically amassed over time (sometimes over a very long time) and as a result can be a strategic asset. Abusing that power may work in the short term but is likely to backfire in the long run, suggesting that judicious power use is the better long-run strategy. Your power and conflict analyses should be ongoing, because your channel is a dynamic organism. You must periodically repeat this analysis exercise and stay in contact with your partners to preserve a relatively conflict-free channel environment.

Chapter 11: WHY DO I NEED A CHANNEL "RELATIONSHIP"?

Most organizational transactions focus on cost efficiency via price negotiations, quantity buys, and performance improvements in various channel functions. Put differently, the focus is on maximizing short-term outcomes, one transaction at a time. However, many B2B transactions are repeated over time. Knowing that you will work with the same vendor or channel member for years to come means that it may be more efficient to establish a level of cooperation or understanding that goes beyond the mere exchange of money for goods or to maintain a focus merely on short-term performance.

Such arrangements can make transactions flow more smoothly or improve the returns to the manufacturer and the channel intermediary, making their activities more mutually beneficial over time. As an example, as Microsoft seeks to establish its footing in cloud services, it will need close relationships with partners such as Rackspace Hosting Inc. to help integrate Office 365 into collaboration technology as customer firms seek to maximize the value from using Microsoft's Azure cloud computing service for their processing, data storage, databases and other services. Rackspace can assist in offering the hosting and security services that firms demand.[52]

Meanwhile, different types of partners are needed to offer highly customized applications in Sharepoint, a collaboration tool which is widely used in many firms. Collaboration can mean securely sharing sensitive information about pricing and demand, or developing new ways of going to market through product bundling or customization. Establishing close relationships with systems integrators and business consulting practices increases partners' willingness to share important information without the risk of exploitation. Systems integrators specialize in bringing together component subsystems into a whole and ensuring that the subsystems function together, and those who understand the combination of IT parts that must be applied to key business practices are key to powerfully leveraging the full technology potential. As a result, Microsoft can accelerate Office 365 implementations by providing the assets that clients are demanding.

However, developing and maintaining a channel relationship is not costless. It requires time, effort and a willingness to coordinate activities and share information. Because of this, you need to understand *when* it makes economic sense to enter into a relationship. Some firms and individuals are averse to this because of the obligations for reciprocity and the mutual "entanglements" that can ensue. There is no doubt that relationships carry risks – most strategic options do. The key for any channel manager is to recognize the possibilities and make a judgment as to whether the benefits outweigh the downsides in any particular case.

Types of Channel Relationships

This raises the natural question: *what type of relationship do I want to have with my channel partner?* The answer to this can vary along a continuum of types from one-off transactional exchanges to extremely cooperative strategic exchanges. Each of these approaches may be typified by the following characteristics:

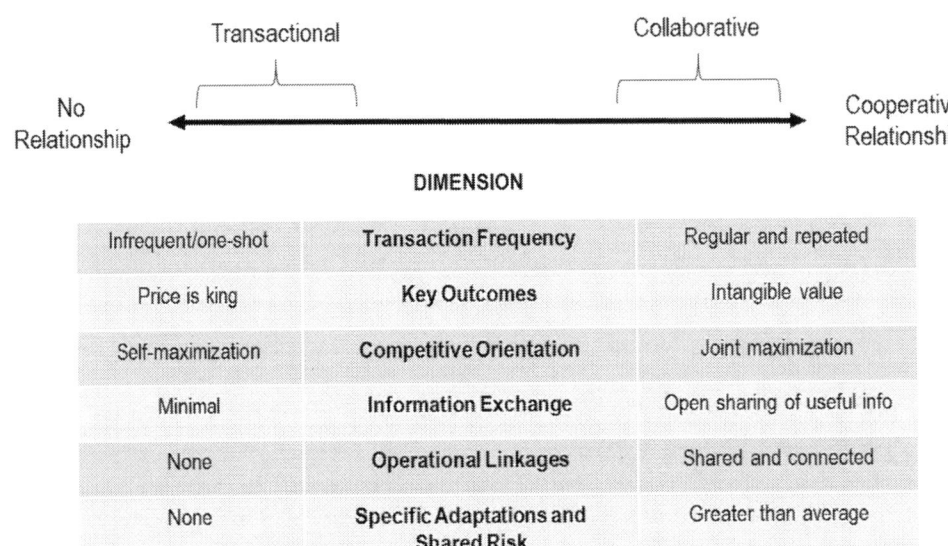

**Figure 11-1:
The Channel Relationship Continuum**

	DIMENSION	
Infrequent/one-shot	Transaction Frequency	Regular and repeated
Price is king	Key Outcomes	Intangible value
Self-maximization	Competitive Orientation	Joint maximization
Minimal	Information Exchange	Open sharing of useful info
None	Operational Linkages	Shared and connected
None	Specific Adaptations and Shared Risk	Greater than average

Transactional relationships are arms-length exchanges in which the focus is typically on money for goods or services. Each firm focuses on maximizing its own position, even at the other's expense, with minimal entanglements, commitments, or time spent on trying to better understand or appreciate the other firm's point of view or its needs and goals for the future. These types of transactions are vitally important, as they promote rapid and efficient exchanges to help achieve a one-period result. It is worth noting that this type of exchange is more the exception than the rule.

Most channel relationships involve repeat purchases, so it makes sense to develop a more collaborative relationship in which you and your channel partner attempt to do more than just pass goods and services for money. For example, it might be worthwhile to exchange information and develop technologies that improve sales forecasting and reduce inventory levels between the firms, or develop unique work flows and processes that benefit the two firms. Typically, the more the firms' people and processes are adapted to support their specific goals and needs, the more likely the two firms will achieve mutual gains and benefits. In other words, the focus of the two firms is less on fighting to divide a shared pie, and more on expanding the pie they will share.

Most channel relationships lie somewhere between these two extremes: some useful information might be shared, some joint benefit creation efforts are investigated, or pure price outcomes are less emphasized. Moving the relationship toward either end of the continuum is a strategic choice that should be systematically made (we will examine this possibility later in the chapter). For now, suffice it to say that channel relationships can be moved from one end of the continuum to the other through increased competition (signals a win-lose orientation that will move the relationship toward a more transactional state) or the development of trust (facilitates a willingness to take joint risks and the sharing of useful or more private information). As you will see, too much or too little competition or cooperation can also work against the exchange and create inefficiency. It's not as simple as taking a "friend or foe" approach; rarely can relationship development be boiled down to simply more competition or more collaboration.

> *Everyone likes to talk about building channel relationships or partnerships.*
> *It is a celebratory, visual process much like a wedding or an engagement.*
> *Rarely do managers consider how relationships break down and dissolve.*
> *Yet this process is not just the reverse of buildup.*
> *It is typically a quiet, isolated process involving suspicion, disappointment and distrust.*

Having said that, a well-working transactional relationship – with reliable and efficient exchange of money for goods – is a necessary condition for the ensuing development of more relational exchanges. Unless both parties know that exchange will happen reliably, there is little incentive to develop trust further through more relational structures or governance forms. Another way to think about this is that mutual channel exchange rests on both equity and performance over time. If the costs of working together are not outweighed by the economic value of doing so, channel exchange cannot persist.

When Does a Collaborative Relationship Make Sense?

Past research has shown that the primary reasons firms enter into collaborative relationships are to better manage uncertainty (e.g. about future demand, technology changes, or competition) and to negotiate their dependence on other organizations. These motivations suggest that the choice of channel relationship type is usually not a stand-alone decision. Various circumstances such as the availability of alternatives, the importance of the purchase, the complexity of supplying it, and the dynamism of the supply market may also determine what type of relationship is most appropriate for your circumstances.[53] As an example, industries that are marked by fast-moving demand and short product cycles can benefit from partner collaboration more than stable industries with fairly predictable demand and time horizons.

Availability of alternatives. When multiple partner alternatives are available to sell comparable goods, price and quality information is readily available to buyers and sellers. However, when there are few suppliers or the goods and services purchased become increasingly differentiated, the lack of readily available alternatives creates uncertainty that is potentially detrimental. As fewer alternatives become available to the firms comprising the channel, they become more motivated to work together to ensure their sources of supply and safeguard their performance.

Importance of the purchase. As the purchase transaction becomes increasingly strategic or has a greater impact on an organization's performance objectives, firms will be more motivated to work closely together. For example, close relationships that ensure that the sourcing of critical raw materials and components is protected into the future can be particularly beneficial. Another way to think about this is in terms of risk and associated stakes: the more costly it is to exchange, or the greater the risk of competitive learning or the payoffs associated with success, the higher the payoffs from close collaboration are likely to be.

Complexity of supply. As the complexity of transportation or provision of goods and services between channel partners increases (e.g. because the supplier wishes to exert more control over the transportation process, or because the management of information is extremely analytical or multifaceted), a closer channel relationship becomes more attractive. Consider the challenges that Dow Chemical might face in its channel structure: it may need to transport explosive or toxic chemicals to distributors or wholesalers who might also need to mix these chemicals with others in order to create the substances required by its downstream customers. These conditions may increase Dow's difficulty of evaluating its purchase choices, performance outcomes, and risk. Thus, when channel exchange itself becomes complex, the firms will be motivated to work closely together to help reduce the ambiguity and risks that arise from their transactions.

Supply market dynamism. Supply dynamism can refer to short-term changes in supply, due to frequent price changes, fluctuations in product availability, and/or long-term forces such as rapidly changing technology or variation in demand. These dynamic factors may motivate firms and their channel partners to develop close bonds to help jointly manage the uncertainties that endanger their sources of supply or their ability to respond to market demand fluctuations. However, firms should weigh these benefits against the locking-in that arises from mutual collaboration, which can make it difficult for these firms to switch away from each other and take quick advantage of a superior alternative.

These four conditions are the most common ones favoring strategic partnerships or close relations between firms. Obviously, this is not an exhaustive list; further, these conditions need not be mutually exclusive. But it provides a useful starting point from which firms can begin to consider whether the development of a closer relationship is worthwhile.

How Do I Build a Collaborative Relationship Over Time?

In the core marketing course, you learned that product sales and development move through a predictable lifecycle. The same can be said of relationships between channel members. The degree of collaboration or closeness can be characterized as the following over time:[54]

**Figure 11-2:
The Relationship Life Cycle Curve**

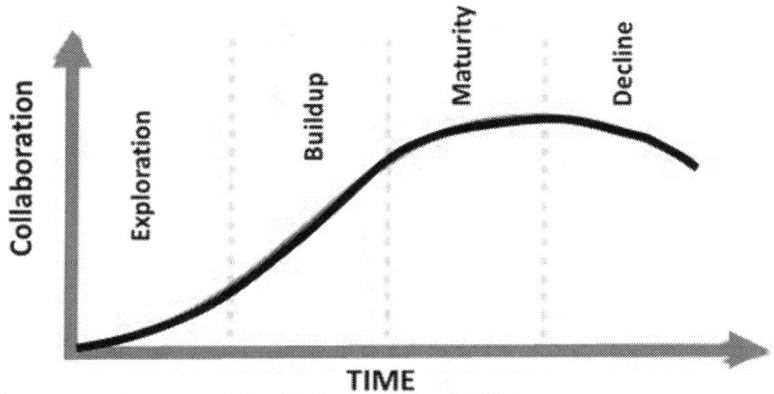

Typically, we would expect sales volumes, joint profits, and any mutual benefits created between the parties to follow a similar curve over time. What's the range of the time span (the X axis)? Like product lifecycles, it can vary from months to years, depending on the industry, the nature of the collaboration, the products and services involved, and the firms themselves. This view of relationship development comes from social exchange theory, one of whose basic premises is that the benefits from having a relationship together must outweigh the costs associated with building and maintaining the relationship in order for mutual effort to persist over time. Equitable investment from both parties is therefore a requirement for continued maintenance and enhancement of the relationship. This framework rests on the premise that equity and performance are important to both firms.

Exploration. The exploration stage is a fragile state in which the firms are "testing the waters" through relatively riskless, but repeated, transactions. During this time, the firms are assessing the ease and intangible benefits of working with each other, such as the development of reliable service, prompt payments, responsiveness to changing circumstances and needs, and mutual trust. This stage reveals whether the firms have compatible goals and can establish cooperative work norms. Like friendships in our personal lives, this stage can (but does not always) lead to the next phase of relationship development.

Buildup. The buildup phase is much like dating in that the firms are increasing their commitments to each other by developing shared patterns of behavior, specific processes, and investments in dedicated assets (e.g. capital equipment, machinery, people, etc.) that are not easily redeployed with an alternative exchange partner (i.e. a competitive supplier or distributor). In this stage, the parties are increasing their mutual trust and willingness to take risks for each other, and are less likely to consider or actively seek alternative partners. Accordingly, as the level of cooperation and close collaboration increases between them, the firms typically also experience higher returns and performance outcomes from their mutual efforts.

Maturity. While collaboration appears to peak in the mature phase of the diagram, research has shown that this phase is not significantly higher in the level of collaboration between the parties.[55] Instead, a better characterization is that the *rate of change* (i.e. the slope of the curve) will drop in the mature phase of relationships although the absolute level of collaboration may not differ greatly from that in the buildup phase. While less activity is targeted toward change and improvement, this phase typically is marked by the harvesting of the firms' efforts – the achievement and enjoyment of improved profitability, increased revenues, or more efficient and cost-effective ways of working together.

Decline. In the decline phase, one or more parties have experienced dissatisfaction with the exchange and have begun to consider or actively explore alternatives. This stage may be protracted and include multiple instances of conflict, or alternatively may exhibit a state of ongoing avoidance and perhaps passive aggression where no move is made to explicitly end the exchange. This stage could also be rapid, with a quick onset followed by the dissolution and termination of the exchange.

Management Implications

The relationship lifecycle is a powerful metaphor for explaining the developmental dynamics that we observe in channel relationships over time. Interestingly, relationships that develop through these phases in the exploration → buildup → maturity → decline sequence are healthier than those that do not. Research has shown that conflict, broken trust, or other incidents that might cause relationships to revert to an earlier phase (e.g. moving from buildup back to exploration, or from maturity back to buildup) result in lower exchange performance.[56]

This means that relationships do not recover well when trust is lost or there is conflict or a breach of confidence between the channel members. Apparently, it is not easy to go back to "business as usual"; channel members do not easily forget past problems, which takes a toll on the exchange. For this reason, channel strategists should not be afraid to switch business partners, as the cost of trying to salvage a broken relationship is likely to outweigh the benefits of doing so.

Above all, it is important to remember that relationship management is never completed or static. Too often, firms will put a great deal of effort and celebration into building long-term or collaborative exchanges. After all, this can be a highly visible, mutual effort that generates a lot of positive word of mouth. However, building a good relationship and then walking away is like abandoning a ship on the water. In order to get the maximum value out of that ship, the captain and its crew must chart new courses, maintain the boat's condition, and regularly benchmark its position over time, or else the boat will never reach new destinations and accomplish all that it was created for. In the same way, building long-term collaborative exchanges with channel partners requires constant attention and efforts in order to make them worthwhile over the long run. For ongoing relationships, this means adopting a strategy that is dynamic and adaptive.

> *Relationships do not recover well when trust is lost or there is a breach of confidence or conflict between the channel members.*

Getting the Balance Right

There are many circumstances under which having a strong channel relationship makes sense. Many pie-expanding benefits can be created with a cooperative channel partner, but it is a fallacy to think that relationships are always beneficial. Some firms go to market with a "relational strategy," in which all of their representatives are charged to build relationships. Their position may in fact be titled, "relationship manager." As an example, ANZ Bank, which holds a leading market share in the banking sector across Australia and New Zealand, refers to its institutional sales force as relationship managers. Its goal is to develop a deep knowledge of a client's business, bringing in relevant product specialists to offer business clients a tailored banking solution for their specific needs.

While the intent of this position is often to reiterate the importance of building strong relationships, it takes a more balanced perspective to understand when developing friendly but "relational" exchanges is truly worthwhile (and when it is not). The energy needed to develop and build long-lasting business relationships is non-trivial and often draws resources and attention from other potential customers, channel members and opportunities. The challenge to the firm is to be able to better identify the circumstances under which such relational investments are worth the costs. To this end, we have created a framework to help firms quantify the potential value from spending their valuable relational energy.

This analysis can be useful even when applied to your "best" or what you believe to be your most valuable channel partners.[57] The framework can be implemented from either the sales or buying side. In this case, we will consider the perspective of a firm which is considering whether it makes sense to develop deeper or more transparent relationships with its channel members. The key to this approach is to diagnose every channel relationship in terms of the degree of relationship equity that has already been built – what we will refer to as the current state of the relationship vis-à-vis its economic potential. These possibilities are graphically illustrated in Figure 11-3.

**Figure 11-3:
A Relational Investment Framework**

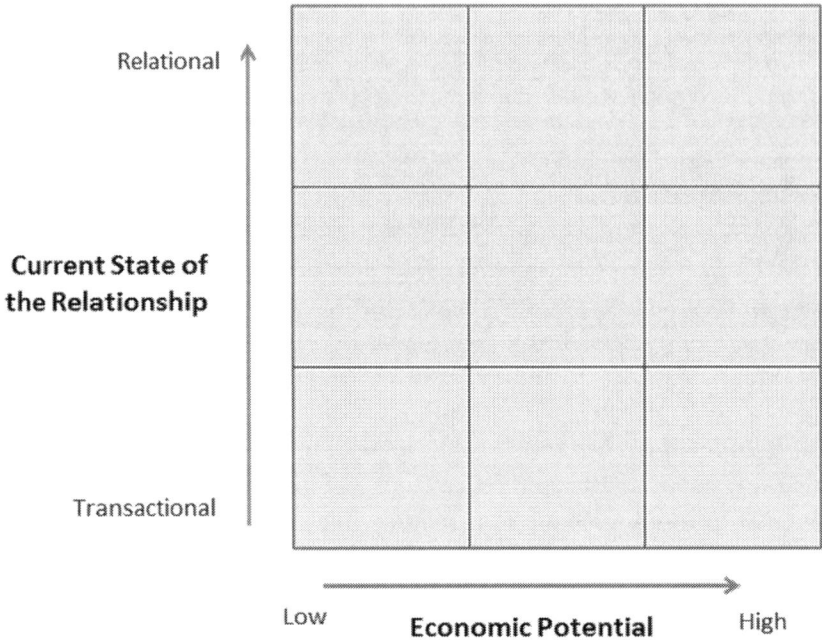

The horizontal axis indicates the potential payoff from building relationships at a given point in time, assessed from the customer point of view. The vertical axis reflects the state of the current relationship that has been built between the firm and the channel member. "Relational" refers to a long-term relationship with social linkages, implicit understandings, and expectations of close exchange in the future. In contrast, the "transactional" end of the graph's vertical axis implies an explicit focus on efficiency outcomes, including equal division or gains for both parties in the short term.

Step 1: Determine the economic potential of a closer relationship

The framework was originally developed to be generalizable to a wide variety of B2B contexts, whether from the perspective of a supplier selling to business customers, or from a procurement group seeking supply from a base of firms. In this chapter, however, we will narrow its scope to that of a supplier who is going to market through a set of potential channel members. Let's imagine that Acme is a manufacturer of metal components and parts, and seeks to determine whether partnerships with wholesalers, distributors, or retailers would be worth developing in order to reach its end users, the various mechanics in mom and pop shops and garages.

The economic potential of developing closer relationships depends on three critical aspects:

- Channel partner positioning
- Acme's sales needs
- Market conditions.

The channel partner's positioning is particularly critical if that organization offers its downstream customers a differentiated value offering. If the wholesaler or distributor is pursuing a differentiation strategy, or has substantial purchasing power, its product may be critical to its downstream customer market in turn. Some distributors' competitive advantage arises not just from their sources of supply, but in the recombination of these supply parts with others, perhaps to create valuable subassemblies or to offer a rounded portfolio of offerings to its customers. In this case, a closer relationship could uncover new opportunities to further differentiate its or Acme's offering to customers. Put differently, the opportunity to co-create and co-develop unique offerings together represents the potential value from forming a closer relationship.

The second thing to consider is Acme's own production and delivery processes. If its product and service line relies on a co-investment by the channel partner, such as specialized storage facilities or intensive handling procedures, or if the product is complex to implement, perhaps requiring customization or substantial involvement from the partner, then a closer relationship would be worth developing. This relationship can reduce frictions in communication and increase channel function efficiencies, as well as strengthen a common goal orientation in the channel. Ultimately, a closer relationship can therefore lead to less opportunistic behavior, greater reciprocation, and a stronger perception of fairness on both sides.

> *The opportunity to co-create and co-develop unique offerings together represents the potential value from forming a closer relationship.*

Finally, some market conditions are more conducive to the development of close relationships than others. For example, if Acme's channel partners were in the agricultural sector, seasonality might create demand fluctuations; in the high-tech sector, strong technological uncertainty would make accurate market forecasts difficult. In either such case, close relationships could help the firms weather these market conditions better than their competitors and safeguard the pair's outcomes and mutual interests.

These three aspects of partnering potential can be measured via a battery of key questions, listed below. This battery of questions assesses the economic potential or value of each channel partner relationship (for example, if Acme uses 20 distributors, then this battery of questions would be answered separately for each distributor relationship), with the response to each being indicated by a 1 to 7 scale.

The Channel Partner's Perspective
1. How critical is your product offering to the channel's downstream markets? (1=not critical, 7= critical)
2. Does the channel member have purchasing power? (1=weak, 7=strong)
3. Is the channel member's position in its downstream markets differentiated? (1=undifferentiated, 7=differentiated)

Acme's Product Needs
1. Do you create value by providing codified knowledge or tacit know-how? (1=codified knowledge, 7=tacit know-how)
2. How complex is the production process of your product offering (i.e. fixed costs)? (1=simple, 7= complex)
3. Does your product offering require customization? (1=low customization, 7=high customization)

Market Conditions
1. How many suppliers could provide an alternative to your product offering? (1=many, 7=few)
2. Is there a great deal of demand fluctuation in your product category? (1=little fluctuation, 7=fluctuates greatly)
3. How much technological uncertainty exists in your product category? (1=very little, 7=considerable)

Sum the scores and divide by nine to get a final score that ranges from 1 to 7; this will place the economic potential of each of Acme's current channel relationships along the horizontal axis of Figure 11-3. Having done this analysis and located the relationship state and economic potential of its relationship, Acme can now assess how altering its relationship development strategy could relocate the relationship and relational efforts to a level that is appropriate for its economic potential.

The closer the final score is to 7, the more important it is to develop and improve the state of the relationship to match its economic potential. Please note that any individual question which scores a "7" can serve as a standalone reason for developing a closer relationship with the channel partner. Conversely, any individual question which scores a "1" is also a sufficient reason *not* to develop a closer relationship.

Step 2: Evaluate the current state of the relationship

In a similar manner, Acme should now assess the state of the current relationship (the vertical axis dimension of Figure 11-3) with the channel member. It is important to estimate this from the channel partner's perspective, not Acme's. This is because it is possible (and not uncommon) for Acme's assessment of the relationship state to be inaccurate. On the other hand, the channel's view of the relationship sets the critical starting point for the direction in which it should be further developing or deemphasizing the relationship in the future. As an example, a channel member may treat Acme as a partner because the individual manager is open and willing to share information, but from an economic standpoint there is little to gain from a closer relationship. Or the channel member may fail to realize the value to be gained from sharing more information or co-developing the next generation of products with Acme. Either scenario carries implications for how Acme should manage the relationship.

The next step is to assess the state of the current relationship with that channel member. Again, a battery of statements can provide a measurement of this. These are listed below; it is important to note that these items focus on the channel member's point of view, not Acme's.

Current Relationship State

Now rate how the channel member treats its relationship with you today, again using the following scale: 1 = strongly disagree; 7 = strongly agree with the statements:

1. We have a close relationship with Acme
2. Acme treats me like a partner
3. Acme shares privileged information with us

Again, average the scores to get a final score that ranges from 1 to 7; this will place the channel relationship along the vertical axis of Figure 11-3. We now have the two key values by which to locate Acme's channel relationship on the graph in Figure 11-3.

Step 3: Analyze next steps

Let's imagine that you conducted this analysis for a group of Acme's channel partners. The results are depicted below in Figure 11-4, based on numerous implementations of this framework with companies like Acme.

Figure 11-4:
Mapping Relational States to Value

The diagonal is desirable. In general, Acme's goal should be to have its relationships aligned on the diagonal. This implies that lower relationship development efforts are exerted on channel relationships with lower economic potential. Meanwhile, channel partners with high economic potential arising from their positioning strategies or market conditions merit efforts to build trust, share useful information, align goals, and collaborate in such a way as to expand the pie of benefits *together*, so that high economic potential is accompanied by high relationship development efforts. Put differently, Acme's relationship development efforts are properly aligned for relationships falling into this diagonal part of the space.

We see that many of Acme's relationships are in fact aligned along the diagonal, with the largest portion of these in a Test the Waters stage. These are relationships for which there is middling economic potential; more understanding is needed in order to identify whether they would be more productive if positioned high or lower on the diagonal.

It is important to note some trends that we observe robustly across many industries and countries. The first is that only 14% of Acme's channel relationships have the economic potential that would benefit from matching the state of the relationship to its economic potential (these are the relationships in the Grow The Pie region.) Another way of thinking about this is that many of Acme's relationships are misaligned (e.g. they have too much or too little relationship investment for their economic potential); by this we are referring to relationships in the Rose Colored Glasses zone, as well as the "Necessary Enlightenment" zone.

This alignment gap between relationship development efforts and economic potential is not uncommon. Given that the Rose Colored Glasses and Necessary Enlightenment zone observations account for nearly 50% of all of Acme's relationships, there is a need for a substantial change in how the parties work together, incentivize, and reward their mutual efforts. Let's now consider each zone more closely.

Rose Colored Glasses. In the Rose Colored Glasses zone, there is too much friendship for the economic potential. Close relationships have been built – this is a costly and time-consuming effort, and its value is questionable given the economic potential. This is an extremely common mistake, and will naturally arise if your firm culture emphasizes the creation of close relationships *at all costs*. In one class discussion, we had a student we'll call Tom, who offered to serve as an in-depth case study to illustrate the framework. Tom worked for a transportation company and proudly told the class about a customer whose average relationship state was a two when he first took over the account. A year later, he had turned that into a six. However, upon further inspection of the economic potential, the class discovered that his efforts were misaligned – he had spent a great deal of time developing a close relationship with a customer for whom the economic potential from partnering was in fact quite low. There were few if any sources of differentiation associated with this customer, the sale of goods and its exchange were relatively straightforward, and the industry was stable with predictable demand.

> *Close relationships have been built – this is a costly and time-consuming effort, and its value is questionable given the economic potential.*
> *This is an extremely common mistake, and will naturally arise if your firm culture emphasizes the creation of close relationships at all costs.*

The management implications of Tom's experience are straightforward. For Acme, the strategy is to enjoy its close relationship with the channel member, but to minimize future relational investments. Relational investments have been made, but should not be continued or should be withdrawn over time. The channel member has likely misperceived the value of a close relationship, and this misperception is working in Acme's favor.[58] The channel partner's relational efforts are enjoyable – it might be willing to share resources and useful information or make investments that benefit their relationship with Acme. However, because of the low economic potential, Acme would be better off redirecting its relational efforts to a more promising channel partner. This is why we refer to this zone as the Rose Colored Glasses area. Acme is in a place of relative enjoyment – the partner has overestimated the value of its relationship with Acme – but the reality is that this is not a relationship that is worth more relational efforts from Acme.

Necessary Enlightenment. If a relationship is plotted in the "Necessary Enlightenment" area, it means that the current relationship state is too transactional, or not "warm" enough. Here, substantial economic value could be exploited if Acme's exchange with this channel member were closer – if more information sharing occurred, trust was built, future goals shared, and a search for more mutual benefit conducted. One way to get started might be to identify a key project that demonstrates the need for closer collaboration. Perhaps this means changing some aspect of a warehouse delivery system, e.g. shipping straight to stores instead of to a distribution center. The implication is a need to marshal the resources – as the supplier, Acme might have to be willing to take on a larger share of this effort – in order to convince the channel partner of the need to work more closely together.

Price is Right. For relationships located in the "Price Is Right" range, the focus should be on operational efficiencies, not on spending resources on relationship building, given the low economic potential of the relationship. This also frees the parties to concentrate their resources on cost minimization efforts and price management. Perhaps undertaking value analysis activities or exploring engineering initiatives to lower the channel's total cost of ownership would make sense. In some cases, systematic cannibalization via the development of a lower cost alternative might also be appropriate. How can costs be lowered between the parties? Employees are often an excellent source of innovation in this area.

For relationships located in the "Price Is Right" range, the focus should be on operational efficiencies, not on spending resources on relationship building, given the low economic potential of the relationship.

Test the Waters. When a relationship is located in the middle, it suggests that increased investments in partnering might have value, but closer consideration is needed. Channel relationships located in this range would benefit from a closer look at the scores for economic potential. For example, it might be that the firms are able to identify an area where tacit know-how or some form of codified knowledge could be mutually beneficial. Or it might be that the firms have engaged in fruitful collaboration in the past and should now consider circumstances under which they could develop additional collaboration. It might also be that their industry has the propensity to change relatively quickly, perhaps because new competitors are entering or there is the potential for demand to become more difficult to forecast. If any of these conditions are present, then Acme's strategy would be to move these current channel relationships toward the "Grow The Pie" region.

It might also suggest that a "middle of the road" strategy really is the best course, in which case continued moderate investments in the relationship would be the best approach. Perhaps it keeps the partners flexible and able to respond quickly to a changing environment if needed. It's worth also considering the stability of this state. If the relationship has been in this "intermediate" state for a number of years, it might be that this is a strategic desire of the channel member – to keep a close, but not too close, relationship.

Grow The Pie. The true strategic partnering situation is only found at the high end of the diagonal. Being located here means that there are compelling reasons to work more closely together, share important information, and seek to expand a joint pie of benefits. The channel member will likely be aware of this, having demonstrated that it is willing to develop a close relationship with Acme. For relationships of this type, efforts to co-develop and co-innovate would be extremely worthwhile. When firms make mutual investments that exploit complementary competencies between them, value grows for both. The focus of the relationship should be on building trust, exchanging useful information, and exploring breakthrough solutions.

Strategic partnering is the quintessential form of relational exchange, requiring both parties to support the relationship in order to expand the efficiency frontier between them. This is where breakthrough advantages and benefits are created. However, successfully creating and managing such partnerships is enormously difficult. It is important that you have a clear understanding of the circumstances under which such efforts are worthwhile, as well as the key ingredients for success. This is the purview of the next chapter, where we again focus on how to "do" strategic partnering better.

The framework we have described is useful for diagnosing your existing partnering strategy at a specific point in time. The relationships might usefully be re-assessed six months or a year later to ensure that your relationship efforts are on track and aligned.

Chapter 12: WHEN SHOULD I TAKE THE LEAP TO STRATEGIC PARTNERING?

Recreating Flower Distribution

For anyone who loves receiving fresh flowers, the emphasis is on *fresh*. Flowers need to feel and appear as if they were just plucked from the plant. However, many flowers can take as long as a week to travel from the grower to a wholesaler, then to a distributor, before finally appearing on a retailer's shelf. This was the dominant route to market for flowers when Ruth Owades decided that this market needed some explosive channel value.

Calyx & Corolla became the first company to increase flower freshness by as much as 80% while delivering them to a doorstep.[59] These flowers were not just the carnations that one would find near the vegetable section of a grocery store. They were fresh anthuriums, orchids, tulips and other exotic blooms. Within a year annual sales reached $4 million, then more than doubled the following year. A little more than 10 years later, the company would generate annual revenues of approximately $16.8 million, with gross margins of more than 50%. Its route to market consisted of 6 million catalogs sent annually, with 40% of its orders taken online.[60]

Moreover, Calyx & Corolla accomplished this without ever holding or owning flower inventory. Instead, it served as the masterful channel captain of a network of strategic partners that jointly managed to provide consumers eight more days of freshness value. At the time, conventional flower delivery occurred at approximately ten days past the day that they were cut at a grower. Under Calyx & Corolla, flowers were delivered from the grower within two days.[61]

How did Calyx & Corolla achieve such stunning success? Via the use of a series of strategic partnerships. What exactly is a strategic partnership? A strategic partnership goes beyond mere cooperation between two channel partners. Instead, it involves significant stakes and risks, trust, and complementary competencies from all partners involved. In particular, it involves a number of *specific adaptations*, including relational, capital, knowledge, and process investments from each partner.

In this chapter we will describe the conditions under which a strategic partnership makes sense. The bad news is that strategic partnering is a difficult endeavor at which more firms fail at than succeed. The good news is that an abundance of research provides guidance on how firms can do it much better.

Conditions for Success

The challenge with most partnerships is that they are more likely to fail than to succeed. For decades, the failure rate of alliances and partnerships has hovered around 50-60%. A 2014 survey of the Chief Marketing Officer council found that 43% of their respondents reported a high failure rate and 45% could not maintain a successful relationship into the long-term. This could have been due to a lack of strategic management: 42% reported that their partnerships are not well-leveraged and 67% did not have a formal partnering strategy.[62]

Strategic partnerships are particularly useful in industries where growth is needed or access to specific resources is critical. For example, high tech startup firms, with their necessary growth focus and a need for partners with specific resources the startup lacks, are natural candidates for strategic partnership formation. In the case of Calyx & Corolla, the supply of flowers was growing at a rate of 10% per year and growers were anxious to identify new sources and increases in demand.

Owades had just sold her first start-up, Gardener's Eden (an upscale catalog company), to Williams-Sonoma and recognized that there was an appetite and willingness to pay for fresh and exotic flowers with a longer shelf life than was currently available through the bricks-and-mortar retail channel.

The existing flower channel's retail level at that time was dominated by FTD shops and local retailers. The only catalog company at the time was 1-800-Flowers and its channel participation consisted primarily of sending purchase leads to FTD-affiliated retail shops for local delivery to consumers. An obvious drawback of this approach is that these deliveries were subject to the local quality of each florist. Put differently, 1-800-Flowers had minimal control over the quality of florists in any town or city, and therefore over the quality of the flowers delivered.

During her MBA program, Owades had studied Federal Express (FedEx) and was aware that they needed to think about how to move boxes in addition to the envelopes and document transportation that was their primary business. Unbeknownst to her at the time, FedEx had also been investigating the catalog business and how they could be doing more in this space with their shipping operations.

Owades recognized that it would not be enough for the channel's members to want to grow their sales. There also had to be a market or appetite for the value they could create together. Based on these insights, her explosive channel innovation was to coordinate Fed Ex to ship directly from the grower to the customer. By bypassing the legacy retailer-distributor-wholesaler channel, Calyx & Corolla was able to increase the shelf life of the shipped flowers by approximately 40%.

Persuading the Channel
One of the biggest roadblocks to building a partnership is finding the right partner. The partner(s) must be firms committed to consistently executing their channel

functions at the right place and time. They have to be willing to control costs and the quality of their outputs for the sake of the channel. Partners must often share sensitive information about costs, margins, and expectations about the future with each other. These are precisely the types of information that most channel members would prefer to keep private. Together, partnering often requires frequent, useful information sharing, as well as compatible goals at the start. There is a great deal of negotiating and learning from each other that must happen before a strategic partnership can occur. Often this means that the partners must have had a successful working relationship in place that gives the firms a sense of the direction each partner is pursuing, and how easy it is to coordinate their work and information sharing activities together.

> *Partners must often share sensitive information about costs, margins, and expectations about the future with each other.*
> *These are precisely the types of information that most channel members would prefer to keep private.*

The Growers

The first partner that Ruth Owades got on board was one she had worked with at Gardener's Eden, Peter Barr of Sunbay Growers in Watsonville, California.[63] Peter was anxious to find ways to grow his business and agreed to donate his time to conduct some test shipments involving different ways of securing flowers and padding assortments into various box sizes. The challenge was that Owades needed the grower to take on a new channel function – picking, packing, and shipping the products. In other words, growers had to adapt from being solely in the agricultural business to entering the upscale-gift business. So instead of shipping 500 stems of flowers to a wholesaler, they would have to wrap a dozen roses in pastel tissue paper, tie them with a bow and add a handwritten note and care instructions before shipping to a single customer.

In February 1988, Owades and Barr dived into learning how to preserve flowers during shipping. They experimented with different sizes of boxes, various ways of securing the flowers, and an assortment of padding. They did test shipments to a dozen sites (family and friends) across the country. Barr wasn't charging for his time, although Owades was picking up the cost of materials. After a couple of weeks the basic concept of shipping bundles of flowers began to seem feasible, but it would require the growers to develop and perform new packaging and shipping processes outside their current experience and capabilities.

Owades summed up the challenge as follow: "It wasn't just finding someone willing to work with me. The growers had to meet certain criteria: quality, specialization in a particular flower variety, and commitment to service. And *then* it was, who will work with me?"

The Shipper

Overnight shippers at that time were not accustomed to handling fresh flowers and oddly-shaped boxes. The dominant overnight shipper, FedEx, mostly shipped flat envelopes. Although Owades considered Airborne and Emery as well as other shippers, most were not able to promise the lift capacity or the space out of specific locations in the farm country where growers were located. They anticipated that some growers would have to ship as many as 5,000 boxes in a single day, and these carriers could not commit at this level.

After navigating the FedEx management maze, Owades was eventually directed to Fed Ex's marketing chief, Richard Metzler, and vice-president of catalog services, Mike Glynn. She needed Fed Ex to offer reasonable prices, provide her with a computerized package-tracking system, and modify their delivery practices (e.g. agree to leave flowers at a customer's door without a signature, or not to leave boxes of flowers by doors in the snow). All of these efforts would be new to FedEx, made specifically to accommodate Calyx & Corolla.

Calyx & Corolla and FedEx had no history of working together, but they had their reputations for business experience and both were eager to grow their business. FedEx had been looking for a way to increase its catalog business and this seemed like a promising opportunity.

Importantly, Ruth positioned Calyx & Corolla as not just a means of enhancing demand around key holidays such as Valentine's Day and Christmas, but as a means of creating increased demand all year long. She knew that the target market that loved fresh and exotic flowers was likely to buy throughout the year on a consistent basis. Some of their most successful offerings would be customer programs that shipped to customers on a monthly or semi-monthly basis all year around.

The Engine that Makes it Work

There is a preponderance of research on the factors that make strategic partnering successful. However, the three most common are the need for complementary competencies, mutual investments and adaptations, and trust. These are the motors that run the partnering engine and together help to create explosive channel value.

Complementary Competencies

A necessary starting point is that partners must have the necessary complementary competencies to create explosive channel value together. Although Airborne and Emery were eager to partner and willing to be very competitive on prices, their inability to guarantee the needed daily capacity in far-flung locations dropped them from serious consideration. The partner must be an expert at the competency that they bring to the table *as well as* have the scale necessary to accommodate the anticipated channel demand.

Without these properties in place, there is no future for a strategic partnership. For example, the Google-Samsung domination of the world's cell phone market share would not have been possible without Google's capabilities in developing the Android operating system and Samsung's manufacturing capabilities and channels of distribution. Whether the competencies lie in transportation, R&D, manufacturing, marketing, or sales force capabilities, these are necessary first steps for pie-expansion.

Mutual Investments

While complementary competencies are a key starting point, there are other essential ingredients to successfully working together. The next most important ingredient in a strategic partnership is that *both* partners must be willing to make specific adaptations and investments for the other. This might include tangible investments such as capital equipment, machinery, and warehouse capacity, or it might include intangible investments such as dedicated human resources, specifically designed processes and practices that support the partnership, or even implicit understandings and a joint knowledge of how to create value together.

In the case of Calyx & Corolla, both the growers and FedEx had to adapt their channel functions specifically to accommodate the business. Growers had to acquire new channel functions of picking, packing, and shipping; instead of packing thousands of flower stems into a box and layering with ice cubes on the top, they now had to pull net caps around rainbow petals of gerbera daisies, rest roses on tiny pillows of iced gel, and insert thirsty plant stems into water vials. These types of skills were outside the purview of most growers, whose focus was typically on shipping volumes of a single flower type to various distributors and wholesalers throughout the country.

FedEx's inventory management system and operations had to be able to accommodate fresh goods in boxes. FedEx also flew teams of people from Memphis to Calyx & Corolla's headquarters in San Francisco to train new Calyx employees before a busy season. Calyx & Corolla developed a formal quality assurance program, complete with incentives and bonuses for Owades' growers to ensure the picking and packing of flowers.

Automated information sharing would be key to all of their joint efforts. Owades envisioned computer linkages between the growers and her company. However, many of the growers didn't even own fax machines at the time. Growers needed to develop an inventory management system by which they could rapidly receive, track and fill orders from Calyx and Corolla. She also needed a foolproof system with FedEx that would allow her to promise exact delivery dates.

Mutual investments create real *risks* on the part of both partners. Economists often refer to this as the "mutual tying of the hands" because these assets and investments would be lost if either partner terminated the exchange prematurely. This helps to align partners' incentives and prevents either from exiting the relationship before these investments can be leveraged for the good of the partnership. The best type of investments are non-fungible, meaning that they are not easily transferred and redeployed to alternative partner relationships. Since the investments are specific to the partners and create a risk from premature termination, they are powerful in motivating the partners to make their joint efforts work.

There is considerable research on the investments made by partners, and one takeaway is clear: a relationship based on investments made by only one side of the partnership is not stable. When only one partner makes a risky investment, that partner becomes subject to "hold-up" or opportunistic exploitation from the other partner. The non-investing partner then has no incentive to stay in the relationship and make it work (other than the continued exploitation of the other's investments). Thus, one-sided investments raise not only the likelihood of exploitation, but also the risk of premature termination.

Research also makes clear that it is not sufficient for both partners to simply put in a fungible resource such as money. Joint ventures based on 50/50 equity positions of the partners have no greater likelihood of success than those that do not involve equity stakes. If ever there was a "golden bullet" in partnering, it would be that non-fungible, or specific, adaptations and investments on the part of both partners are the most effective means of safeguarding their mutual outcomes. This has been underscored by empirical research involving hundreds of ongoing partnering relationships between suppliers and their distribution channels. Mutual, specific investments have been shown to be more effective than the development of interpersonal trust between firms or the cultivation of common goals.[64]

> *If ever there was a "golden bullet" in partnering, it would be that non-fungible, or specific adaptations and investments on the part of both partners, are the most effective way of safeguarding their mutual outcomes.*

It was in this manner that the trio of partners – growers, Calyx & Corolla, and FedEx – would create a new route to market for flower delivery that would fundamentally change the type of products that could be received at home (exotic, high-end flowers) with substantially longer shelf lives, at a premium price point.

Trust Between Partners

The final key ingredient that every strategic partnership needs is a sense of trust between the partners. Trust involves both the ability to reliably predict what your partner might do and the belief that your partner will act in your best interests – i.e. that the partner is not opportunistic. Ultimately, Peter Barr said of Owades, "Ruth is working to promote flowers, and we appreciate that. As a result, she has the top priority for getting flowers if we're running short."

Managing, developing, and growing trust is not a topic that is widely taught in business schools, yet it is fundamental for any transaction. In 1972, Kenneth Arrow, a Nobel Prize-winning economist, noted that virtually *every* commercial transaction contains an element of trust. A buyer must trust that the seller will release goods upon payment and a seller must trust that the buyer will release the payment. If trust is needed for a single transaction, how much more trust is needed for building a risky partnership where the returns are unknown, the processes are untried, and there are real stakes in place? Trust is critical for greasing the partnership engine.

From a legal standpoint, trust can be thought of as the means by which all the non-contractual elements of work are governed. In other words, since it is not possible to create a contract that can account for every possible contingency that might arise between two transacting parties, a sense of trust or solidarity can help "fill in the gaps."

Importantly, trust is not built overnight, although it can be easily lost. One way to think of this is to consider the metaphor of water levels in a bathtub. A bathtub is not filled instantaneously, but with the constant addition of water over time. However, the stock of water can be quickly drained by opening the plug. In Chapter 11 ("Why Do I Need a Channel Relationship?") we talked about research that shows that the well can be poisoned – i.e. trust once lost is difficult to regain. Bad experiences, relationship failure, or conflict are hard to recover from and often plant the seeds of suspicion, distrust, and acrimony that will ultimately undermine the partnership and exchange.

This was the precisely the experience of Oracle and Hewlett-Packard, whose relationship went into a downward spiral after each lost trust in the other. During the 1980s these partners had together won over 140,000 new customers across various industries as a result of combining Hewlett-Packard's capabilities in manufacturing with Oracle's abilities as an up-and-coming software developer. In 2009, Oracle became interested in Sun Microsystems after learning that Intel was looking to acquire it. The partners originally considered the purchase together, and ultimately Hewlett-Packard declined the opportunity.

> *Importantly, trust is not built overnight, although it can be easily lost.*

In a surprise move, Oracle acquired Sun outright, thus becoming a direct competitor to Hewlett-Packard. Hewlett-Packard's response was to hire two well-known Oracle enemies: Ray Land, a former Oracle executive, and Leo Apotheker, a former SAP chief executive. This downward spiral between Oracle and Hewlett-Packard might never have occurred if trust had not been broken over the Sun Microsystems acquisition. Empirical research on partnership management has shown that this phenomenon of lost trust being difficult to regain is common to the management of organizational relationships in general.[65]

Having said this, it is also important to realize that trust is not blind. The partners must continue to monitor each other, or as Ronald Reagan famously put it, "Trust but verify." In the case of Calyx & Corolla, Ruth had to regularly monitor FedEx. When they said that they left flowers at a doorstep, she would often verify that they really were left there. This was not a typical channel function performed by FedEx, but it was critical for the sake of the partnership.

Ruth also monitored the flower quality and shipping practices of her growers. She had to drop one of her key growers in the first few months of the startup because of inconsistent quality. Gift certificates and letters of apology were sent to the hundreds of customers who had received flowers from that particular grower. Importantly, she did not allow the problem to fester, but cut ties early.

The Dark Side of Partnering

While complementary competencies, mutual investments and trust are necessary for experiencing and receiving the tremendous joint benefits of partnering, these are paradoxically the same factors that contribute to the stubborn failure rate of partnerships. This phenomenon, which has been dubbed the "dark side of relationships," proposes that the characteristics that make partnering relationships successful are the same means by which they dissolve and fail.[66]

The downside risk of mutual investments is that they can create an inertia that prevents the partners from moving on to new opportunities or alternative partners. Their efforts can grow stale, and innovation can lag. Consider the Italian construction industry during the late 1980s and early 1990s. Forty-nine contractors created a network to aid the control and distribution of resources and diffuse risk

> *While complementary competencies, mutual investments and trust are necessary for experiencing and receiving the tremendous joint benefits of partnering, these are paradoxically the same factors that contribute to the stubborn failure rate of partnerships.*

among them. They operated like a cartel, protecting each other from competitive pressures by restraining and controlling competition among themselves. But over time this network developed destabilizing properties. By insulating themselves from market pressures, they unwittingly removed the external pressure to innovate and progress, slowing the pace of the entire industry, and ultimately Italy's entire construction industry suffered. In this manner, the competitive advantage that was created by these mutual investments paradoxically became the weakest links.

Similarly, Toyota has recently announced that it would go outside its traditional keiretsu network of parts suppliers (led by Denso Corp) to source a cutting edge crash prevention system from German parts maker Continental AG.[67] Japanese parts suppliers are losing their edge, particularly in next-generation software technologies for safety and autonomous driving.

Strategic Partnerships as a Source of Competitive Advantage

At its startup in 1989, Calyx & Corolla consisted of a staff of 8 people and quickly grew out of its startup stage, exceeding its break-even goal by 1992 and posting profits greater than 5% on sales in excess of $10 million. The average order size at that time was $65. By the time of its sale in 2003 to Vermont Teddy Bear, it had grown to 25 full-time workers. Twenty-five growers supplied Calyx & Corolla and Fed Ex used 18-wheel trailers to service their business. During busy seasons, growers could fill six trucks, booked in advance, with packages.

Calyx & Corolla entered a large but competitive market. Flower sales from the dominant competitors of TeleFlora, FTD, and 1-800-Flowers topped over $9 billion in total. Competitors have tried to duplicate what Calyx & Corolla has done, but the partnership that was created is not easy to observe or replicate. One startup lasted about a year before shutting down: Harry & David, a fruit and catalog company, attempted a flower catalog in 1991, but then left the market. All of this suggests that building a strategic partnership is not easy to do; however, once built, the endeavor can serve as a huge source of competitive advantage for all its participating parties.

A Checklist for Strategic Partnering Management

Creating and managing partnering relationships must involve thoughtfully strategic choices on the part of both channel members. Not only can the payoffs from such endeavors substantially outweigh the individual outcomes of any single partner alone, but partnering relationships can also serve as a key source of sustainable competitive advantage.

The channel strategist does not need to enter into partnering relationships blindly, as much is already known about how to successfully partner over time. Below is a brief checklist of the criteria behind good answers to the key questions in channel relationship creation and management.

Table 12-1:
A Checklist for Channel Relationship Creation

Questions to Ask	Criteria to Consider
How do I select a partner?	Successful partnerships occur between partners with different skills, and *complementary competencies*.
How should I build a partnering relationship?	1. Build trust through repeated and consistent actions that signal an interest in mutual benefits. 2. Put in place contracts that provide broad protections and considerations for both partners, but avoid getting bogged down in very specific details or contingencies. 3. Be very explicit about the short- and long-term goals of each partner. Mutual information sharing is critical to this endeavor.
What keeps the partnership strong?	1. Frequent, communications on a weekly basis as well as regular "pulse check" efforts where strategies and goals are compared and updated. 2. Mutual, specific investments on the part of both partners that support their joint effort.
When should I exit?	1. When organizational goals and strategies are no longer served by the mutual effort 2. When trust has been irreparably lost or broken and suspicion is rampant and unavoidable

PART 3: HOW DO I INCENTIVIZE THE CHANNEL?

Chapter 13: HOW DO I PRICE THROUGH THE CHANNEL?

Much has been written about pricing: on willingness to pay, segmented end-user demand and price sensitivity, competitive pricing, dynamic pricing, and pricing methods such as cost-based, target-return-based, and demand-based.

End-User Price Generally Cannot be Set by the Manufacturer

These discussions are useful, but tend to ignore a fact that fundamentally affects most channel pricing strategies: absent a contract, the manufacturer typically cannot dictate the downstream price of its products. This lack of control occurs whenever the manufacturer sells to intermediaries that take title to the products sold at any number of steps removed from the manufacturer. Lack of pricing control is also likely when a manufacturer sells its B2B components to an OEM buyer, who in turn prices the whole product it sells to its channel. The multiple prices being set throughout the channel as a product passes hands from one channel partner to another raise a host of challenging problems.

The market price seen by the final customer is an important cue that strongly affects purchase choice. If the price is extraordinarily low, customers may be dissuaded from buying – particularly when they are unable to assess the product's quality. In such situations, price may offer a strong (whether true or untrue) signal of quality, with too low a price signaling a "cheap" product rather than a "good buy." For example, we learned that a colleague's friend was shopping for a big-screen TV, wanted a very high-quality product, and did not know how to determine what to buy other than by highest price. Our colleague did his best to advise his friend, so that he would purchase the *right* product, not just an *expensive* product.

Conversely, if the price seems too high, the customer may also be dissuaded from buying what would otherwise be a valued product. The brand's positioning may be affected: the Mazda Miata was so popular at product launch that dealers were charging prices thousands of dollars higher than suggested list price, placing the Miata into a higher-priced competitive sports car category than the original strategy and product design warranted.

If the manufacturer were always able to set the final market price for all its products, market research could reveal the price that maximizes total channel profit. Indeed, much of the advice available on pricing focuses on this very question of the right end-user price to set. Numerous research techniques and statistical models assist in the estimation of price elasticity of demand to this end. A direct-to-consumer channel can set the *coordinated* price suggested by these techniques, meaning a price with no distortions from intermediary price-setting practices. However, coordinated pricing policies may not be the most profitable ones for every intermediary. For example, a direct-to-consumer channel that fails to work with intermediaries that are more efficient at executing on the channel design (e.g. lower-inventory-cost distributors) suffers from a higher *total* channel cost than one that benefits from best-in-class functional technologies. Higher total channel cost leads to higher end-user prices and lower demand, whose negative profit effect can dominate the benefit of coordinated price-setting in the total channel profit equation. The ideal, of course, would be the ability to go to market directly, with the most efficient channel functional technologies – thus enjoying both pricing coordination through the channel and lowest cost to go to market. Because the channel manager typically cannot have both elements of this ideal, the goal becomes to balance coordination with efficiency in channel pricing strategies.

This chapter identifies and explains the management problems created by the transfer of pricing authority to a channel partner. We then discuss an array of commonly-used strategies and tactics for improving (or completely re-acquiring) control over downstream prices. Often, more than one possible strategy may help manage a given channel problem, and conversely, a strategy may be useful in controlling more than one type of problem. In each case, the channel strategist must weigh the benefits against the costs of re-acquiring pricing control. Control is rarely low-cost, so while attractive it may not always be the right solution to the challenge.

Developing a Channel Pricing Strategy

One possible channel pricing strategy is to seek to always set the wholesale price below the end-user's willingness to pay. Although transparent and somewhat useful, this simple policy does not promise to motivate channel intermediaries to perform the needed functions and services, compensate them appropriately, or result in a demand-optimizing end-user price. Instead, what is needed is a general process to guide you in identifying the wholesale pricing strategy that properly incentivizes and rewards desired channel behaviors. A process for effective channel pricing management is presented in Figure 13-1:

Figure 13-1:
The Channel Pricing Process

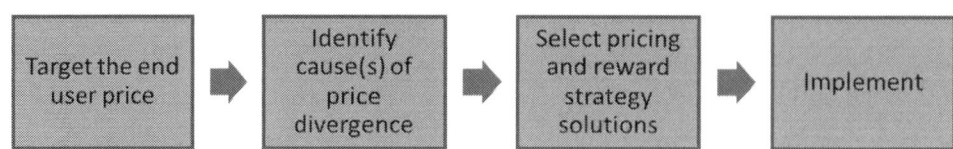

Identify the ideal end user price - Identify what end-user price you would set if you had the right to do so, and compare it with the actual end-user price(s) in the market for your product.

Identify cause(s) of price divergence - Diagnose why the actual end-user price diverges from the goal price – there are several possibilities, as discussed below.

Select a pricing and/or reward solution - Consider the available solutions, including pricing and reward strategies used by your competitors or in other industry analogues. Decide which one or ones are applicable and implementable in your situation.

Implement - Finally, implement your channel pricing strategy.

The most critical step in developing a wholesale pricing strategy is to first identify the sources of mis-pricing in your channel. Don't jump at the first possible action you think of (remember to "aim" before you "fire"!). The key goals of channel pricing are (a) to create the right incentives for behavior among channel partners, and (b) to split channel profits reasonably amongst the channel partners. Thus, our discussion of incentives in the channel in the previous chapter informs the management of channel pricing as well.

Pricing Challenges

Using the channel pricing process requires knowledge of the major drivers of channel pricing and margin-taking, as well as the challenges commonly faced by channel captains and the set of available tools and solutions. Your channel pricing toolkit includes not only mechanisms for setting a wholesale price to downstream channel members, but also evaluation of the prices your channel partners charge and the compensation/rewards they demand for performance of their functions. Pricing and compensation are fundamental to coordinating channel activity. We therefore discuss some incentive and reward practices, as well as various pricing practices, as solutions to the challenges of channel pricing in general. Table 13-1 summarizes the key challenges and related examples discussed in the following sections.[68]

**Table 13-1:
Pricing Challenges and Related Examples**

The Challenge	How It is Observed in the Channel	Related Example
Ownership transfer	Product title and ownership – and thus end-user pricing authority – must often be transferred to independent partners	DigiGadgets
Channel margin math: the tendency toward double marginalization	A partner's gross margin requirements create a "double marginalization" problem, that successively and increasingly distorts pricing away from the level that would maximize total channel profits	Dogear Publishing and the "self"-publishing author
Asymmetries among partners	All channel partners do not perform the same set of functions, and differ in their abilities to deliver on them at a fair cost	Standard book publishing channel through large and small retailers
Channel function allocation	Some partners may be expected to execute on multiple desired functions	Selling health insurance to corporations and their employees

Retaining Ownership: Vertical integration

A seemingly obvious solution to all of these pricing challenges is to eliminate intermediaries and vertically integrate downstream. Selling direct to end-users avoids *transferring ownership*, and clearly gives the manufacturer the right (indeed, the imperative) to set price to that end-user. It gets rid of the *double marginalization problem*, because only one margin (the difference between cost and price of the manufacturer) is set. No *asymmetries* in channel partners occur. And who better to internalize the incentives to perform all the right (and right amount of) channel activities than the manufacturer! This is the only option that affords full control over the pricing strategy to the manufacturer.

But if vertical integration solves every channel pricing problem, why don't manufacturers own the channel more often? There are both cost-side and demand-side reasons for this. It is usually more costly for a manufacturer to sell direct, especially if it is careful to partner with intermediaries that can perform one or more valued channel functions more efficiently. For example, you may not have enough "feet on the street" – the employee sales force – to blanket the market, and particularly for profitable sales to small accounts. Sales force management is a complex process, and the manufacturer may not have the capabilities to handle it cost-effectively. Or you may not run a standard production line that generates the steady inventory to merit a full-time employee sales force. Or end-users prefer one-stop shopping across a wider variety of products than you can provide.

A more common approach that straddles both points of view is the use of a hybrid or multi-channel structure, where the manufacturer sells direct to a subset of its clients, but also retains an independent channel that offers both a lower cost and benefits that direct selling cannot provide to all end-user segments. In the B2B realm, a customer account that has been handled by an independent distributor may be brought in-house to be handled instead by the employee sales force when it becomes big enough or strategically important enough. In-house channels also allow the service and product experience to be controlled at a very personalized level.

In the B2C realm, an important reason for Apple's development and ownership of its own retail stores was to improve the representation of its products to end-users and to support full retail price levels in the market. Similarly, Niketown stores were created precisely because Nike wanted to gain better control over how their products were presented, merchandised, and explained to consumers. When end-users demand it, or when even the best intermediaries fail to perform at the best effort levels, that extra cost of centralization may be worthwhile because of the accompanying improvement in channel benefit provision.

In the following sections, we discuss the channel pricing challenges of Table 13-1, along with the non-vertical integration solutions that are commonly used to handle them.

Challenge #1: Ownership Transfer

DigiGadgets: End-User Pricing Chaos

A U.S. company that we'll call DigiGadgets[69] makes and sells electronic consumer products, most of which were low-priced. It has sought the broadest possible distribution for these products, because profits depend on volume and market share. Authorized routes to market include independent distributors selling to medium and small retailers; direct sales to big-box retailers like Best Buy; and both direct and indirect routes through online mega-retailers like Amazon.com and Tiger Direct. Unauthorized (gray market) resellers also sell DigiGadgets products, as shown below:

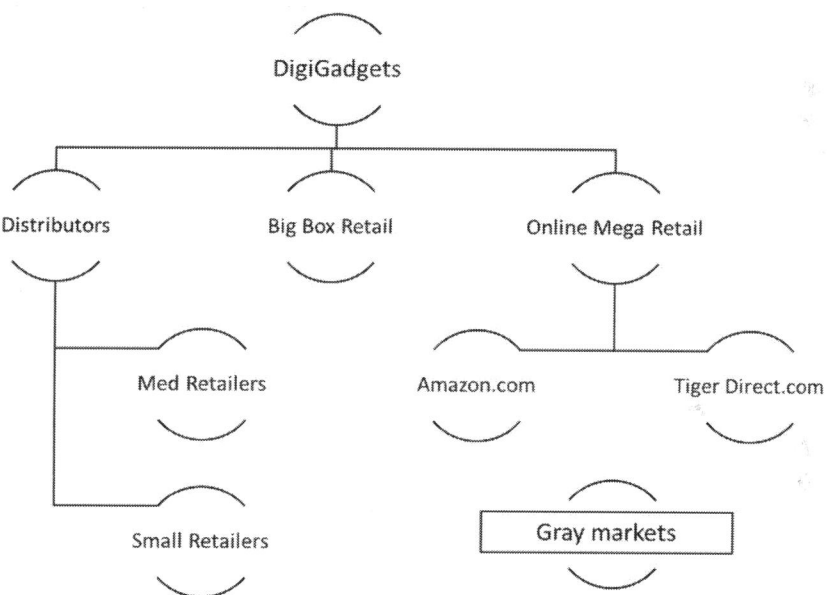

Figure 13-1: DigiGadget's Channel Strategy

Imagine this distribution channel system as a many-branched tree: some branches with distributors buying from DigiGadgets and then reselling to retailers; others with large retailers buying direct from DigiGadgets and selling through their bricks-and-mortar stores; and other branches involving online retailers.

DigiGadgets never tried to control pricing through its many channel partners, and with the relatively low margins on its product lines, prevailing price variations hadn't been extreme. Every channel member was required to purchase DigiGadget's products before reselling them downstream or to any other channel members. All members accepted as a fact of life that some price discounting and unauthorized distribution occurs through gray market channels.

However, recently DigiGadgets acquired two other companies that each produced a higher-end product line of home electronic products whose prices were as much as five times higher than those of the company's legacy products. These new products were sold by their former companies through higher-end, exclusive distribution, not mass merchandisers and e-tailers. DigiGadgets wanted to broaden the distribution for the new lines into traditionally lower-priced channels, but needed to keep their high-end retailers happy because their service provision (both pre- and post-sale) was key to happy high-end consumers. The stakes were high, as the company acquisitions were costly and a poorly executed strategy could decimate the value of the acquired product lines.

Why Is Ownership Transfer a Problem?

DigiGadgets needed a pricing strategy that maintained and reinforced its products' brand image and attractiveness in a wide range of end-user markets. So what's the problem? To start with, each channel member sought a downstream price that ensured what each saw as a "fair" margin. Some set their prices based on the competition. Others set theirs based on the cost of performing needed functions like merchandising and financing. Different members faced different economies of scale and overhead cost structures. All of this led to inconsistent pricing across the broad channel system.

Even worse, DigiGadgets found its legacy products for sale in the Amazon Marketplace, being offered by unauthorized third-party resellers at deep discounts. The distribution VP had no idea initially how their products were reaching these outlets. But he did realize that his authorized resellers were irritated by the larger competitive set and the price pressure they brought. The retail price erosion problem was bleeding into Amazon's prices itself, since Amazon's pricing algorithm checks for price drops and chooses when to match them. A buyer at Tiger Direct, a major reseller, was only halfway joking when he told the DigiGadgets VP that it had dominant market share in its legacy lines, but somehow seemed to be involved in a retail price war... **with itself!**

These instances of price-cutting, inconsistent price offerings, and the ease with which downstream customers could compare prices across channels and purchase DigiGadgets' products in both unauthorized and authorized channels demonstrated to the company how delegating retail price-setting to downstream channel partners could derail an otherwise strong and coherent branding and go-to-market strategy.

Solutions to Loss of Pricing Control

What can DigiGadgets, or other firms in this position, do to better balance the desire for broad distribution with the wish to control channel pricing and the end user's final price? We consider three common solutions to this problem, the last of which DigiGadgets (and other manufacturers in a similar multi-channel strategy situation) actually implemented:

(a) Using sales representative firms
(b) Selling on consignment, make-to-order, or drop-shipping
(c) Implementing a Minimum Advertised Pricing (MAP) policy

The Use of a Sales Representative Firm

Suppose you are a manufacturer that just isn't as adept at some functions as your partners are. Vertical integration can be a very costly strategy for regaining price control. Fortunately, the widely used option of engaging an independent representative (or rep firm) is a lower-cost way to enjoy many of the benefits of vertical integration. Rep firms may sell a complementary product line to your own, which is beneficial when customers value one-stop shopping. Importantly, a rep firm (unlike an independent distributor, for example) typically does not take title to your products, nor does it inventory them for downstream delivery. Since it neither holds nor owns products, it does not set the final price – you do. This solves the problem of loss of downstream pricing control. Using a rep firm has the added benefit of giving you control over a database of downstream customer names and order quantities – information that few distributors or retailers are likely to spontaneously share with you. Because a rep firm does not make profit from markups on wholesale-priced inventory, the channel pricing and reward structure typically involve the manufacturer paying a rep firm a commission and/or bonus instead.

Note that when using a rep firm, your downstream pricing control comes at a cost: you are now responsible for inventory holding, ownership, and attendant risking costs that would otherwise be borne by an independent distributor or other inventory-carrying downstream intermediary. You also carry the responsibility to ship ordered product to the downstream customer, often in small lot sizes with poor economies of scale. Your choice to use a rep firm rather than vertically integrating should therefore weigh the benefits of pricing control and possibly superior sales and promotional skills against the costs of inventory holding, ownership, and shipping to downstream customers.

The reward structure offered to the rep firm – commissions, bonuses, or some combination – ideally is designed to motivate its salespeople to devote sales time and promotional effort to your products.

Sell on Consignment, Make-to-order, or Drop-ship

Under consignment, the manufacturer transfers inventory-holding responsibility to a downstream partner, but retains product title. Thus, the manufacturer retains control over downstream pricing, and the downstream partner avoids the costs of ownership, including inventory financing, until a sale occurs. The channel partners must agree on how the inventory is held and displayed, and on insurance to protect against loss through damage or theft.

Artists frequently use consignment to distribute their work through galleries. The downstream partner – the gallery owner – is unlikely to be willing to take on the financial and other risk of buying an artist's works outright, given the uncertain time until a sale (unless the artist's work is in high and reliable demand). After all, even with a consignment process, the gallery owner will give up valuable display space to show this artist's work – space whose opportunity cost is the value of displaying other, potentially better-selling, work. Thus, the artist who offers to take these functional costs off a gallery owner's shoulders improves the attractiveness of her art in the eyes of the gallery owner.

Interestingly, even though the artist retains inventory ownership, the retail price may still be negotiated with the gallery owner, who is interested in selling the work sooner rather than later. However, the gallery owner shares the incentive to set a profitable price, because the reward structure in a consignment sale (as in the rep firm channel) involves a percentage commission on retail price to the gallery. The higher the retail sales price, the greater the commission to the gallery, which creates an alignment of channel pricing incentives between artist and gallery.

Similar channel pricing arrangements are possible when products are made to order, or when the manufacturer arranges to drop-ship orders directly to the end-user. Buyers' identities and order quantities are naturally known to the manufacturer, as in the consignment situation, and the non-inventory-holding status of the intermediary opens the door to retaining pricing control.

MAP Policies and Unilateral, Voluntary Price Maintenance Agreements with Channel Partners

Minimum Advertised Pricing policies improve pricing coordination in situations where the channel *transfers title and inventory holding to downstream channel partners*, and when it includes partners with *asymmetric performance of key channel functions*. Unilateral, voluntary price maintenance agreements are a variant on MAP where a channel manager dictates not just minimum price but also maximum price or even exact resale price. Such agreements are legal when properly written.[70]

DigiGadgets opted to implement a MAP policy for its newer, high-end products that involves setting up a formal authorized dealer network (thus distinguishing authorized from unauthorized resellers); serializing all product units, to facilitate tracking of unauthorized channel activity; firing resellers that do not comply with the MAP policy; and using a third-party web price tracking service to find MAP violators among both authorized and unauthorized resellers.

MAP policies make sense when the manufacturer relies on channel partners to perform important – but costly – functions such as service or education. Resellers may provide varying levels of service effectiveness, which creates asymmetries in their functional performance. Asymmetries create an opportunity for free-riding resellers to fail to perform some functions (such as keeping ample inventory in stock or providing pre- and post-sale customer service). Such resellers might seek to avoid these functions' costs, and therefore set lower prices than the outlets of channel members who perform the costly functions.

As discussed in Chapter 4, showrooming is a common consumer behavior outcome in channels with reseller free-riding. Showrooming consumers physically examine a product in a store and become educated on its options, but then purchase it at a lower-priced outlet, e.g. an online store that fails to offer the valued customer service. In this case, the online retailer books the purchase, but the physical retailer incurs all the location and service costs – thus suffering both higher costs *and* lower revenue. Left unchecked, showrooming tends to drive high-service providers out of the market, leaving only the discounters that fail to support the product, its price, and the brand's image.

How does a MAP policy mitigate this problem? The manufacturer unilaterally[71] declares a MAP policy that holds equally for all of its resellers, and includes a penalty for noncompliance. The MAP policy of GoPro, a manufacturer of mountable and wearable cameras, states:

> "GoPro, in its sole discretion, reserves the right to discontinue doing business with any reseller that advertises any product(s) covered by this MAP Policy at a price lower than the MAP...."

GoPro enforces this policy by monitoring the advertised prices of its dealers through both direct and third-party means. Its MAP policy allows GoPro to modify, or suspend, one or more products' MAP prices for a specified period of time, or to pass on a manufacturer's rebate to consumers; but GoPro specifies the time period in advance and the MAP policy is re-established at the end of the promotion period.

GoPro's policy shows the key elements that make it possible to improve its pricing control. First, it unilaterally states its policy in clear terms and communicates these terms to all authorized resellers. Second, it states the penalty for non-compliance. And third, it invests in (costly) monitoring to detect violations of its MAP policy and punishes all violators equally. Without all of these mechanisms in place, a MAP policy is ineffective: stating policy and penalties but failing to monitor partners' pricing behavior does not lead to pricing control because partners will see that violators are not controlled. Similarly, a MAP policy and enforcement process without clear penalties does not motivate compliant downstream pricing behavior and may be perceived by channel partners as merely capricious.

Even a well-crafted MAP policy may not completely solve the problem of controlling downstream pricing in the manufacturer's channel. Research on MAP price violations and enforcement[72] shows that violations may still be observed by authorized resellers, with even more violations by unauthorized resellers. By definition, unauthorized resellers are not subject to the manufacturer's MAP policy, so an uncontrolled "gray market" for goods can lessen the impact of a carefully implemented MAP policy.

Happily, research also shows that authorized resellers are less likely to become non-compliant by observing unauthorized resellers' non-compliance than by observing *other authorized* resellers' non-compliance. A low price from a similar (also authorized) reseller may be more threatening, and this may trigger a faster response than one from a more dissimilar (unauthorized) reseller. It is therefore imperative that the channel strategist institute and follow through with a program of persistent enforcement in the authorized channel in order to improve downstream pricing control.

Note that merely *stating* a MAP policy is not enough. Monitoring and enforcement, with penalties, is necessary to make your MAP policy stick. This control preserves authorized channel partners' gross profit margins and their ability and motivation to provide value-added channel benefits to end-users. The brand image is thus reinforced through consistent end-user pricing and provision of the full combination of product and benefits to end-users.

Challenge #2: Channel Margin Math, or the Tendency Toward Double Marginalization

The "Self"-Publishing Author's Dilemma: DIY, or Use a Channel Partner Like Dogear Publishing?

Every go-to-market decision must resolve the tradeoff between the costs and benefits of using a partner versus doing it yourself (i.e. vertical integration). Jack is considering whether to self-publish his book, and faces a choice among several channel options. Self-publishing avoids using intermediaries, with the exception of selling directly through online retailers such as Amazon.com. Jack also has the option to use a third-party agent (thus outsourcing manufacturing, some product design, and some marketing functions); a wholesaler; and a retailer (bricks-and-mortar or combined with an online channel) to sell to the end consumer.[73] Variations on these options are also possible.

Dogear Publishers (www.dogearpublishing.net) is a third-party agent that offers channel pricing advice along with other functions such as editing, publishing, printing, and marketing to the author.

Should Jack use a channel partner, or go it alone? On the one hand, Dogear could increase market reach – but at what cost? Jack must consider the following to resolve this dilemma:

1. Set the book's retail price. Dogear suggests a retail price that is at least 2.5 times the single-copy printing cost, to cover Dogear's fees, trade (retailer, wholesaler) discounts, and Jack's net income per unit.
2. Assess the wholesale cost-benefit tradeoff. Wholesalers typically offer levels of breadth of coverage, albeit at a cost. For example, if Jack is willing to grant a 55 percent discount off retail price to the wholesaler, he will gain access to small and large bookstores and online book sellers. At a 40 percent discount, he may lose access to the small bookstore channel, but retain access to large chains and online retailers.

These calculations enable Jack to assess the benefits of using a channel partner versus the costs of doing it himself.

What's the Problem Here? ... The Tendency Toward Double Marginalization

Jack's example illustrates several key points in channel pricing:

- The vertical integration option lets Jack avoid high discounts, but requires him to do the work himself and likely limits the book's distribution breadth
- The use of channel partners implies that his net revenue or profit per unit will be reduced to a fraction of his target retail price
- The use of an intermediary moves downstream pricing discretion into the hands of the channel partner

- The more intermediaries that are used, the more margins will be taken on the product. As a result, increasing the number of channel members involved will "squeeze" Jack's pricing ability as well as his profits. It may also reduce his visibility into the determination of the final retail price.

This phenomenon of successive margin-taking by each channel member results in what is widely referred to as the "double marginalization" problem.[74] Multiple successive channel margins distort end-user prices upward to a higher level than would otherwise be charged, resulting in lower demand than would otherwise be enjoyed, all else equal. Intuitively, each successive member faces a marginal cost of acquiring the product that includes its production cost, *plus a margin taken by all members above it in the channel structure*. This effective higher cost of goods sold (COGS) leads it to set a yet higher downstream transfer price (since price is a positive function of costs). Together, the successive margin-taking creates an upward bias in the COGS facing the retailer and hence in retail price itself.

> *Successive margin-taking creates an upward bias in the COGS facing the retailer and hence in retail price itself.*

Even a simple channel with just one intermediary creates a double marginalization problem. This is because the manufacturer setting a simple wholesale price per unit is trying to accomplish two tasks with that one price: (1) induce a more coordinated downstream channel price, and (2) reap a share of channel profits. These are competing outcomes, and stretching one instrument to do two tasks leaves neither well done. As a result, both goals are thwarted – the retail price is ultimately higher than the vertically-integrated level, and unit sales and profits are lower than those in a vertically-integrated channel.

How to Solve the Double Marginalization Problem

Double marginalization plagues any manufacturer transferring product ownership to an intermediary, because the manufacturer's markup over its COGS is internalized into the intermediary's COGS, triggering a cascading markup problem in the disintermediated channel. Note that this tendency exists *regardless of the relative cost to operate a vertically-integrated versus a disintermediated channel*.

That said, double marginalization's price escalation effect can be *mitigated* if the indirect intermediary enjoys a lower channel function cost than would the direct-selling manufacturer. This is not unusual, since most channel members specialize in the performance of their allocated channel functions. For example, Home Depot has learned how to run a cost-effective and profitable retail operation that allows it to benefit from economies of scope across its product lines. Its marginal cost of retailing is therefore lower than the manufacturer's marginal cost of retailing would be in a vertically-integrated channel. If this discrepancy is great enough, the channel profit pie can increase sufficiently to award the retailer a fair margin and still leave the manufacturer better off than selling direct.

Dogear appeals to Jack because it sets different fees in return for performing different channel functions, including book production, promotion, printing, and website services. Dogear's menu of prices makes salient the value it can provide to Jack. Jack can pick and choose the subset of services most beneficial to him.

Dogear Publishing's offer is an example of a multi-part tariff, a common channel pricing strategy. In general, a multi-part tariff is a pricing policy that includes multiple components, designed to incentivize and reward various channel behaviors, while also generating an acceptable split of channel profits. If the problem is not enough tools – both to incentivize proper pricing and to take profits – one solution is to apply more tools. This is the heart of the benefit of multi-part tariffs for pricing and performance control in the downstream channel.

> A multi-part tariff is a pricing policy that includes multiple components, designed to incentivize and reward various channel behaviors, while also generating an acceptable split of channel profits.

A fully bundled price that did not separate out performance of individual valued functions (e.g. expedited production) would fail to create an incentive for Dogear to invest in quicker production, and would include a profit-making markup from Dogear as well. The multi-part tariff therefore benefits Jack as well as Dogear, because it makes explicit Jack's demand for, and reward for the performance of, incremental channel functions, while holding down successive margin-taking on Dogear's part.

In sum, the tendency of prices to rise with the number of channel partners is solved by careful choice of cost-effective partners, combined with pricing strategies such as multi-part tariffs. These strategies blunt the problem of loss of control over end-user prices.

Challenge #3: Asymmetric Partners

Pricing to Asymmetric Partners in the Retail Book Industry

Not all partners are created equal: every channel system likely includes partners at the same level (say, retailers) that differ in their capabilities as well as their willingness to perform the functions they are assigned. These asymmetries in partner ability and willingness pose a challenge to the channel captain seeking a consistent, efficient, and effective execution of the channel strategy.

As an example, consider small and large book retailers. Publishers often supply large retailers like Amazon or Barnes & Noble direct, shipping full pallets of a single book title at a time to their wholly-owned distribution centers. Further, the large bookseller is very likely to be a good credit risk, and adopts state-of-the-art technologies for ordering, invoicing, and payment. In short, serving such booksellers is an exercise in channel efficiency, and publishers therefore distribute directly to them.

In contrast, the small book retailer has no warehouse and requires mixed-pallet shipments of several titles, which increases the publisher's cost to sell through them. These retailers may not be technologically savvy and may pose a higher credit risk as well. To serve this channel, the publisher typically uses a book wholesaler that can purchase full pallets of a single title from the publisher, hold speculative inventory, use state-of-the-art ordering and payment systems, and supply mixed pallets to small retailers. They also manage the myriad smaller retail accounts and their non-payment risks, so that the publisher does not have to.

Not surprisingly, different pricing and discount structures have sprung up to compensate channel members for the functions they perform. Wholesalers earn a discount off list price from the publisher in return for function costs borne on behalf of the small retailer. Similarly, publishers' recognition that some – but not all – of their retailers could cost-effectively relieve them of several channel functional costs leads them to offer incentives for the performance of those functions by large retailers, including discounts for running distribution centers, for ordering large quantities, for early payment, and for promotional activities at retail.

What's the Problem with Asymmetric Partners?

Clearly, one simple wholesale price offered equally to all channels does not incentivize specific performance by the different channel partners, and a more sophisticated pricing structure like the one publishers use is better able to reward valued partner activities.

Big does not always mean more functionally capable, however. As discussed in Chapter 10, Home Depot is happy to sell John Deere riding lawnmowers, but makes no investment in the ability to prep the vehicle for the buyer or to provide after-sales service; smaller John Deere dealers do have these servicing capabilities, but not the same "shelf space" or market size to match Home Depot's. Asymmetries in partner capabilities have to be analyzed on a case-by-case basis to establish which partners can (or cannot) perform which functions.

Further, partners may differ not only in their capability, but also in their *willingness*, to perform various functions. Without specific incentives for functional performance, this means that the manufacturer itself may have to fill that role in order for end-users to be fully satisfied with their purchase through any of the manufacturer's multi-channel offerings.

Solution to the Asymmetric Partner Challenge: Functional Discounts Linked to Performance of Valued Functions

When dealing with potential asymmetries in different parts of one's overall channel system, a MAP policy as discussed above could help in some situations, but would be unlikely to fully motivate the performance of specific functions. Quantity discounts, with a lower per-unit wholesale price for buyers of larger quantities of product, can be an effective motivator if the main driver of cost to serve a channel is economies of scale (rather than a desire to motivate specific financing, payment, or promotional activities, for instance).

Instead, the publishers' solution profiled above is an example of a *functional discount* policy. Such a policy starts with a baseline discount off list price (that is, a wholesale price equal to a certain percentage of the suggested retail price) offered to all resellers; it then augments this with a menu of discounts off the list price, each based on the performance of a specified function. Any reseller that performs a particular value-added function earns the associated discount. A partner can earn multiple functional discounts if it performs multiple functions. Those that don't choose to perform such functions do not receive the discounts. A functional discount schedule is thus a specialized form of a multi-part tariff, where discounts rather than prices are set, and where the discounts specifically link to channel function performance.

> *A functional discount schedule is a specialized form of a multi-part tariff, where discounts rather than prices are set, and where the discounts specifically link to channel function performance.*

Examples of functional discounts include discounts for *early payment; carrying sufficient or speculative inventory; favorable placement of product, or favorable sales mentions; electronic rather than paper ordering;* or *completing training programs*. In all of these functional discount cases, the seller offers the discount to the buyer in return for the buyer's willingness to take a cost off the shoulders of the seller. This approach levels the downstream pricing playing field by compensating partners for the costs they may asymmetrically bear, but which can benefit all in the channel structure.

Challenge #4: Motivating Multiple Partner Behaviors

Selling Health Insurance to Corporations and Their Employees

Even if a manufacturer chooses to use just one channel partner, a simple wholesale price is still insufficient to motivate the partner to do multiple specific activities. Consider an insurance company offering health insurance to a corporation, which then offers this benefit to its employees. An insurance broker connects the insurance company and the corporation seeking health insurance for its employees. The corporation chooses which insurance company's plan to adopt on behalf of its employees. The corporation's human resources group educates employees about the plan and its benefits and encourages them to sign up for insurance (if it is not automatically offered).

Setting the right price – that is, the right premium to charge the corporation and its employees – requires knowledge of the cost to serve these customers. This is a function of how many individuals will be insured and the risk involved in insuring them. For example, insuring employees who work at an office-based firm is different than insuring those at a skyscraper construction contractor, because of the different physical injury risks. The insurance company's cost is also affected by the family status, number of dependents on each policy, and demographics of the population to estimate the incidence of claims against the policies. Taking account of these factors, the insurance company typically sets the insurance premium (i.e. the price of the insurance) with the help of its underwriter, an employee expert in risk assessment and price-setting. A price quote is then offered to the firm, which may include multiple levels of deductibles and insurance premiums.

This example illustrates several management problems:

- The insurance company may not be able to control how strongly the broker promotes its plan to the corporation, risking the loss of business to a lower-priced rival (even if this insurance firm's offer is superior in its coverage)
- The underwriter may not acquire full and accurate information on the population of employees to be insured, increasing uncertainty around the expected cost of the program
- The corporation's human resources (HR) department may not promote the insurance plan (versus open-enrollment policy options under the U.S.'s Affordable Care Act, for example), leading to uncertainty about the ultimate number of employees who will choose this policy
- Employees may not take care of their health once they know they have health insurance, leading to higher claims than estimated at the underwriting stage (known as the *moral hazard* problem).

The General Problem: Creating the Right Incentives for Performance of Multiple, Specific Functions

These difficulties arise because the insurance firm relies on its partners to perform functions that help close the sale, and measure and manage the costs of covering insured employees after the initial sale is made. The broker is expected to collect full and accurate data on the population to be insured, in order to maximize the quality of the underwriting (price-setting) effort. The broker is also responsible for promoting this insurance firm's policy versus those of competitors, since a corporation usually seeks multiple health insurance quotes before deciding on one to adopt. It relies on the HR department of the corporation to promote the adoption of its policy by employees, even after having won the business. And it relies on the insured employee to manage his/her health after choosing this company's policy, in order to control claims costs.

A single policy quote is a blunt instrument to create the right incentives for performance by the corporation and its employees. Commissions paid to the broker are more precise tools to incentivize promotional activity, although not to induce careful collection of the relevant data for good underwriting. All in all, the standard pricing elements in the corporate health insurance market fall short of incentivizing the multiple behaviors required for an efficient and coordinated channel, particularly in a market focused on the management of risk and uncertainty.

The insurance industry example shows that the more complex the set of activities the manufacturer delegates to its channel partners, the less effective a simple pricing policy will be. If the manufacturer does not create appropriate incentives for the performance of the specific activities delegated to each partner (including the end-user!), it may find its costs of business to be higher than optimal and may lose business along the way as well.

Solutions to the Problem of Incentivizing Performance of Multiple Functions: Vertical Integration, Functional Discounts, and SPIFFs

As in the previous examples, effective incentive mechanisms involve the thoughtful unbundling of channel functions and associated channel pricing. Partial vertical integration of the channel can overcome many problems. One company, Guarantee Mutual, used this approach to deal with problems of adequate communication about the population to be insured, risk management and quote generation, and satisfaction of insured employees with claims service. Guarantee Mutual left the sales function with insurance brokers in the field, because their standard compensation structure (set at a percentage of the premiums paid) directly incentivized sales efforts. Brokers focused intensively on exerting selling effort – at which they excelled – and Guarantee Mutual removed their obligation to service the account post-sale. Instead, it vertically integrated key underwriting and post-sale functions by making significant investments in big data management systems that improved speed and accuracy of quotes, enrollment of insured employees, and claims processing. This also lowered the cost of managing these activities. In this case, vertical integration of these specific functions worked well because it improved functional performance, reduced channel execution costs, and gave Guarantee Mutual strategic control over the customer's post-sale claims service.

When partial vertical integration is not feasible or optimal, functional discounts (discussed above) can coordinate action as well.

Finally, when the manufacturer uses an independent intermediary whose sales force is a key contributor to sales generation, an array of sales incentive policies may be used by that intermediary to induce the right type and amount of sales effort from the sales force, on behalf of the manufacturer. However, the manufacturer might further benefit from direct access to those salespeople, rather than relying on a channel intermediary to act (typically, imperfectly) on the manufacturer's behalf. In these situations, a common solution is the use of SPIFFs.[75] The acronym SPIFF stands for "Sales Promotion In Field [Sales] Forces,"[76] and refers to (usually cash) incentive payments made by a manufacturer directly to a salesperson employed by the manufacturer's intermediary. SPIFFs are commonly used as short-term incentives to promote the sale of a new and thus harder-to-sell product. For example, a sales rep might receive a $100 cash bonus for every new product or service adoption by customers. SPIFFs can also direct a sales rep's efforts to accelerate sales of a declining product that the manufacturer would like to retire from the market, or to improve the competitive positioning of its brand versus others in the market. A sales rep might thus receive a cash bonus to promote sales of Brand A refrigerators this month, and Brand B refrigerators next month.

SPIFFs thus play a useful role in intensifying short-term and well-directed promotional (selling) efforts for a particular set of products. Like SPIFFs, sales contests for field sales forces are often used to increase sales effort over a specified period of time. Research has shown that sales force motivation is multidimensional:

sales reps exert additional efforts because they are motivated by (1) rational needs, such as the acquisition and attainment of more money, or to defend and keep existing reward levels, and (2) emotional needs such as a desire to bond with an employer or its sales group, and make use of opportunities to grow, learn, and make meaningful contributions.[77] Sales contests and incentive programs incentivize a sales rep's effort to succeed and increase overall sales substantially. Many types of rewards can be offered; non-cash rewards, such as trips and experiences, or non-cash rewards bundled with cash, are offered more often than cash-only awards.[78]

Summary of Pricing Challenges

The four challenges profiled here suggest that channel pricing is inherently difficult – precisely because the most efficient channel structure usually entails partnership with one or more intermediaries outside the direct and total control of the manufacturer. Their ability to set final price to the end-user and to add on markups to maximize their individual profit (rather than total channel), their heterogeneity in the channel system, and their responsibility for multiple functions combine to make simple channel pricing strategies simply inadequate to coordinate the channel. The channel captain needs more sophisticated pricing tools in order to create the right set of incentives for a varied and task-laden set of partners.

We return to the mapping laid out at the beginning of the chapter to synthesize our analysis:

Table 13-1 (Reprise): Pricing Challenges and Solutions

The Challenge	How It is Observed in the Channel	Solutions
Ownership transfer	Product title and ownership must often be transferred to independent channel partners	• MAP (minimum advertised price) policies • Unilateral, voluntary price maintenance agreements • Retain ownership (vertical integration)
Channel margin math: the tendency toward double marginalization	A partner's gross margin requirements create a "double marginalization" problem, that successively and increasingly distorts pricing away from the level that would maximize total channel profits	• Multi-part tariffs • Retain ownership (vertical integration)
Asymmetries among partners	All channel partners do not perform the same set of channel functions, and differ in their abilities to deliver on them at a fair cost	• Functional discounts • MAP (minimum advertised price) policies • Quantity discounts • Retain ownership (vertical integration)
Channel function allocation	Some partners may be expected to execute on multiple desired channel functions	• SPIFFs • Sales contests • Retain ownership (vertical integration)

There is no one-to-one mapping from a particular channel pricing problem to the one, ideal solution, as the above examples and discussion illustrate. Any given channel pricing challenge has more than one possible solution, and the various solutions discussed in this chapter can be used to mitigate more than one of the challenges. Indeed, the number of solutions undoubtedly exceeds the set presented here, and is limited only by the ingenuity of the clever channel strategist. Importantly, the channel pricing analysis process in Table 13-1 (Reprise) directs you to proceed to first identify the ideal end-user price, then to identify causes of divergence of actual from ideal price, next to analyze possible pricing and reward strategy solutions, and only then to implement as the final step after a thoughtful analysis of *why* your channel and end-user prices and rewards do not properly incentivize your partners and cause end-users to flock to your products.

> *There is no one-to-one mapping from a particular channel pricing problem to the one, ideal solution.*

Chapter 14: HOW SHOULD I COMPENSATE MY SALES FORCE?

Wells Fargo's Cross-Selling Scandal

On September 8, 2016,[79] it was announced that Wells Fargo would be fined a total of $185 million for aggressive and fraudulent sales behavior, which had been occurring since 2011. $100 million was to be paid to the CFPB (Consumer Financial Protection Bureau, a U.S. federal agency), $35 million to the Office of the Comptroller of the Currency, and $50 million to the City and County of Los Angeles, as well as $2.6 million in refunds to customers for fees on accounts they had not authorized. Wells Fargo was found to have opened up to 1.5 million checking and savings accounts, and over 500,000 credit cards, without the account holder's permission, affecting a notable percentage of its 40 million retail customers. It was the largest fine to date levied by the CFPB, although it amounted to a very small fraction of Wells Fargo's total profits in 2016. It was unclear how many customers' credit ratings had suffered long-term damage by Wells Fargo salespeople's behavior, or how they could be compensated for it.

CFPB Director Richard Cordray said, "Wells Fargo built an incentive-compensation program that made it possible for its employees to pursue underhanded sales practices, and it appears that the bank did not monitor the program carefully." He added that "Today's enforcement actions against Wells Fargo likely could have been prevented if the bank had a stronger compliance risk management program that fostered a more healthy culture, in which incentives aligned behaviors properly."

The Sales Compensation Breakdown

Wells Fargo, like all other banks and indeed most other consumer goods companies, was interested in creating retail sales incentives for *cross-selling*: once a Wells Fargo consumer had bought *one* of the firm's products, cross-selling meant the attempt to sell *other* of its products to this consumer as well. This is a common sales goal because it is easier to sell another unit to a current consumer than to land a new consumer, given the reasonable assumption that the current consumer already likes the company. At its heart, the encouragement of cross-selling efforts is not the core issue in the Wells Fargo scandal.

> At its heart, the encouragement of cross-selling efforts
> is not the core issue in the Wells Fargo scandal.

Instead, this is an example of a *poorly-designed and improperly-implemented sales compensation plan*, fed by a combination of demand-side and supply-side issues. On the demand side, the aggressive goals in Wells Fargo's retail sales compensation plan indicated an over-estimation of the underlying consumer demand for various bank products as well as an over-estimation of the consumer's appetite for purchase of multiple products provided by one bank. On the supply side, channel design and implementation failures built upon a cluster of factors, including the allocation of responsibility for sales to bank selling employees, an aggressive-target compensation plan with significant compensation kickers for meeting quotas, threats of job loss for lack of quota achievement, the same types of incentives and threats for first-level branch and regional managers, and a failure at the central management level to monitor sales behavior. A 2013 lawsuit argued that managers "constantly hound, berate, demean and threaten employees to meet these unreachable quotas," and that the bank had "done little, if anything, to terminate these practices, nor to reform the business model it created that has fostered them." In May 2015,[80] the city of Los Angeles sued Wells Fargo for pressuring employees to engage in fraud in order to meet sales goals and for using the same tactics first exposed in 2013.

The Wells Fargo retail sales compensation plan was an example of a *salary plus quota/bonus plan*. It offered a baseline salary, with bonuses earned only if the salesperson reached quota. Branch bank tellers were paid mainly in salary, with about 3% of potential incentive pay based on sales and customer service. Personal bankers, also employed in branch offices and carrying out sales functions, earned about 15-20% of their pay from sales incentives. Base salaries for branch employees were approximately $30,000 annually, with bonuses of $500 to $2,000 per quarter for those who hit their sales quotas; district managers' bonuses could total $10,000 to $20,000 per year.[81]

Both personal bankers and tellers were expected to generate sales, with tellers expected to make at least 100 sales of bank products per quarter, directly or by referring the customer to a personal banker. Branch managers faced hourly phone conferences with regional supervisors concerning progress toward daily quotas for new accounts and cross-selling to existing bank customers. An employee who missed the quotas would be required to stay after hours or work weekends. Management threatened to fire those who did not meet goals after two months. This threat of being fired if quota is not met is an example of a *forcing contract*, meaning a compensation formula that penalizes non-achievement not only by withholding incentive pay, but by terminating employment. The forcing contract and the quota-bonus structure in the Wells Fargo case were not inherently poor compensation choices; after all, they did provide a powerful incentive to achieve the firm's goals of increasing sales through more intensive sales per bank customer.

The problem instead lay in the unreasonably high quota levels. Wells Fargo relied on its branch employees to generate retail sales, with the expectation that 80% of customers would be sold at least four financial products each – with the ultimate goal of the "Great 8," meaning an average of eight products per household. Not only were herculean or even godlike efforts required to meet quota, but failure over a short two-month period to do so resulted in losing one's job. Wells Fargo employees also filed lawsuits in 2013, alleging that the bank forced them to work overtime without pay to meet sales targets. It was this extreme pressure to meet sales goals that led retail employees to open accounts a customer did not need or ask for; order credit cards without a customer's permission; and forge customer signatures on required paperwork. A branch manager even found to her dismay that her employees had convinced a homeless woman to open six (!) checking and savings accounts, with total fees of $39 per month.

Repercussions Throughout the Business

The salesperson was left with two options: to quit (as some did), or to "find another way" to meet quota. The Wells Fargo story shows that *both* paths were followed. Wells Fargo employees "pinned" (assigned personal identification numbers, or PINs) bank customers' credit cards without their permission so that they could open an online banking account in the customer's name, helping them meet sales quotas. In order to conceal this fact from the customer, the employee would then provide false customer contact information, such as an email address of "noname@wellsfargo.com". Former employees described setting up sales stations outside blood banks in the Denver, CO area and targeting poor people who gave blood to make money as potential bank customers, even though "The majority of the time we knew…the account would be frozen."

> *The problem with Wells Fargo's retail sales compensation plan isn't its use of a quota-bonus structure and forcing contract, but its unreasonably high sales quota levels.*

One might counter-argue that at least Wells Fargo got the aggressive sales results it sought. The bank's average number of financial products per household was 6.17 in 2014 and 6.13 in 2015, consistent with its very high 2013 numbers. And indeed, Wells Fargo did have the highest number of bank products sold per household in the industry – by a factor of two. However, this came with several serious drawbacks that collectively are likely to more than wipe out any benefit. The first is the fact that *Wells Fargo did not benefit – indeed, it lost – from retail salespeople's misbehavior.* New accounts were often fake or chimerical – to be deleted once the salesperson got credit for the "sale." Such "sales" were not really sales at all. Given that its community banking segment (including retail banking products and services at the center of the scandal) accounted for 57% of Wells Fargo's revenue and net income in 2016, losses of revenue in this segment stood to affect the company overall, not just the retail segment.

Further, irate banking customers inflicted service costs on the bank when they found out about the unauthorized accounts made in their names, which then had to be closed with reimbursement of prior fees paid.

Wells Fargo also incurred the loss of good sales employees who gave up and left the bank. The large fines assessed in September 2016 were the most immediately visible cost of the unfortunate sales compensation program. While no firm is happy to pay $185 million in fines, this amount was a small fraction of Wells Fargo's profit in 2016, and did not change its ability to continue doing business. But worse was the blow to its reputation – something much harder to repair. Wells

Fargo had been one of the country's most admired banks, having weathered the Great Recession and built an apparently robust retail business since then.

> *Wells Fargo not only did not financially benefit from its poorly conceived retail sales compensation strategy, but it also lost good employees and incurred reputational risk.*

Wells Fargo's mistakes in sales force management and compensation affected the entire firm in both the short and long term.[82] Getting compensation right not only helps motivate your channel's sales force to carry out promotional functions in your channel – their most salient purpose – but also can set the tone for the culture of the sales organization and even for the company as a whole.

Implications For Channel Design and Implementation

The exertion of power and leverage is clear in the Wells Fargo example, with Wells Fargo playing the powerful channel partner role and the retail sales employee endowed with relatively little power. In particular, Wells Fargo had strong *reward power* over a retail sales employee, through its offer of compensation related to the performance of desired functions (in this instance, cross-selling of Wells Fargo products). More generally, sales compensation plans reward salespeople for exerting selling effort, closing a sale, reaching a daily/weekly/monthly sales goal, acquiring new customers, and the like.

The reward power inherent in Wells Fargo's incentive compensation plan was accompanied by *coercive* power in the form of threats of losing one's job. In a strong job market, the threat of losing your job is not very serious, since you can find a comparable job fairly easily. This was evidently not the case for many Wells Fargo retail banking sales employees: when the alternative earnings opportunities are few or not lucrative, the coercive power of the employer is increased.

Clearly, the employee retail sales force was a key element of Wells Fargo's go-to-market strategy. Motivating them to sell was and is a major focus of their channel efforts. This meant that *as a body*, the retail sales force was a very important channel partner to Wells Fargo. In some channels, this statement implies that the sales force exerts reward, expertise, and coercive power of its own. But because Wells Fargo had thousands of retail salespeople across the U.S., and because individual salespeople were replaceable (thus lacking *scarcity* power at the individual level), the firm could coercively pressure individual salespeople despite its dependence on them collectively.

The right compensation plan clearly has a strong influence on the firm's ability to engender enough (and the right kind) of sales effort to achieve its sales and profitability goals. The compensation plan's motivational aspects arise from its choice of key parameters:

- *Total pay offered* (in the Wells Fargo case, baseline salary was modest, but incentives made the potential total pay level much higher)

- The *elements* of the plan put in place (salary, commissions, and other incentive compensation elements): the presence of different compensation elements creates different motivations for behavior, effort, and performance
- The *leverage* in the plan – that is, the percentage of total pay that can be earned in incentives versus in straight salary (leverage could be high in the Wells Fargo case, creating a strong incentive to sell)
- *Other higher-order incentives* (such as the promise of a promotion in rank) or *disincentives* (such as the threat of losing one's job)
- The *relationship between lower-level employees'* ability to reach sales goals and *higher-level employees'* (bank managers, regional managers) compensation and likelihood of losing *their* job (disincentive). When the threat point is high, pressure from sales managers may exacerbate the underlying retail selling situation.

More generally, a channel manager should expect salespeople to figure out how to "game the compensation system" because their goal is to make the maximum in income, given the effort they exert. If there are few or no external monitoring processes in place (as was true with Wells Fargo), salesperson behavior may therefore subvert the goals of some otherwise very effective sales compensation practices. Governance processes are as important when working with internal sales employees as they were in the direct selling channel example from the previous chapter.

How to Use Compensation Effectively

Salary and bonus above quota comprises just one compensation plan type. We summarize some other commonly-used compensation elements here, and discuss their motivational purposes, contexts, and goals; the ways in which a salesperson can subvert them or the plan can otherwise fail to achieve its motivational objectives (i.e. the possibility of the "law of unintended consequences"); and mechanisms for monitoring and preventing the subversion or failure. The channel manager should think of these elements as jointly managing the performance of desired functions by channel partners; the total cost of getting those functions done; the detection of potential conflictual behavior by a channel partner; and the implementation of control systems to disincentivize such behavior and promote the desired behaviors.[83]

Table 14-1
Sales Compensation Elements and Incentive Effect

Component	Definition	Incentive Effect
Salary	Fixed payment independent of current performance	Risk avoidance; future salary adjustments award current performance (lump-sum)
Commission	Payment of *x*% of sales or gross margin	Effort to sell product units or highest-margin products
Bonus	Lump sum awarded for sales over minimum quota amount, or awarded from a pool of fixed quota size when salesperson meets quota	Effort to reach quota
Sales Contest Award	Lump-sum payments/awards for performance relative to other salespeople	Short-term effort, competitive in nature
SPIFF	Sales commission paid by manufacturer *directly* to partner's salespeople, not to the partner firm itself	Shift effort to specific spiffed products
Team Selling Award	Commission or bonus based on performance of *team* of salespeople; or of cross-functional, cross-geography team	Exertion of *team* effort; may reduce risk through diversification as well

Salary is a very common element in sales compensation plans. It offers a fixed and guaranteed per-period payment regardless of the salesperson's performance and thus reduces a salesperson's risk in taking on the sales job. Pure-salary plans do not create strong immediate incentives to exert sales effort, although the promise of annual salary changes based on the past year's performance do encourage sales productivity and relationship management with the firm's downstream partners and customers.

Commission can be based on unit sales, sales revenue, or gross margin (to name the most common metrics). Obviously, the metric on which commissions are based is the output measure the salesperson seeks to maximize, so a unit-sales commission may fail to meet a firm's profit goals if it results in high unit sales of low-profit goods. This suggests the superiority of a gross-margin-based commission metric. However, implementing this commission requires revealing the gross margins of the firm's products to the sales force; some firms are reluctant to share this information, given the risk that it may reach members upstream or downstream and trigger demands for better partner margins.

Bonuses are like commissions in their metric bases, but are typically lump-sum payments predicated on reaching a quota, that is, a minimum level of performance against the metric. They can be offered only sporadically (e.g. in the first quarter of the year), or throughout the year on a monthly, quarterly, semiannual, or annual basis. The firm faces opportunistic sales force behavior with a sporadic or time-limited bonus, because the effective income earned from a given sale is larger within the bonus period than just before or just after the bonus period. Salespeople therefore have an incentive to "sandbag" sales: delaying processing a sales order received shortly before the beginning of the bonus period. They may also seek to accelerate sales by pressuring customers to order early, in order to book sales before the bonus period ends. These behaviors cost the firm more compensation than is warranted, and can also irritate customers whose orders are not promptly processed or who are pressured into accelerated buying.

A further implementation risk accompanies the *fixed bonus pool*, and also affects *sales contests*: salespeople now realize that they are competing with others, not just trying to increase their own performance. The incentive value of the fixed-pool bonus is negatively related to the number of *other* salespeople who qualify for the bonus pool. Similarly, the number and relative sizes of contest prizes define the limits on number of salespeople earning the incentive. Setting quotas too low may cause many salespeople to exert extra effort to qualify for the bonus, but also leads to smaller awards for success. Giving many, but small, prizes may similarly fail to incentivize salespeople to increase effort during a contest; offering few, but large, prizes can also backfire when the probable winners are known early in the contest period. A good contest therefore has to be a "good horse race" where many competitors are motivated to exert effort to excel. Care in calibrating quota levels and the size of the bonus pool, as well as the number and amount of contest prizes, is therefore warranted to preserve a strong incentive to sell during the award period.

SPIFFs are an incentive award (either a commission per unit sale, or a bonus) used by manufacturers using the sales force of a channel partner, such as an independent distributor firm or a sales representative firm. Specifically, the SPIFF differs from an incentive payment offered to the intermediary firm because it is awarded directly to the salespeople of the intermediary instead. SPIFFs are designed to increase effort and thus sales of new-to-market products that require some education of the customer, or alternatively to incentivize sales of a soon-to-be-retired product in order to get it out of the channel system. Its great benefit is its ability to reach *through* the channel partner to the salesperson who actually closes the sale – it is an extremely well-placed compensation element. Some intermediaries may welcome the help in covering their sales force compensation costs that comes from SPIFF payments as well. However, savvy intermediaries often refuse to allow a manufacturer to use SPIFFs, because they alter the salesperson's incentive to sell across the product line, e.g. by diverting the salesperson's efforts from selling the intermediary's most profitable product to selling the manufacturer's dying product. The firm wishing to use SPIFFs therefore must not only design them to appeal to the salesperson, but also to the intermediary employing the sales force.

Team incentives are also common, based on the joint performance of multiple people. They are attractive when multiple types of effort are needed to close a sale, whether those efforts are geographically or functionally diverse. Team incentives can produce higher output than individual incentives when team members encourage *each other* to exert more effort, above and beyond any exhortations by the firm itself. However, team incentives are subject to free-riding by some team members; when this type of opportunism is easy to engage in (e.g. because it is difficult to detect), morale and thus effort across the whole team can suffer. Thus, a team incentive may not be a good single incentive tool, and may best complement other compensation components instead.

Consumer-goods firms selling through multi-channel systems find they are inadvertently facing more and more "team selling" – though not of their own devising. This is driven by consumers' multi-channel shopping behavior, for example with one route to market offering pre-sales customer service in the form of education and "touch and feel" opportunities, and another offering quick delivery and low price through online sales (see Chapter 13's discussion of DigiGadgets and pricing through the channel). Most firms do not have an adequate "team incentive" in place in these instances, resulting in the opportunistic free rider extracting the entire retail selling margin while the cost-bearing, service-providing channel partner receives no share of retail profits. The incentive problems with this lopsided award system are obvious. The principle of functional discounts or a team incentive can ameliorate this free-riding problem.

> *Consumer multi-channel shopping behavior creates the need to think about "team selling" awards for selling partners in all channels shopped by the consumer, not just the one where purchase occurs.*

In sum, sales compensation is the management of the firm's *reward* and *coercive* power sources to incentivize the performance of desired functions by its salesperson channel partners – whether those salespeople are employees of the firm or of its intermediary channel partners. The Wells Fargo example shows that miscalibrating the compensation plan not only fails to properly motivate the sales force to sell, but may disastrously motivate salespeople to game the system and even harm customers and the firm through their behaviors, with repercussions for the firm and its reputation as well as for short-term sales response. As in any channel function and compensation analysis, appropriate sales compensation instead involves choosing the right tool to encourage the specific behavior desired, as well as choosing the threshold for earning compensation, and the compensation amount, to induce appropriate and strong efforts by its salespeople that will increase the firm's profitability.

ENDNOTES

Preface Notes

[1] 2015 State of the Wholesale Distribution Industry, *National Association of Wholesale Distributors*, https://www.naw.org/about/industry.php, accessed on October 22, 2016.

[2] 2015 US Retail Sales to Near $5 Trillion in 2016, eMarketer, http://www.emarketer.com/Article/US-Retail-Sales-Near-5-Trillion-2016/1013368, accessed on October 28, 2016. 2015 The World Bank, http://data.worldbank.org/indicator/NY.GDP.MKTP.CD accessed on October 28, 2016.

[3] "US Foods to Cut Jobs Amid Corporate Restructuring," *Wall Street Journal*, October 21, 2016. http://www.wsj.com/articles/us-foods-to-cut-jobs-amid-corporate-restructuring-1477051386 accessed on October 24, 2016.

Chapter 3 Notes

[4] http://www.bedbathandbeyond.com/store/page/College , viewed on 12-17-2015.

[5] …And just about every company has more "legacy" products than innovative, new-to-market products, making it crucial to effectively manage the go-to-market strategy for all parts of the line.

Chapter 4 Notes

[6] We routinely ask executives and students to report on their channel benefit assessments in specific shopping experiences, and the following discussion shows the typical information gathered in this type of exercise and how it can be used to improve channel targeting and management.

[7] Applying this idea to a B2B context, a customer's demand for quick delivery for a piece of original equipment (say, a machine on an assembly line) may be moderate if the buyer is simply upgrading the line. But once the machine is in place, that buyer's channel benefit demand for quick delivery of post-sale service and parts is generally much more intense, because uptime of the production line is crucial and the line cannot operate when a part is broken.

[8] Viewed at www.fleetfeetsports.com; www.zappos.com; and www.6pm.com, on December 18, 2015.

[9] As in the usual calculation of a GPA, the conversion of grades to points is: A=4, B=3, C=2, D=1, and F=0. A 4.0 GPA is a perfect score for a retailer/channel, where the provision of all channel benefits at that particular retailer was found to be excellent.

[10] Of the 17 New Balance SKUs offered by FFS, 11 were also offered by Zappos.com and only 4 by 6pm.com.

Chapter 5 Notes

[11] Even higher-level relationships call for SAMs (Strategic Account Managers) or GAMs (Global Account Managers), all of whom also have responsibility for maintaining a smoothly operating channel and customer relationship.

[12] See www.paymode-X.com , accessed on August 12, 2014.

Chapter 6 Notes

[13] A simple, linear metric would assign a value of 1 to "Low," 2 to "Medium," and 3 to "High"; sum up all the point totals to get a grand total for the whole channel; and calculate the share for each function as the ratio of its point value to the grand total point value across the whole channel. For instance, if inventory holding/transport is rated "High" (3 points) and the sum of all functions' points is 14, then the estimated share of inventory holding/transport costs to total channel costs would be (3/14), scaled as 21 points out of 100. Non-linear metrics could also be applied if the channel analyst finds this useful.

[14] For example, Darren's company's weighted cost share borne equals (25*[0.3]+10*[1]+15*[1]+25*[.5]+5*[.5]+5*[.25]+10*[.16]+5*[.2])%.

[15] We omit Darren's company's R&D cost-bearing from this commentary not because it is unimportant – on the contrary, the company is very intent on making back the significant R&D costs it incurred to launch the new product. Rather, these R&D costs are "sunk" from an economic point of view and the channel cost-bearing discussion naturally focuses more directly on channel-specific, ongoing costs.

Chapter 7 Notes

[16] Adapted from Gary Gebhardt (1992), "Achieving Maximum Marketing Efficiency," Frank Lynn Associates, Inc. Client Communique, Vol. 4 (January), p. 3.

[17] These fees hold for an order of less than $35.00.

[18] Note that if segment B's willingness-to-pay function were curved rather than a step function, we could also conclude that drugstore.com could provide a slightly slower delivery speed for the $12.99 fee and still attract segment B – an example of *overprovision* of this channel benefit, relative to willingness-to-pay.

[19] Lele, Milind (1986), "Matching Your Channels to Your Product's Life Cycle," Business Marketing, December, pp. 61-69 discusses at an aggregate level how the optimal channel form might change as a product moves from introduction through maturity to decline in its life cycle; as well, each segment and each market's bounds and gaps may vary at different paces over time, with the need to respond individually to these different changes.

Chapter 8 Notes

[20] Flanders Wallcovering is a pseudonym used to protect the real retailer's identity, although the events described in this example are real.

[21] For more information, see Coughlan, Anne T. (2004), *Michaels Craft Stores: Integrated Channel Management and Vendor-Retailer Relations,"* Kellogg School of Management case number KEL036.

Chapter 9 Notes

[22] "Direct Selling's Economic Footprint Continues to Expand in United States, According to New National Survey," Press Release, Direct Selling Association, June 8, 2016.

[23] These are some of the top 20 Direct Selling Association member companies, measured by net sales in 2014. See Direct Selling Association, *2015 Growth & Outlook Report: U.S. Direct Selling in 2014*, published July 2015.

[24] This literature is often applied within the contexts of law enforcement, but is equally applicable in the channel implementation context. See for example Becker, Gary S. *(1968)*, "Crime and Punishment: An Economic Approach," Journal of Political Economy, 76 (2, March-April), 169-217; and Stigler, George J. (1970), "The Optimum Enforcement of Laws," Journal of Political Economy, 78 (3, May-June), 526-536.

[25] www.rodanandfields.com .

[26] R+F requires its Consultants to include this statement with any income claim: 'For information regarding earnings under the R+F Compensation Plan, see the Income Disclosure Statement [URL provided], and a copy of the Income Disclosure Statement should be handed out if speaking about lifestyle claims during in-person meetings."

[27] Rodan + Fields Policies and Procedures, Rule 16a., pp. 40-41.

[28] www.usana.com . USANA's distributors are called "Associates."

[29] USANA Annual Report 2014, p. 18.

[30] Becker (1968, p. 174) notes: "It would be cheaper to achieve any given level of activity [i.e. enforcement]... the more highly developed the state of the arts, as determined by technologies like fingerprinting, wire-tapping, computer control, and lie-detecting." Similarly, investment in today's state-of-the-art databased screening mechanisms allows either a lower cost to achieve the same level of detection as previously, or a more effective level of detection from the same cost as previously.

[31] 2013 Mannatech Annual Report, p. 10, section on "Management of Independent Associates."

[32] Mannatech 2012 United States Policies & Procedures, p. 16.

[33] Direct Selling Association Code of Ethics, 2016, p. 12.

[34] http://www.vorys.com/services-650.html.

[35] See Chopra, Sunil and Peter Meindl (2001), *Supply Chain Management: Strategy, Planning, and Operation*, Prentice Hall: Upper Saddle River, NJ, Chapter 9, pp. 221-257 for details.

Chapter 10 Notes

36 http://www.cinnabonfranchising.com/bakery-franchise-the-sweet-difference, accessed on October 12, 2016.

37 http://www.brandingstrategyinsider.com/2011/11/brand-licensing-case-study-cinnabon.html#.V_z3dvkrLmE, accessed on Oct 11, 2016.

38 http://www.cinnabon.com/blog/post/frosted-cinnasweeties, http://www.cinnabon.com/blog/post/better-call-saul, accessed on Oct 11, 2016.

39 de Dreu, C. K., & Van Kleef, G. A. (2004). The influence of power on the information search, impression formation, and demands in negotiation. *Journal of Experimental Social Psychology*, 40, 303–319. doi:10.1016/j.jesp.2003.07.004

40 Briñol, P., Petty, R. E., Valle, C., Rucker, D. D., & Becerra, A. (2007). The effects of message recipients' power before and after persuasion: A self-validation analysis, *Journal of Personality and Social Psychology* 93, 1040. doi:10.1037/0022-3514.93.6.1040

41 Galinsky, A. D., Magee, J. C., Gruenfeld, D. H., Whitson, J. A., & Liljenquist, K. A. (2008). Power reduces the press of the situation: Implications for creativity, conformity, and dissonance. *Journal of Personality and Social Psychology* 95, 1450–1466.

42 Chen, S., Lee-Chai, A. Y. and Bargh, J. A. (2001), "Relationship Orientation As a Moderator of the Effects of Social Power," *Journal of Personality and Social Psychology*, 80:173-187.

43 Schmidt Mast, M., Jonas, K., and Hall, J. A. (2009), "Give a Person Power and He or She Will Show Interpersonal Sensitivity: The Phenomenon and Its Why and When," *Journal of Personality and Social Psychology* 97, 835-50.

44 Mead, N. L. and Maner, J. K. (2012), "On Keeping Your Enemies Close: Powerful Leaders Seek Proximity to Ingroup Power Threats," *Journal of Personality and Social Psychology*, 102, 576-91.

45 Rucker, D. D., and Galinsky, A. D. (2008), "Desire to Acquire: Powerlessness and Compensatory Consumption," *Journal of Consumer Research*, 37, 257-67. Rucker, D. D., and Galinsky, A. D. (2009), "Conspicuous Consumption Versus Utilitarian Ideals: How Different Levels of Power Shape Consumer Behavior," *Journal of Experimental Social Psychology*, 45, 549-55.

46 Frazier, Mya, "John Deere Cultivates Its Image," *Advertising Age*, July 25, 2005. These observations are consistent with information provided to the authors by channel managers at Deere.

47 "The Home Depot® and Deere & Company Announce Agreement to Sell New Series of John Deere Lawn Tractors," John Deere press release, Moline, IL, June 17, 2003.

48 "The Home Depot® and Deere & Company Announce Agreement to Sell New Series of John Deere Lawn Tractors," John Deere press release, Moline, IL, June 17, 2003.

49 Frazier, Mya, "John Deere Cultivates Its Image," *Advertising Age*, July 25, 2005.

50 Bloomberg News, "Lowes to sell riding mowers next year," *Chicago Tribune*, June 4, 2005.

[51] Gombossy, George, "John Deere Denies Big Store Items Are Inferior," *Hartford Courant*, April 25, 2009.

Chapter 11 Notes

[52] "Microsoft and Rackspace Form Cloud Alliance," *Wall Street Journal*, July 13, 2015. http://www.wsj.com/articles/microsoftandrackspaceformcloudalliance1436799601

[53] Cannon, Joseph P. and William D. Perreault Jr. (1999), "Buyer-Seller Relationships in Business Markets," *Journal of Marketing Research*, 439-60.

[54] Dwyer, Robert F., Paul H. Schurr and Sego Oh (1987), "Developing Buyer-Seller Relationships," *Journal of Marketing*, 51(April), 11-27.

[55] Jap, Sandy D. and Erin Anderson (2007), "Testing a Life-Cycle Theory of Cooperative Interorganizational Relationships: Movement Across Stages and Performance," *Management Science*, 53(2), 260-75. Figure 11-2 depicts the hypothesized collaboration levels across relationship stages; this later research fine-tunes the collaboration level differences from buildup to maturity.

[56] Sandy D. Jap and Erin Anderson (2007), "Testing a Life-Cycle Theory of Cooperative Interorganizational Relationships: Movement Across Stages and Performance," *Management Science*, 53(2), 260-75.

[57] Dalsace, Frédéric and Sandy Jap (2015), "The Friend or Foe Fallacy or Why Your Best Customers Don't Need Your Friendship," working paper.

[58] Vosgereau, Joachim, Erin Anderson and William T. Ross (2008), "Can Inaccurate Perceptions in Business-to-Business (B2B) Relationships be Beneficial?" *Marketing Science*, 27(2), 205-24.

Chapter 12 Notes

[59] Calyx & Corolla is a classic case from 1989 whose challenges face many firms today. Fortunately, enough time has passed so that its strategic partnering relationship development story has been made public, in contrast with the confidentiality that surrounds recent examples.

[60] *Multichannel Merchant*, "Vermont Teddy Bear Purchases Calyx and Corolla" October 1, 2003. http://multichannelmerchant.com/news/vermontteddybearpurchasescalyxcorolla01102003/[60] *Multichannel Merchant*, "Vermont Teddy Bear Purchases Calyx and Corolla" October 1, 2003. http://multichannelmerchant.com/news/vermontteddybearpurchasescalyxcorolla01102003/

[61] Salmon, Walter J., and David Wylie. "Calyx & Corolla." Harvard Business School Case 592-035, November 1991. (Revised October 1995.)

[62] "Grow from the Right Intro: A Report on the Strategic Value of Business Alliances and Compatible Partner Matching," September 2014, BPI Network and the CMO Council.

[63] "28 Steps to a Strategic Alliance," by Leslie Brokaw, Inc.com, April 9, 1993 http://www.inc.com/magazine/19930401/3493.html. "In the Mailbox, Roses and

Profits," by Stephanie Strom, Feb 14, 1992, http://www.nytimes.com/1992/02/14/business/inthemailboxrosesandprofits.html

64 Jap, Sandy D. and Erin Anderson (2003), "Safeguarding Interorganizational Performance and Continuity Under *Ex Post* Opportunism," *Management Science*, 49(12), 1684-1701.

65 Wang, Qiong, Ujwal Kayande, and Sandy D. Jap, (2010) "The Seeds of Dissolution: Discrepancy and Incoherence in Buyer-Supplier Exchange," *Marketing Science,* 29(6), 1109-24.

66 Anderson, Erin and Sandy D. Jap (2005), "The Dark Side of Close Relationships," *MIT Sloan Management Review,* Spring, *46(3)*, reprint 46314.

67 "Toyota Shakes Up a Japanese Tradition," by Yoko Kubota and Eric Pfanner, *Wall Street Journal*, Oct 28, 2015.

Chapter 13 Notes

68 This assortment of solutions is almost certainly not exhaustive, since channel managers innovate new methods of incentivizing and pricing to their channel partners as needed in various market circumstances. However, the set discussed here are the most well-known and broadly-used behaviors.

69 The company's name is disguised for confidentiality reasons, but the channel pricing challenge is entirely true – and, unfortunately, experienced by many other firms as well.

70 Outside the U.S., laws may be different and the interested reader should check to see what types of vertical price policies are allowed. See Zelek, Eugene F., Jr. (2011), "Legal Tools that Support Value Pricing," Freeborn & Peters LLP Contemporary Legal Issues White Paper, September, for a cogent discussion of downstream channel price maintenance and how to implement it.

71 Unilateral action by the manufacturer is crucial to avoid allegations of conspiracy in the channel, an antitrust violation.

72 See Israeli, Ayelet; Eric T. Anderson; and Anne T. Coughlan (2015), "Minimum Advertised Pricing: Patterns of Violation in Competitive Retail Markets," *Marketing Science*, forthcoming; and Israeli, Ayelet (2015), "Channel Management and MAP: Evidence from a Natural Experiment," working paper.

73 The "Jacks" of the world often consider themselves "self"-publishers even when they use these partners to reach final consumers, because they have not contracted with an established publishing house to take their book to market.

74 "Double" stands in for any number of intermediaries, not just one.

75 See Caldieraro, Fabio and Anne T. Coughlan (2007), "Spiffed-Up Channels: The Role of Spiffs in Hierarchical Selling Organizations," *Marketing Science*, Vol. 26 (1, Jan.-Feb.), 31-51, for an analysis of the effectiveness of SPIFFs.

76 Other definitions (and spellings!) of SPIFF include "Special Payment Incentive for Fast Sales" (SPIFFS) and "Sales Promotion Incentive Fund" (SPIF).

77 "Employee Motivation: A Powerful New Model," by Nitin Nohria, Boris Groysberg, and Linda-Eling Lee, *Harvard Business Review*, July-August 2008, p. 78-84.

78 "Do Channel Rep Incentives Really Work?" Insights from 2013 Maritz Channel Market Study, 2014.

Chapter 14 Notes

79 See Glazer, Emily (2016), "Wells Fargo to Pay $185 Million Fine Over Account Offerings," *The Wall Street Journal*, Sept. 8, downloaded on Sept. 13, 2016 from http://www.wsj.com/articles/wells-fargo-to-pay-185-million-fine-over-account-openings-1473352548 ; Merle, Renae (2016), "Wells Fargo boots 5,300 employees for creating accounts its customers didn't ask for," *The Washington Post*, Sept. 8, downloaded on Sept. 13, 2016 from https://www.washingtonpost.com/news/business/wp/2016/09/08/wells-fargo-fined-185-million-for-creating-accounts-its-customers-didnt-ask-for/; Associated Press (2016), "Wells Fargo Fined $185 Million for Improper Account Openings," *The New York Times*, Sept. 8, downloaded on Sept. 13, 2016 from http://www.nytimes.com/2016/09/09/business/dealbook/wells-fargo-fined-for-years-of-harm-to-customers.html; and Koren, James Rufus (2016), "Wells Fargo to pay $185 million settlement for 'outrageous' sales culture," *the Los Angeles Times*, Sept. 8, downloaded on Sept. 13, 2016 from http://www.latimes.com/business/la-fi-wells-fargo-settlement-20160907-snap-story.html.

80 Rudegeair, Peter (2015), "Los Angeles Sues Wells Fargo Over Sales Tactics," *The Wall Street Journal*, May 5, downloaded on Sept. 22, 2016 from http://www.wsj.com/articles/los-angeles-sues-wells-fargo-over-sales-tactics-1430849801 .

81 Glazer, Emily (2016), "How Wells Fargo's High-Pressure Sales Culture Spiraled Out of Control," *The Wall Street Journal*, Sept. 16, downloaded Sept. 22, 2016 from http://www.wsj.com/articles/how-wells-fargos-high-pressure-sales-culture-spiraled-out-of-control-1474053044.

82 Both the bank's CEO, John Stumpf, and the leader of the banking group overseeing retail banking, Carrie Tolstedt, lost their jobs as a result of these events. Glazer, Emily (2016), "Wells Fargo CEO John Stumpf Steps Down," *The Wall Street Journal*, Oct. 12, downloaded on Oct. 15, 2016 from http://www.wsj.com/articles/wells-fargo-ceo-stumpf-to-retire-1476306019 .

83 For more detail on sales compensation plans, please see Coughlan, Anne T. and Kissan Joseph (© 2012), "Sales Force Compensation: Research Insights and Research Potential," in <u>Handbook on Business-to-Business Marketing</u>, Gary L. Lilien and Rajdeep Grewal, Editors, Edward Elgar Publishing, pp. 473-495.

BOOK INDEX

1 in 5 before 5, 17, 18
1-800-Flowers, 148, 154
6pm.com, 31, 46, 49, 50, 51, 52, 53, 54, 55, 56, 185
Acme relationship example, 138–45
Activity-based costing, 59, 64, 70
AdvoCare, 105
Aidpod, 18, 21, 22
Air Canada, 55
Airborne, 150
Airborne and Emery, 150
Alignment analysis, 12, 20, 22, 79, 81, 82, 83, 84, 85, 86, 87, 143, 166
Amazon.com, 2, 7, 68, 113, 163, 164, 168, 170
Amount, 37, 39
Amway, 105
Anderson, Eric T., 190
Anderson, Erin, 189, 190
Android, 150
ANZ Bank, 137
Apotheker, Leo, 153
Apple, 162
Arbonne, 105
Ariana Huffington, 68
Arrow, Kenneth, 152
Ashford, 92, 93, 94, 95, 96, 98, 99, 100, 101, 102, 103
Assortment, 21, 25, 37, 38, 39, 45, 47, 48, 49, 50, 51, 54, 55, 82, 92, 94, 128, 149, 190
Asymmetric partners, 170, 171
Asymmetric power, 117, 118
Auntie Anne's, 117
Australia, 137
Autotrader, 61–62
Availability of alternatives, 133
Azure, 131
B2B, 10, 31, 32, 36, 51, 57, 60, 62, 69, 70, 71, 72, 73, 74, 85, 131, 138, 159, 162, 185, 189

B2B flooring channel functions, Darren, 57, 62–64, 71–76
Bargh, J. A., 188
Barnes & Noble, 170
Becerra, A., 188
Becker, Gary S., 187
Bed Bath & Beyond offers channel benefits, 35–36, 37–39, 40–41
Benevolent dictator, 104, 118, 121, 122
Best Buy, 41, 42, 163
Block tower analogy explained, 8, 14
Bloomingdale's, 102
Bonus, 106, 108, 151, 165, 174, 178, 179, 181, 182, 183
Branded variants, 22, 101
Brick-and-mortar, 25, 28, 40, 49, 51, 83, 94, 148, 163, 168
Briñol, P., 188
Buildup stage of the relationship life cycle, 135
Caldieraro, Fabio, 190
Calyx & Corolla, 147, 148, 150, 151, 152, 153, 154, 189
Calyx & Corolla example, 147–53
Cannon, Joseph P., 189
Carvel, 117
Cell phone channel benefit demands, 41–42
CFPB (Consumer Financial Protection Bureau, 177
Channel asymmetries, 22, 23, 117, 118, 162, 166, 170, 171
Channel benefit analysis process, 45, 46, 54
Channel benefits, 20, 21, 22, 23, 31, 36, 37, 40, 41, 42, 43, 45, 46, 47, 48, 49, 50, 51, 53, 54, 56, 57, 58, 60, 65, 67, 79, 82, 84, 85, 91, 93, 94, 98, 106, 167, 185
Channel conflict, 9, 12, 14, 23, 91, 92, 93, 94, 95, 96, 104, 105, 107, 123, 124, 126, 127, 128, 129, 130, 136, 137, 153

Channel coordination, 10, 83, 91, 93, 96, 98, 103, 104, 118, 160, 166
Channel design, 7, 12, 35, 65, 77, 86, 87, 91, 103, 105, 107, 160, 178
Channel functional cost analysis, 76
Channel functions, 11, 12, 22, 28, 57, 58, 60, 62, 63, 64, 67, 68, 69, 70, 71, 74, 75, 77, 79, 83, 85, 99, 100, 101, 103, 131, 149, 151, 162, 166, 169, 170, 174, 175
Channel power, 14, 91, 93, 94, 95, 103, 118, 128, 130
Channel value proposition, 81, 85, 97
Chen, S., 188
Chopra, Sunil, 187
Cinnabon example, 117–21
Coca-Cola, 18
Coercive power, 76, 95, 125, 126, 180, 184
COGS (Cost Of Goods Sold), 169
Coke, 18, 21, 23, 32
ColaLife in Zambia channel strategy, 17–23
Commission, 182
Complementary competencies, 145, 147, 150, 151, 153, 154, 155
Complexity of supply, 134
Compliance, 12, 100, 107, 108, 109, 111, 112, 113, 167, 177
Conjoint analysis, 42, 46
Consignment selling, 165
Continental AG, 154
Cooperative advertising, 99, 101
Coughlan, Anne T., 1, 2, 4, 187, 190
Customer segments, 26, 41, 45
Customer service, 37, 39, 45, 47, 48, 50, 51, 52, 53, 54, 57, 92, 94, 106, 124, 127, 166, 178, 184
Dalsace, Frédéric, 189
de Dreu, C. K., 188
Decline stage of the relationship life cycle, 136
Delivery Time, 37, 39, 47, 48, 50, 54
Dell, 123
Demand-side alignment, 80, 81

Denso Corp, 154
DigiGadgets, 161, 163–64, 163, 164, 166, 184
Direct selling, 105, 106, 112, 113
Direct Selling Association's Code of Ethics, 113
Distance, 37, 39
Dogear Publishing, 161, 168–69, 168–69, 170
Domain conflict, 94, 95, 126, 127
Double marginalization, 161, 162, 169, 175
Dow Chemical, 134
Downlines, 108, 109, 110, 111
Drop-ship, 165
Drugstore.com alignment example, 80–82, 85, 186
Dwyer, Robert F., 189
eBay, 68, 113
Economic impact of channel activity, 10
Emery, 150
Enforcement, 97, 102, 104, 106, 107, 112, 113, 114, 115, 167, 177, 187
Equity Rule, 57, 64, 70, 76
E-tailers, 101
Etsy, 68
Exploration stage of the relationship life cycle, 135
Explosive Value, 23, 26, 31
Explosive Value creation checklist, 30
Explosive value creation levers, 27
Externalities, 99, 100
Facebook, 68
Federal Express, 148
Flanders Paint & Wallpaper, 91
Flanders Wallcovering Inc., 91
Flanders Wallcoverings example, 91–96, 99–100, 100–102
Fleet Feet Sports, 49–55
Focus Brands, 117
Focus groups, 42, 46
Forcing contract, 178, 179
Frazier, Mya, 188

free-riding, 53, 93, 97, 101, 102, 103, 166, 183, 184
friend or foe, 133
Frito-Lay, 99
FTD, 148, 154
Functional discount, 171, 172, 174, 184
Galinsky, A. D., 188
Gardener's Eden, 148, 149
Gebhardt, Gary, 186
Glazer, Emily, 191
Glynn, Mike, 150
goal conflict, 93
Goal conflict, 103, 126, 127
Gombossy, George, 189
Google, 39, 68, 150
GoPro, 167
governance strategy, 106, 107, 111, 113, 115
Governance strategy, 107
GPA (Grade for the channel), 49, 50, 51, 52, 54, 185
Gray market, 102, 163, 167
Grewal, Rajdeep, 191
Grow The Pie, 142, 144
Groysberg, Boris, 191
Gruenfeld, D. H., 188
Guarantee Mutual, 174
Hall, J. A., 188
Harry & David, 154
Health Insurance, 172
Herbalife, 105
Hewlett-Packard, 153
Home Depot, 124, 125, 126, 127, 128, 129, 169, 171, 188
Houzz.com, 91
How customers want to buy, 9, 11, 19, 25, 26, 31, 33, 35, 36, 41
HP, 68
Huffington Post, 68
IBM, 68
Importance of the purchase, 134
Income Claims, 108, 109
Information and Education, 37, 39
Information asymmetry, 98
Infrastructural environment, 86

Intel, 153
Internalize the externality, 99
Isagenix, 105
Israeli, Ayelet, 190
Jap, Sandy D., 189, 190
John Deere example, 123–29, 171, 188, 189
Jonas, K., 188
Joseph, Kissan, 191
Kayande, Ujwal, 190
Koren, James Rufus, 191
Land, Ray, 153
Lane, Robert W., 128
Lee, Linda-Eling, 191
Lee-Chai, A. Y., 188
Legal constraints, 86
LegalShield, 105
Legitimate power, 125
Lele, Milind, 186
Leverage (sales compensation), 37, 41, 91, 93, 94, 104, 118, 125, 129, 130, 180, 181
Lifetime value, customer, 40, 55, 115, 126, 127, 128
Lilien, Gary L., 191
Liljenquist, K. A., 188
Locational convenience, 94
Lockheed-Martin, 40–41
Macy's, 102
Magee, J. C., 188
Managerial constraints, 86
Maner, J. K., 188
Mannatech, 112, 187
MAP policy, 102, 164, 166, 167, 171
Mary Kay, 105
Maturity stage of the relationship life cycle, 136
Maximum resale price maintenance policy, 102
Mead, N. L., 188
Meindl, Peter, 187
Melaleuca, 105
Merle, Renae, 191
Metzler, Richard, 150
Michaels Craft Stores, 100, 187

Microsoft, 68, 131, 189
Middle of the road, 144
Minimum advertised price policy (MAP). *See* MAP policy
Moe's, 117
Monitoring, 97, 101, 103, 104, 106, 107, 111, 112, 113, 115, 122, 167, 181
Moral hazard, 97, 100, 101, 103, 173
MSRP, 99
Multi-Channel, 42, 53, 55, 125, 128, 129, 162, 164, 171, 184
Multi-part tariff, 170, 172
Mutual Investments, 151
Necessary Enlightenment, 142, 143
New Balance, 47, 48, 49, 50, 51, 53, 55, 185
New Zealand, 137
Nike, 162
Nohria, Nitin, 191
Nu Skin, 105
Office 365, 131
Oh, Sego, 189
Omni-channel (see also Multi-channel), 52
Opportunism, 12, 23, 93, 104, 107, 183
Oracle, 153
Oreos, 119
Owades, Ruth, 147, 148, 149, 150, 151, 152
Ownership transfer, 161, 175
Package size, 37, 39
PayPal, 60, 68
Perceptual conflict, 113, 126, 127
Perreault Jr., William D., 189
Peter Barr, 149, 152
Petty, R. E., 188
Pick-and-pack, 87
Pillsbury, 117, 118, 119, 120, 121
Pirates, 92
Price Is Right, 144
Price, Coordinated, 130, 159, 160, 169, 173
Price, versus channel benefits, 42
Price-matching guarantee, 101
Quota (sales), 178, 179, 181, 182, 183

Rackspace Hosting Inc, 131
Ralph Lauren, 102
Realignment, 85, 86
Referent power, 119, 125, 126
Resale price maintenance (RPM), 102
Reward power, 100, 125, 126, 180
Risk Mitigation, 108
Rodan + Fields example, 107–11
Ronald Reagan, 153
Rose Colored Glasses, 142, 143
Ross, William T., 189
RTM, 27, 28, 31, 33
Rucker, D. D., 188
Rudegeair, Peter, 191
rules of conduct, 12, 104, 106, 107, 111, 115
Ruth Owades, 149
Safeguarded, 93, 96
Safety inventory, 114
Salary, 181, 182
Sales Contest, 182
Sales representative firm, 70, 165, 166
Salmon, Walter J., 189
Samsung, 150
Sara Lee, 99
Scarcity power, 119, 125, 126, 180
Schlotzky's, 117
Schmidt Mast, M., 188
Schurr, Paul H., 189
Scotts, 124
Sears, 118, 129
Channel margin math, 161, 175
Segmentation, for channel design, 28, 31, 35, 37, 41, 42, 45, 46, 47, 48, 49, 51, 52, 53, 55, 56, 80, 81, 82, 83, 84, 85, 87, 98, 101, 123, 124, 126, 127, 128, 179, 186
Sephora, 83
Sharepoint, 131
Showrooming, 53, 55, 93, 96, 98, 101, 102, 166
Simon Berry, 17, 18
SKUs, 25, 50, 114, 185
Slotting allowances, 99
SPIFF, 174, 182, 183, 190

Sponsoring Responsibilities, 108, 109
Stigler, George J., 187
Stockout, 114
Strategic assets, 120
Strategic skeptic, 12, 96, 105
Stumpf, John, 191
Sun Microsystems, 153
Sunbay Growers, 149
Supply and Demand Principles of Channel Strategy, 19
Supply market dynamism, 134
Supply-side misalignments, 80, 82, 83, 84, 85, 107
Target, 46, 47, 48, 49, 50, 99, 106
Team Selling, 182
TeleFlora, 154
Test the Waters, 135, 142, 144
Tiger Direct, 163, 164
Time horizons, 133
Tina Turk, 102
Toyota, 154, 190
Tragedy of the commons, 99
Transactional relationships, 132
Trucking company, explosive value creation, 31–33
Unauthorized channel, 113, 163, 164, 166, 167, 179
under-pricing, 82
United Parcel Service, 119
USANA, 111, 187
Valle, C., 188
Van Kleef, G. A., 188

Variety, 8, 17, 21, 25, 27, 31, 35, 36, 37, 39, 41, 45, 47, 48, 49, 50, 51, 54, 85, 92, 94, 98, 104, 119, 138, 149, 162
Vermont Teddy Bear, 154, 189
Vertical integration, 103, 162, 165, 168, 174, 175
Vorys, 113
Vosgereau, Joachim, 189
Wallpaperdirect.com, 92, 93, 94, 101, 102
Wal-Mart, 60, 99
Wang, Qiong, 190
Weight, channel benefit, 48
Weighted cost, 70, 74, 76, 186
Wells Fargo, 177–81
Whitson, J. A., 188
Williams-Sonoma, 148
Willingness to pay, 35, 36, 42, 80, 83, 148, 159, 160
Wood block tower, 8
www.wallpaperdirect.com, 92
Wylie, David, 189
Zappos and 6pm.com shoe purchasing - how, not just what, 25–26, 28, 31, 46–55
Zappos.com, 25, 31, 46, 49, 50, 51, 52, 53, 54, 55, 56, 185
Zelek, Eugene F., Jr., 190
Zero-based channel, 65, 77, 79, 80, 86, 87
Zero-based model, 87

finis

NOTES

NOTES

Made in the USA
Columbia, SC
28 November 2017